NOW THE DUST HAS SETTLED

Memories of War and Peace, 1939-1994

Freddie De Butts

TABB HOUSE
Padstow

First published 1995
Tabb House, 7 Church Street, Padstow, Cornwall, PL288BG

Reprinted 1995

ISBN 1 873951 13 2

British Library Cataloguing-in-Publication Data
A catalogue record of this title is available from the British Library

Printed and bound by: Short Run Press, Exeter

For my wife, loyal companion over fifty years,
and our children and grandchildren

_____

MY family persuaded me to write this book whilst my memory was
still reasonably good, and this is the result.

Directly descended on my father's side from four generations of
soldiers and completing my education just before World War II, it was
inevitable that I should go into the Army.

Much of my story is about deserts: the North African desert in
World War II, and the periphery of the Arabian Peninsula at Aden and
the Gulf Shaikhdoms during the 1950s and '60s. By way of contrast I
was involved in End of Empire in India, Malaya and Cyprus, and had
an odd habit of arriving just as a state of emergency was declared.

During thirty-six years in the Army, I spent a total of twenty-six
overseas in the Middle or Far East and was never stationed in Germany;
an unusual balance for a British service officer but full of interest,
excitement and fun. I have no regrets, as I hope will appear from the
pages that follow.

Hoggeston
1995

CONTENTS

LIST OF ILLUSTRATIONS

ACKNOWLEDGEMENTS

I AM most grateful to the following friends from my Army days and since retirement who helped in different ways:

Glen Balfour-Paul, CMG, for his very valuable comments on Chapter 22;

Gordon Beningfield for his encouragement and advice;

Lieutenant Colonel Ronnie Borradaile, MBE, MC, for the description of his escape from an Italian POW camp;

Emma Bradshaw for transferring the original typescript onto a word processor and accepting endless amendments with such good grace;

Major-General Bala Bredin CB DSO MC DL for his memories when commanding 2 Para in Cyprus;

Jack Briggs, OBE, for bringing me up to date on the UAE;

Brigadier James Brind, DSO, for checking Chapter 15;

Ken Burrage for the enormous help that he has given me over preparing several versions of the typescript;

Sara Dodsworth for taking on the original typing, editing much of it and persuading me to have it published;

Major David Goddard, MBE, for his help with Chapter 15;

Veronica Goonewardene for drawing the seven sketch maps in such a clear way;

Sir Donald Hawley, KCMG, MBE, for permission to quote from his book *The Trucial States*;

Bill Heeps, CBE, for his interest and encouragement;

Sir David Hunt, KCMG, OBE, for kindly writing the Foreword, giving valuable advice on the text and writing out *Lili Marlene* in German;

Colonel Colin Huxley for his account of the Malayan ambush just after I left;

Eric Jones for his interest and help;

Rear-Admiral Michael Kyrle Pope, CB, MBE, DL, and his wife Suzanne who read and re-read the manuscript and gave much advice;

Peter Mann, former General Manager of ADMA on Das Island, for memories of 1966;

Ann Mitchell, my cousin and an author herself, for her help and advice;

Paul Odgers, CB, MBE, for his valuable advice on drafting the original script, and reminding me of Monty's Tac HQ at Zonhoven;

Georgina Palmer, JP, for her interest and help;

Brigadier John Platt, DSO OBE, DL, for his encouragement and help;

Major-General Sir Digby Raeburn, KCVO, CB, DSO, MBE, for his help on the Western Desert chapters;

David Shepherd for permission to reproduce the cover painting, in my possession, and to quote from his book *The Man Who Loves Giants*;

Jill Simmons for acting as my unofficial unpaid agent;

Major Hugo White, DL, for his research on Ralph Rivers-Bodilly; and

Lord Wright of Richmond, GCMG, for his valuable comments on Chapters 24 and 25.

FOREWORD

I AM grateful for the privilege of contributing a foreword to this fascinating autobiography by my old friend Brigadier De Butts. I feel that I am introducing the general reader to a thrilling story of a kind that used to be more common some fifty years ago and which is about to disappear. The hero moves from one adventure to another. Most of them take place overseas, in romantic places. In his youth he fights in the British army in the Egyptian desert, later in life in command of Arab troops in the deserts of Arabia on the fringes of the Empty Quarter, and in between in the Malaysian jungle. At the beginning of his career in the profession of arms he takes part in the defeat of the German bid for world power, to which defeat he contributes both on the staff and in the field. As he bids farewell to the profession he can reflect that he has witnessed, and participated in, the closing days of the British Empire, in India, Malaysia and the Middle East. He belongs to the last generation in Britain that lived through the experience of the End of Empire, and he is among the few who can describe it from personal experience.

The story starts slowly and conventionally. Freddie De Butts is from an old-established Army family. He does not seem to have thought of taking up a different career, but his progressive-minded father insisted on one variation to the usual course: his son should enter the Army, not through Sandhurst but by graduating at Oxford. Three years at Oriel and an honours degree in Modern History both gave him greater maturity than the average young army officer and also endowed him with a command of good English to which the engaging and lucid style of this book bears witness. No sooner had he graduated than he was posted overseas to the first battalion of his regiment, the Somerset Light Infantry, which was then stationed at Poona. It sounds the sort of place they would be; it sounds equally typical of the army that when, in August 1939, the first troops were sent from India to reinforce the thinly-held Imperial position in the Middle East the young subaltern was sent with them as, of all things, a Field Cashier. As the convoy drew into Suez he might have had a foreboding, but at the age of twenty-three pretty certainly did not, that his future was to be linked with Arabs and deserts. It did not take long for his superiors to realise that there were talents here that could be put to better use than supervising the arrangements for troops' pay. To be frank, at that time in the Middle East, there was so great a demand for competent officers to carry out the staff duties called for by the rapid expansion of the Middle East base that almost any reasonably sensible officer was eagerly snapped up. An intellectual from Oxford was a fine catch. It was not long before he was posted as Intelligence Officer to the Headquarters of British Troops in Egypt under the very experienced Staff Officer, Intelligence, Major Priest. I served under Bob Priest myself a year later; he was thoroughly well informed both about the nature of the Western Desert, the one which separated Egypt from Italian Libya, and about the Italian Army, on which he was the greatest British expert. Freddie De Butts proved a first-class pupil. He learned everything he could from his mentor and soon surpassed him. I shall argue later that he was the ideal type of Intelligence staff officer.

Let me in the meantime point out the virtues of the necessity that was forced on those who were organizing the command structures of the headquarters and formations in the Middle East. I shall concentrate on the Intelligence staffs because this is the field in which Freddie De Butts was first engaged and in which we first knew each other. There was no-one in the Middle East who had been on any of the courses on Intelligence in the Field which had proliferated back in Britain. This was an advantage. Those courses − I also never went on one, but I knew enough about them from studying their products − were of little practical use, being based on experience in the First World War and theories inapplicable in practice. The officers who were plucked from regimental duties to be conscripted into Intelligence posts on the General Staff in the Middle East were not confused by any of this stuff and were forced to apply common sense and experience to the problems of appreciating enemy strength and intentions. This was greatly to the advantage of their commanders. Military Intelligence is not an arcane mystery. It can be learned quite quickly by persons of average intelligence, and the regular army contained far more men of superior intelligence than was popularly supposed. Of course a knowledge of foreign languages is useful, but interpreters are cheap and plentiful. What counts is practical experience of actual operations of war. That is the only thing which gives you the instinctive feeling for what the enemy is likely to get up to next. The purpose of these remarks is to lead up to a brief appreciation of the period when I first met the man who was to instruct me in staff duties and in the nature of Military Intelligence which thereafter was to be my speciality until the end of the war. I had arrived in the Middle East in June of 1940 and precisely a year later I was sent off to the Western Desert, having just returned after serving for the previous seven months in Greece and, most recently, in Crete. I had had three months in Western Desert Force Headquarters, under Bob Priest, and in September 1941, when Eighth Army came into existence, was posted to 13 Corps Headquarters where

I was number two in the Intelligence section under Major De Butts. It was my most valuable military experience.

In spite of his polite and kindly references to me I don't think he had any need to learn anything from me. I, on the contrary, learned everything from him and it is from this period of June 1941 to August 1942 that I date my feeling of admiration and friendship. He had in the previous year not only taken part in O'Connor's great offensive, in which our small forces had destroyed the better part of two Italian Armies, but had also fought as a regimental officer in the sharp but bitterly contested Syrian campaign. He was in consequence admirably equipped for his task. Showing a cool courage in circumstances of difficulty and danger, for in the quickly-moving battles which were characteristic of the Western Desert, staff officers often became involved in close-quarter tactical clashes, he retained his intellectual poise and grasp of the facts of the situation. Throughout my further service I maintained my opinion of his outstanding capacities and regard him as one of the best of the many masters of Intelligence that were produced in the course of the Mediterranean campaigns.

So much I must say on the basis of a year's experience during which we were engaged together in a series of battles with various fortunes. For the rest I depend on what I heard of his military exploits and on the account which he gives in his book. His subsequent career was based on the reputation he had gained in war. It was a career distinguished by accelerated promotion in which operational experience and staff duties were combined. It began gradually to direct itself towards that co-operation with the defence of British interests in the Arab countries which has always romantically attracted the best British military minds. I shall leave him to recount, in his modest and entertaining fashion, his service with the Levies in Aden, the Trucial Oman Scouts and his final senior commands in the Gulf, in what is now called the United Arab Emirates, whose prosperity and stability owe so much to his wise guidance. The final stages of what has been called 'Britain's moment in the Middle East' are described here with affection and humour.

It would not be in accordance with the facts of history to echo Froude and proclaim: 'And now it is all gone, like an insubstantial pageant faded'. The work of British officers who have laboured to bring into existence the Independent states of Arabia maintains its solid worth. They are still influenced by the memory of the integrity, good humour and loyal cooperation of men like Brigadier De Butts.

David Hunt.

PART 1, 1916-1939

CHAPTER 1

Early Days

THOUGH the records are somewhat obscure I believe that the De Butts family were Huguenots living in Holland in the seventeenth century, who emigrated to Ireland about the time that the Dutch Prince William of Orange and his English wife Mary became King and Queen of England in 1689.

Two brothers of the third generation are interesting: John became Provost of Sligo and several of his descendants emigrated to America in the mid-eighteenth century, settling in Maryland and Virginia where they still live. Seven generations later another John De Butts, born in 1915, became Chairman of American Telephones and Telegraph (A T & T), one of the largest companies in the world, and a grand-daughter of General Robert E. Lee, the famous Confederate leader in the American Civil War, Mary Custis Lee, married Hunter De Butts in 1925. My wife and I dined with her, a charming old lady, in Virginia in 1981.

The other brother, Elias, was Rector of Castlemaine, Co. Kerry. His son, another Elias, is on record as chairing the 'goff' club in Bray in 1762, the first known reference to golf being played in Ireland.*

I am directly descended from Elias. He had five sons of whom the fourth, Augustus, became a General, Colonel Commandant of the Royal Engineers and a Knight. Augustus had twelve children of whom surprisingly only the youngest, John Cromie Blackwood, had any male heirs. John was also a sapper, became a major-general and had nine children, of whom the sixth, Frederick Robert McCrea, was my grandfather. He was a mountain gunner in India and was killed in action on the North-West Frontier in 1897 whilst commanding his battery. My father, Frederick Cromie, born in India in 1888, was his only son. My grandmother, daughter of Captain James Dalgairns Travers, 17th Foot, who had twenty-three first cousins in the Army or Navy, found herself widowed in India with six small children, three of whom died when quite young.

*Early Irish Golf, William H. Gibson, 1988, Oakleaf Publications, Naas, Co. Kildare.

1

My father was originally destined for Christ's Hospital, the Bluecoats school where boys whose fathers had been killed in action could be educated almost free. At the last moment he was made a Foundationer at Wellington at a greatly reduced fee. He went on to Sandhurst and was commissioned in the Indian Army (55th Cokes Rifles) in 1907. In World War I he first served in France with the 31st Division Signal Company and was badly wounded and awarded the MC in 1915. I remember him telling me that he was evacuated to Sister Agnes Hospital, then at 17 Grosvenor Crescent near Hyde Park Corner, and visited by the King who walked up many flights of stairs (there being no lift) as my father was on the top floor. The following year he was transferred to Mesopotamia (the modern Iraq) and won the DSO there in 1917. After the War he was awarded a place on the first peace time staff college course at Quetta in 1920, and served in a series of staff appointments before commanding his regiment, now re-named the 1st Battalion 13th Frontier Force Rifles. At the outbreak of World War II he was GSO 1 Peshawar District North-West Frontier Province, and in 1940 was given command of the Kohat Brigade, also on the frontier. In 1943 shortly before he retired he was awarded the CB, an honour seldom given below the rank of major-general.

My mother, Kathleen Primrose O'Donnell, was the elder daughter of Octavius O'Donnell, descended from another Protestant Irish family. She was born in India where her father was for many years overseer of the opium crop in the United Provinces. He had hoped to enter the Indian Army but his eyesight was not good enough. Despite this, he was an excellent shot with both rifle and shotgun and a good cricketer. He retired in 1911 and settled at Hintlesham in Suffolk. Though he was fifty-four, in 1914 he joined up and went to France to look after Indian pioneers who were digging trench systems.

My parents, having met in India, were married in 1915, when my father was on leave from France. I was born on April 17th, 1916 in a nursing home in Ipswich, by which time my father was in Mesopotamia. Tragically my mother died eight days later. My father's two sisters, Kathleen (known as B) and Charlotte (Sharlie), were then living in Guernsey with their mother, Sha being already a war widow with a daughter, Patsy, six months older than me. It was agreed that B and Sharlie would look after me in Guernsey until the War was over.

In 1920 my father married Sybil Katherine Beauchamp, my godmother, whose parents had lived near the O'Donnells in Suffolk. Her father, Canon Beauchamp of Copdock, died before the War and her mother 'Katie' moved to Oxford where she had a very comfortable Victorian house in Rawlinson Road. I was a page at the wedding which took place in Oxford. Sybil was to be a wonderful step-mother to me.

Later that year we sailed for India complete with a governess, Miss Oakley, who was engaged to look after me, then aged four. I have vague memories of her being rather severe.

I remember little about Quetta. My father was then posted as Brigade Major at Jhansi in the United Provinces where he was to spend three years. The brigade commander, Gilbert Cassels, and his wife were close friends of my parents and they had a daughter, Lavender, who was my age. We used to be led out on ponies together.

In 1923 my father was due for home leave and decided that I should go to school in England and not return to India. In the event I spent most of that year at Lavender's aunt's house in Sevenoaks, sharing lessons with Lavender whose parents had also decided that she should not return to India.

In 1924 I spent a year at Melbreck pre-prep school at Tilford in Surrey. My only memories of Melbreck are that there was a happy atmosphere and that I somehow got into the cricket XI. Peter Studd was Captain, aged nine. He later captained Harrow and became Lord Mayor of London.

My father always intended that I should follow him at Crowthorne Towers, the main prep school for Wellington and actually located in the grounds, and then go on to Wellington itself. This I duly did, and was to spend the next nine years boarding at two schools within spitting distance of each other in Crowthorne, a rather unattractive village on the edge of heathland and with more than its fair share of pine trees.

Throughout this very formative period of growing up I had no proper home as my parents were in India, apart from eight months to a year's home leave every three years. They rented three houses during that time, two near Reading and one at Pewsey in Wiltshire. I have happy memories of those houses though no sooner had I come to regard them as home than it was time to pack up. For the rest of the time I spent my holidays with my O'Donnell grandparents, first at Holbrook in Suffolk (where they had moved from Hintlesham) and later at Great Fransham in Norfolk. They were kind and did everything they could to make me feel at home. Both were in their sixties and it cannot have been easy for them coping with one small boy.

Crow Towers was a fairly tough school, certainly by present day standards. The academic level under Guy Powell, the headmaster, was high. I was not particularly happy there but put this down to lack of a home environment as much as anything else. I did reasonably well both at work and games and sat a scholarship for Wellington which I failed, but was awarded a place and duly went there in January 1930.

The move was exciting and an important step forward in growing up. I had of course seen lots of Wellington boys in the grounds when

I was still at Crow Towers and had longed to be one of them. Wellington had over many years built up a reputation for being the public school that provided more officers for the Army than any other. F.B. Malim, the Master, was a classical scholar and though a strict disciplinarian never pushed the army down our throats; if anything, the reverse. He was widely respected and it was difficult not to listen to his addresses in chapel.

The 'fagging' system was universal in those days (last boy to reach the prefect when he shouted 'fag' did the job). I don't remember resenting it; probably being fairly quick on my feet I usually managed not to be last. Almost total immersion for a matter of seconds in a tub-bath full of cold water was compulsory every morning and failure to turn up was automatically a beating offence.

In those days no boarding school allowed a boy to spend a night away during term time (except Eton which was of course a law unto itself). I think there was sense in this since although I looked forward to being taken out for the statutory three times a term, I was always very unsettled when the outings were over.

I think it was a foregone conclusion that I would go into the army. I can't remember considering any other career except that of an engine driver, like most boys in the era of steam locomotives, but I grew out of this. The OTC was very active at Wellington, and I joined as young as possible and worked my way up to sergeant. In the sporting world I was fairly good at hockey, running and boxing but disappointing at the two major games, rugger and cricket. My only individual achievement was to win the Little Kingsley at the age of fifteen, a cross-country race for all boys under sixteen over about one and a half miles, involving crossing the Blackwater River twice and a bog known as the 'slough of despond'. I don't know how this came about, but I didn't continue with cross-country except to go beagling, which I did principally to get away from college for an afternoon in the country.

In due course I became a dormitory (equivalent to house) prefect, and went into the sixth form, initially on the classical side as I was quite good at Greek and Latin. However, as an 'army candidate' I was transferred to the Modern Sixth. My father was very keen that I should if possible go into the army through Oxford and not Sandhurst, which he regarded in those days as a 'sausage machine' for turning out officers.

I was equally keen on this plan and it was decided that I should apply for Oriel, a relatively small college where one of great-great grandfather Augustus's sons had been a Fellow. My sixth-form tutor thought that it was worth trying for a scholarship, which I duly sat in Christchurch Hall — an inspiring setting but not enough to turn me into a scholar. I duly entered Oriel as a commoner in October 1934.

The switch from school to university is a much greater jump in education than that of prep school to public school. I suddenly found myself on my own, required to attend lectures and write essays for my tutor, and invited to participate in sport 'if I felt like it'. There was virtually no supervision; it was up to me to work and participate in the life of the college. Oriel was at that time Head of the River at rowing and on almost my first day there was a polite knock on my door from the rowing secretary, who said, 'You will of course row, won't you'. Though Wellington was not a rowing school and I weighed only just over ten stone, I weakly said yes. Looking back I do not regret that decision at all. I was taught to row properly, there was a tremendous spirit in the college rowing club and I gradually progressed from 3rd eight to 2nd eight to 1st eight over three years.

Christopher Pepys was another 'fresher' with me; he had been born in the Argentine and after Winchester had just completed a year's service in their army to allow re-entry if he wished. Christopher already knew more about life than most of the rest of us put together. He was ordained after leaving Oxford and later became a very popular bishop.

Twenty-two of the old colleges were for men only in my day; there were five women's colleges and All Souls which was (and still is) for Fellows only. Today all the former men's colleges admit women and the overall ratio in the University is three men to two women. For me Oxford was a continuance of my single-sex education. Having no sisters I had only met girls occasionally during the holidays and was naturally shy with them. Today's mixing of the sexes throughout school and university life was unheard of in the '20s and '30s.

I read modern History, which started at 55 BC. Two of my lecturers were well known in different ways; Sir Ernest Swinton was Chichele Professor of Modern History and had played an important part in inventing tanks in World War I. He lectured on Clausewitz and in particular his theory that 'war is a continuation of policy by other means'. This was all highly relevant to what was happening in Germany under Hitler, although I don't think many of us except Churchill realised it at the time.

The other personality was a don at Exeter named Atkinson, whose speciality was the Peninsula War and Wellington's defeat of Napoleon. Atkinson was a misogynist, refusing to allow women to attend his lectures. He was, however, so good that those women from LMH, Somerville and St. Hughs who were reading that period always turned up in the hope that he might relent, and even sat in the front row only to be told that he flatly refused to start until they had left. Imagine what the Equal Opportunities Commission would have to say about that today!

I joined the Cavalry squadron of the University OTC, not because I aspired ultimately to join a cavalry regiment but because it was an extremely cheap way of riding under expert supervision. My father was an excellent horseman and always wanted me to ride. In fact he had arranged for me to have special lessons when I was still at Crow Towers. This was not a success as I had several falls and became quite scared. Once during the holidays my pony had bolted and charged through a narrow archway which was both alarming and painful. On another occasion, when aged fifteen, I was following the local hunt on foot when a member had a bad fall and volunteers were called for to ride his horse some five miles home. I volunteered and found myself riding an extremely fresh hunter which immediately took off on a public road and didn't stop for several miles. All I could do was to stay in the saddle. Fortunately we did not meet a single car. The horse eventually stopped of its own accord and I walked him back to where he belonged. The owner's wife was surprised to see me so soon but didn't ask any questions and gave me a ten bob tip. I did also have a few days' hunting in Norfolk on hirelings.

The cavalry squadron at Oxford was fun. Nobody took the military aspect at all seriously though at summer camp we were worked quite hard. I can remember some of my more dashing and moneyed fellow-troopers arriving back in camp at Tidworth at 6 a.m. from London in white tie and tails and straightaway joining us grooming the horses.

My most dramatic experience as a member of the OU OTC was lining the route outside St George's Chapel, Windsor, on a very cold day in January 1936 for the funeral of King George V. After a minimum of practice we were required to stand absolutely still with our rifles reversed and our heads down for what seemed a very long time. The funeral cortège came to Windsor by train, and I remember the first indication we had that the climax was approaching was hearing the bands playing funeral marches. The music sounded quite close, then faded away as the procession wound round Windsor, and finally got louder and louder as it entered the castle. We of course were not allowed to look up, and all one could do, as the gun carriage with the King's coffin on it under a Union Jack passed within a yard or two, was to squint upwards. All the crowned heads of Europe were there, together with the entire British Royal family. It was a sad and moving occasion, and one in which I felt privileged to participate.

Less than a year later, on December 10th, I was in a cinema in Oxford when King Edward VIII's abdication was flashed on the screen. I remember feeling sad and almost stunned by the news. 'Teddy' was enormously popular with my generation. I had watched him ride, fall and remount in a point-to-point in Norfolk, and heard much about his 'common touch' with working-class people. A day or two later I boarded a bus in London and heard the conductor saying that he remembered seeing Teddy on the Western Front in the War talking to the men in the trenches. Like so many people he was saddened by news of the abdication.

I don't remember any particularly rowdy behaviour when I was up. The proctors, accompanied by their faithful 'bulldogs'*, visited likely trouble spots fairly regularly.

On one occasion a group of us were in the Clarendon and must have been making too much noise as suddenly someone said; 'Look out, the progs', and we just managed to walk out of one side of the revolving doors into the Cornmarket as the University authorities walked in the other side. It was a close shave.

I think that I only climbed into Oriel once over the wall from Magpie Lane. If, when living in, you were out after midnight the alternatives were: climb over the wall, or knock on the College front door, give the porter a fiver and hope that he would not report you to the Dean. If you were in digs your landlady was likewise supposed to report if you came in after midnight. There were of course ways of persuading her to keep quiet.

During my second year (1936), as I was now officially an army candidate, I was required to complete a six-week attachment to a regular unit in the summer vacation. I was duly granted a temporary Territorial Army commission on the General List and ordered to report to the Oxfordshire and Buckinghamshire Light Infantry at Colchester. The officers' mess was already full so I was given a room in a barracks about a mile away. Every evening I bicycled (I couldn't afford a car) in white tie and tails to dine in the mess. I had to wear these extraordinary clothes because it was the equivalent of mess kit, which all the other officers were wearing. I felt a complete fool and little attempt was made to ease my embarrassment. In fact hardly anybody spoke to me.

The training (or lack of it) that we did was ludicrous when one

*The proctors were two University dons (a senior and a junior) who during their term of office were responsible for discipline among undergraduates outside Colleges. They were accompanied by two toughish men known as bulldogs who were employed by the University to assist them in their duties. In the event of trouble the Proctor was required to say to the miscreant: 'Are you a member of the University' before taking the matter further.

There are stories of undergraduates being chased over ploughed fields by perspiring 'bullers', who had to wear dark suits and bowler hats. Fun for the undergraduate who might be a cross-country blue; not so funny for the bullers.

remembers that World War II was only three years away. I repaired to the Colchester Club most days in the early afternoon to play tennis. There wasn't much else to do. At the end of my six-week attachment the CO was required to say whether or not I was likely to make a suitable regular officer. He obligingly said yes though I had hardly met him.

During two summer vacations I spent a month or two staying with families in France and Germany, theoretically to improve my French and German. The French family lived near Montauban in the south-west; it was fun but a waste of time as there were two young Britons of my age also staying in the house, and we of course spoke English to each other. I came back by cargo boat from Bordeaux to Southampton for the princely sum of £5.

The German trip was a more serious affair, as might be expected at that time. It was 1936, the year of the Olympic games in Berlin. I was met at Cologne station and it was German all the time as the family spoke no English. A son and daughter of about my age went off in uniform most evenings to Hitler Youth meetings. They were very friendly and I suspect tried to convince me that Hitler meant no harm to Britain. After six weeks in Cologne I went on to Frankfurt and stayed a week with friends of my stepmother. They were German Jews, though the significance of this meant nothing to me at the time, and I fear 'disappeared' during the War as I never heard of them again. From Frankfurt I went to the Wagner festival at Bayreuth and saw *Lohengrin*. Hitler, who was known to be a Wagner fan, was said to be there.

I don't remember being even vaguely aware that the lights were to go out all over Europe only three summers later. I think Hitler must still have thought (as advised by Ribbentrop, his ambassador in London) that Britain would not fight if he quietly continued 'annexing' chunks of Europe. To quote a recent Times leader: 'By 1933 pacifism had so swept the intellectual elite that the Oxford Union passed a motion that "this House will in no circumstances fight for its King and Country"'. It was therefore important that English tourists were made welcome.

There were many distractions at Oxford and it was probably as well that rowing was a very serious commitment; failure to turn up for the regular outing every afternoon throughout the term meant that you were likely to lose your place in the boat. We rowed in all weathers; on one occasion, when the river was in flood and we were entering Osney lock, our cox, an Indian whose command of English was not all that good, gave the 'easy all' too early and instead of entering the lock we were swept broadside against the weir. All four oars on stroke side snapped off and the boat began to turn over. As one man we all stepped out onto the weir and watched our old clinker break up.

In 1937, my last year, Oxford won the Boat Race for the first time for thirteen years amid enormous jubilation and Brian Hodgson the stroke was an Oriel man. His photograph was on the front page of most of the National Dailies. I was then stroking the college 2nd eight. For the last week of the Easter vacation our first two crews used to stay at the Star & Garter Hotel at Putney and train on the Tideway. On our last day we rowed the full boat race course, the first crew giving us a substantial start. They rowed past us somewhere near Barnes bridge.

Oriel had now been Head of the River in Eights for four years and no college had ever managed five consecutive years. With Hodgson at stroke we were all set to break the record. About three weeks before Eights Week began, Hodgson was badly bruised in a car accident and was not allowed to row. I was brought in at two and the whole crew reorganised. We rowed over the first evening with New College almost overlapping. Sadly, they caught us the second evening and we lost another three places, finishing fifth. Hodgson rejoined the crew for Henley, I retained my place, and we had high hopes but were beaten by Corpus Christi Cambridge in the Ladies Plate.

Henley Week and a Commem Ball tended to interfere with my Finals, and I like to think that a deep commitment to rowing contributed to my only achieving a Class III when the results were finally published. My parents were on home leave and we were actually in Ireland when I was summoned back to Oxford for a viva. It was recognised that a long viva meant one was a borderline case between two classes. Mine went on a long time and I came away feeling that I had not done well. My tutor told me afterwards that I had got a 'high third'.

CHAPTER 2

An Army Unprepared for War

HARDLY had I gone down than the War Office informed me that I was commissioned Second Lieutenant in the Somerset Light Infantry and ordered me to report to the 2nd Battalion, then at Colchester, at the end of September 1937. I was twenty-one. My father had finally recommended the Somersets as he knew the then Colonel, General Sir Walter Braithwaite, and it proved a very happy choice although I had no connection with Somerset or the West Country.

I duly reported at Colchester, having visited the regimental tailors, then Hawkes of Saville Row, and ordered what uniform was required. On commissioning one received a uniform allowance of £50, and I was able to have made a suit of service dress and red mess kit for not much more than this sum. I was also issued with an Edward VIII sword as my commission was dated January 30th, 1936, ten days after he became King. Unfortunately it was destroyed with the rest of my kit in a Bombay warehouse fire during the war.

Two other young officers joined the same day as I did, both straight out of Sandhurst and eighteen months younger than I. University candidates received an ante-date of seniority as the degree course at Oxford was three years and Sandhurst only eighteen months. My commission was therefore backdated. I felt that I might be at a slight disadvantage on first joining as my soldiering in the Oxford OTC had been child's play compared to Sandhurst. However, I need not have worried too much as we three were all immediately put under the Regimental Sergeant Major to be taught Light Infantry drill and I managed to get a higher mark than either of them on passing out. I suspect that they were fed up with drill whereas it was almost a novelty to me.

The adjutant David Maud was very strict. He would not allow us to go anywhere near the men until he had personally inspected us in our rooms every morning to see that we were correctly dressed, down to the last button. I did not take to him in those early days but later he was to become my closest friend in the regiment and godfather to my son David.

10

I spent only three months at Colchester as I was told almost on arrival that I would be posted to the 1st Battalion at Poona, India, early in the New Year. The other two new arrivals were to stay at home a little longer. I felt it almost appropriate that the Somersets should be stationed in Poona. The name epitomised India and the Raj in music hall jokes, and it happened that my father was born there in 1888. I left England by troopship in January 1938 for Bombay. The voyage was uneventful; I shared a cabin with three other young hopefuls, all just commissioned. We had to wear red mess kit every night as far as Suez which meant starched shirts and collars; very uncomfortable in that confined atmosphere. It was a relief to change into white.

I was not to return to the UK for almost exactly six years.

From what I have read and heard the Indian Raj changed little between the wars. The lessons of the appalling Amritsar massacre in 1920 had been learnt, and we were carefully drilled in 'Aid to the Civil Power'. However the British community, both civilian and military, hardly mixed at all with the Indians. As a British army unit in a predominantly military station we kept ourselves to ourselves. Apart from my excellent Hindu bearer, Krishna, (who had been sent to Bombay to meet me) and regimental tailors, contractors and syces, we met very few locals. The picture painted by E.M. Forster in *A Passage to India*, published in 1924, is accurate in this respect. Outside our very British barracks we tended to spend our leisure time at the Gymkhana Club, which in those days was not open to Indian membership.

I shared a bungalow with three other officers, one of whom kept a cobra in a cage in the back garden. I cannot imagine why; I have hated snakes ever since.

'Soldiering' was taken a good deal more seriously than at home. One of the problems was to keep the men fit in a hot climate; we did a lot of marching and shooting on the range and generally showing the flag, much of it ceremonial. In those days a soldier's tour in India was six years, and some volunteered to do even longer. Sergeant Cotton served twenty-one years abroad with the battalion from 1926 to 1948 without going home to England. When he arrived at Taunton he was frightened to leave barracks. There were compensations; for instance, contractors' men would shave you in bed every morning, one going down the row of men, dormitory-style, with a brush followed closely by another with a razor, and probably a third with a cup of 'char', all at about 6.30 a.m.

Every two or three months we went out on a company march which involved several days away from barracks on a carefully arranged route, perhaps ten to fifteen miles per day, and camping each night. I remember that we all wore pith helmets (not to be confused with

'Bombay bowlers' which tended to be worn by Eurasians), and the column was followed at a discreet distance by an ambulance to pick up those who couldn't make it.

The only problems were the heat and the dust which we created. Company marches were rather fun; we got away from barracks, saw some of the outlying villages and slept in the open under the stars listening to the barking of pie-dogs and the shrill chirping of cicadas.

In the autumn of 1938 I was sent on a two-month small arms course at Pachmarhi in the Central Provinces. We were taught all the finer points of the basic infantry weapons, the rifle and light machine gun. Apart from the work my main interest was that Pachmarhi was well known as a centre for big game shooting, particularly tiger. The drill was that two of us would hire a *shikari* (hunter) who bought a young buffalo and tied it to a tree at a carefully chosen spot in the jungle. If everything went according to plan, a tiger would kill the buffalo, the shikari would immediately inform us and at the same time build a hide known as a *machan* up the tree. We would then take it in turn to sit over the dead buffalo, and hopefully shoot the tiger when it returned, usually at night, to continue its meal.

Sure enough the *shikari* was on our doorstep in no time reporting a kill. My friend Tony and I immediately went out to a *dak* (Urdu for shooting lodge) bungalow nearby and tossed for first go up into the *machan*. He won, and went out before dark to get as comfortable as possible while he could see. I went to bed. At about first light the shikari came running in, saying that the tiger had come, the sahib had shot it but it was not dead and had got away. This was the worst possible scenario as walking up a wounded tiger is recognised as being a very dangerous game. I went straight to the scene armed with my twelve-bore shotgun loaded with buckshot, and found Tony very stiff and tired still up the tree. He said that the tiger was badly wounded and we must walk it up, which we proceeded to do. The pug marks were very clear and there was quite a lot of blood about, particularly where the tiger had lain down and rested, but we didn't catch up with him despite following the trail all day. We heard afterwards that the tiger was found dead some distance further on. That was my first and last experience of shooting tiger.

On another occasion I managed to shoot a black buck which had a fine head with long straight spiral horns. I had it mounted by a taxidermist but lost it during the War when all my kit was lost in the Bombay warehouse fire.

The Munich crisis occurred whilst we were at Pachmarhi (September 1938) and Chamberlain returned with the famous piece of paper declaring 'peace in our time'. I think like most people we were relieved.

My father was then GSO 1 Peshawar District on the North-West Frontier and I took Christmas leave to spend with him and my stepmother. I travelled on the Frontier Mail, one of the famous Indian expresses, which took forty-eight hours from Bombay to Peshawar via Delhi and was very comfortable but slow and boring. Christmas at Peshawar was delightful — the climate superb with a hot sun but snow on the mountains all around. My father had a lovely hunter named Grey Dawn which I was allowed to take out for a day with the Peshawar Vale. I also drove up to see the famous Khyber Pass, the main route from India into Afghanistan. Otherwise it was parties and then time to board the Frontier Mail for the long haul south. I was not to see my parents again for nearly six years.

Early in 1939 the regiment organised a run-a-mile, walk-a-mile, ride-a-mile competition round Poona Racecourse for those officers who wanted to have a go. I was still quite quick on my feet and was well backed to win though much depended on the horse that you drew for lap three. After the run and walk I was well ahead but my pony was not exactly a racehorse and Charles Howard, a fine horseman and mounted on a fit hunter, overtook me on the final straight. It was a fun event. Little did I know that eight years later I was to take over from him in Deolali just up the road as acting CO.

Poona Racecourse was also used for ceremonial parades and I remember on the King's Official Birthday, which must have been in June (the date of this imperial function was and still is no respecter of the Monarch's actual birthday), our entire brigade was drawn up in front of HE The Governor of Bombay, Sir Roger Lumley, who was mounted and accompanied by several of the top brass.

For two months' summer leave in 1939 I arranged to go to Australia by P & O. My stepmother had relations living in Adelaide and I was invited to stay with them. I booked on the *Strathmore*, a most comfortable modern liner; a first class single berth cabin close to the swimming pool cost £50 return Bombay — Adelaide. My pay was then about £25 per month and I was allowed to draw two months' advance of pay before leaving, which just paid for my ticket.

I boarded the *Strathmore* early in May. She was full of German Jews escaping from Nazi Germany. Apparently those who could afford it were allowed to spend as much as they liked on the passage but not transfer funds overseas. All the state cabins were, not surprisingly therefore, full. There were some Myers on board who were to start the Myers Emporium in Melbourne and elsewhere.

After an extremely comfortable voyage spent in the swimming pool, eating sumptuous meals or in bed, I was met in Adelaide by Brigadier A.M. Martyn, his wife Stella and two daughters Joan and Merris aged twenty and eighteen. Martyn had fought at Gallipoli and was in charge of all army units in South Australia. They had a nice house and were kindness itself. After a week I travelled to Melbourne by train and stayed in a service club. There I met somebody who, when I said that my next stop was Sydney, gave me the keys of his flat there and said, 'be my guest'. Such was Australian hospitality to a rather gauche young Pom. In Sydney I met the man who claimed to have opened the famous Harbour Bridge in 1932. I have dined out on this story many times because surprisingly few young Aussies know what happened. Apparently the Prime Minister of New South Wales, a Mr Lang, and his Government were very unpopular but let it be known that the bridge would be opened in their name. De Groot, a prominent member of the New Guard and masquerading as a member of the mounted bodyguard for the Prime Minister, rode forward just as Lang was about to cut the ribbon with a pair of scissors and, drawing his sword, slashed the ribbon and shouted 'I open this bridge in the name of the people of New South Wales'. He was immediately pulled off his horse, arrested, declared to be insane and locked up. However, such was the outcry to release him that the Government had to give in, and De Groot became a national hero overnight. He showed me an album full of press cuttings from all over the world, together with presents from admirers which included a gold cigarette case.

After Sydney I decided to sample Australian skiing. It was late June and there was said to be good snow on Mount Kosciusko on the New South Wales-Victoria border at 6,000 feet. I took a bus and eventually arrived at the snow-line to find that I was virtually the first winter sports enthusiast of the season. I stayed in a wooden hut called Betts Camp, hired some hickory skis and made my own tracks. There were no lifts in those days. Having had three 'seasons' in Switzerland when I was at Oxford (each one lasting only one week) I knew the rudiments of the sport but it was long before the days of safety bindings and my skis were at least two metres long. Fortunately I did not break anything as casualty evacuation might have been slow.

After a week I hurried back to Adelaide to say goodbye to the Martyns and catch the *Strathmore* on her return voyage to Europe. But I literally missed the boat — she had sailed. So I summoned up my last pennies and flew in a Dakota to Perth (it took eight hours) and caught the good ship *Strathmore* at Fremantle. My first class cabin, complete with a cabin trunk which I had been allowed to leave on board, was awaiting me (all included in the £50!).

PART II, World War II

CHAPTER 3

With Wavell's Thirty Thousand — 'Never has so much been surrendered by so many to so few'

LOOKING back on that summer and my return to Bombay in July after leave in Australia, I don't remember sensing that war was imminent. Life in Poona seemed not to have changed, yet within a week or two I was sent for by the acting Commanding Officer and told that I was to accompany Force Heron to the Canal Zone as Field Cashier. We would sail by troopship in early August.

I had never heard of the appointment of Field Cashier and was told that it would involve paying the entire Force on a weekly basis and keeping a pretty detailed Imprest* account. I would draw funds from an Egyptian bank and an Indian pay clerk would accompany me to see that I did not make too many mistakes.

Force Heron consisted of the 11th Indian Infantry Brigade of three battalions (the Cameron Highlanders from Ahmadnagar and two Indian battalions). We were to be the first reinforcements to sail from India to the Middle East. It all sounded rather exciting at the time — regimental soldiering in Poona was not, and even though the job of Field Cashier was a very odd one for a young infantry subaltern aged twenty-three, I went quite happily. I think the Somersets had been detailed to provide an officer to fill this post and I was the most readily available.

I remember little of the voyage to Suez except that we passed at sea another troopship taking my parents and John Harding out to India. My father was returning to his job as General Staff Officer Grade 1 Peshawar District, and John Harding was on his way to Poona to take command of the battalion that I had just left. Of course my parents had no idea that I was sailing the other way, and I had no means of letting them know. I had scarcely heard of John Harding and little did I think that within barely a year I was to serve under him in the Western Desert, the war theatre where he was to make his name.

On arrival at Suez, Force Heron moved into camp at Fayid on the Great Bitter Lake through which the Suez Canal passes, and I set about my duties. My clerk did virtually all the detailed accounting; I merely had to draw the cash, pay out unit representatives, sign the books and

*An account dealing only with public funds.

15

accept financial responsibility. However, within a week or two I decided that the job was not for me and was lucky enough, on a visit to the fleshpots of Cairo, to be offered a job on the cypher staff at HQ BTE (British Troops Egypt) provided that I could relinquish my duties as Field Cashier. This proved easier than I expected, and by the end of August I had left Force Heron and was staying in Bodmin House, a *pension* in Gezira, Cairo, where I learnt the mysteries of cypher work. It was there on September 3rd that I heard Neville Chamberlain telling the nation on the radio that we were at war with Germany. I found myself one of a small team of young officers hastily recruited to deal with the flood of traffic between Whitehall and the newly-formed Middle East Command under General Wavell at the outbreak of war. Our work was all highly confidential and 'most immediate priority'. We worked shifts and I was several times called out in the middle of the night to go to the office, open the safe, get out all the necessary books and decipher a telegram which would begin 'Personal for General Wavell from the Prime Minister'. I would then have to decide whether the contents required me to contact a senior member of the C-in-C's staff, which might mean ringing him at his flat, discussing the telegram in guarded language, and perhaps sending a car to fetch him. It was heady stuff and a far cry from being Field Cashier of Force Heron!

I'm not sure how long I did this job but it wasn't for more than a month or two, because trained cypher staff arrived, I believe from the United Kingdom, and I was then fortunate to be appointed an Intelligence officer on the staff of the GOC-in-C HQ BTE General Sir Maitland Wilson. My immediate boss was Major Bob Priest* and he in turn was responsible to Major Victor Paley.** My duties were to learn all about the Italian Army, and in particular that part of it serving in Libya. Italy had not of course entered the war at this stage (October-November 1939), Mussolini having decided to wait and see how Hitler fared against the combined might of France and the British Empire. However, there was a huge Italian presence in Libya under Marshal Graziani: two armies, the Fifth in Tripolitania and the Tenth in Cyrenaica facing us in Egypt, totalling over a quarter of a million men, 1,400 guns and 450 tanks. It outnumbered us by eight to one.

So I had quite an absorbing job. Cairo was great fun during the 'phoney' war; there were no restrictions like blackouts and coupons, and though most of us had to work hard, there was time for relaxation, such as tennis and swimming at the Gezira club and dinghy sailing on the Nile. I bought an old Riley tourer for about £20 and later changed

---

*Later Brigadier R. T. Priest, CBE
**Later Major General Sir Victor Paley, KBE, CB, DSO

it for a fairly new Ford Ten which cost £50. I moved into a flat with four other officers: Squadron Leader Paddy Dunn,* RAF; Major Alan Goodwin, Suffolk Regiment; Captain Sholto Douglas, Royal Scots and Major Claude Dredge, Dogra Regiment, Indian Army. Over the Christmas break Claude and I together with Henry Huth,** 8th Hussars, and John Prentice, Poona Horse, drove in two cars across the Sinai Peninsula to Aqaba. On the way we shot two bustard, members of the turkey family which were eminently suitable Christmas fare. Aqaba was then a tiny village of mud huts and date palms at the head of the Gulf of that name. Eilat, Mecca for winter tourists, did not of course exist, nor for that matter did Israel! I think we were the only visitors that first Christmas of the War and it was a very peaceful place.

The tempo of life gradually increased during the early months of 1940. It was fairly clear that Mussolini was going to order his huge army in Libya to invade Egypt and seize the Delta. It was merely a question of timing. The British 7th Armoured Division (the famous Desert Rats) were patrolling the frontier from Sollum to the Siwa Oasis some 150 miles to the south, and we in the Intelligence branch in Cairo were building up as accurate a picture as possible of our potential enemy. A Maltese officer who spoke fluent Italian joined our team, as did Brian Emery, already a well-known authority on ancient Egypt. Brian was our draughtsman-cum-mapping expert. At Easter he and his wife Molly took me in their Buick up the Nile to Luxor where Victor and Susan Paley joined us. Little did I realise at the time that we were privileged to have in Brian a guide who was to become one of the foremost Egyptologists of his time. We were to meet again in Cairo in 1970. After a day or two in Luxor we drove through the barren hills to the Red Sea and back up the coast to Suez. I remember we met some Italians. I think they were consular officials (probably spying), but they were very friendly and it was difficult to believe that they would be our enemies in a month or two.

And so the sands were running out; Hitler launched his blitzkrieg in north-west Europe on May 10th, and Churchill became Prime Minister on the same day. Exactly a month later, on June 10th, Mussolini declared war on Britain, having seen the fall of France and the evacuation of Dunkirk.

Within days the Western Desert Force (WDF) was established in the sand dunes at Maaten Bagush about twenty miles east of Mersa Matruh and 150 west of Alexandria. My boss Bob Priest was appointed GSO 2 Intelligence to the Force, and our small section of Intelligence officers

*Later Air Marshal Sir Patrick Dunn, KBE, CB, DFC
**Later Lieutenant Colonel H. Huth, DSO, MC

moved out there at once. Victor Paley stayed in Cairo on 'Jumbo' Wilson's staff as did Brian Emery. I found myself promoted to acting Captain and GSO 3, which was exciting at the age of just twenty-four.

Our new GOC was Lieutenant General Dick O'Connor, who had commanded a brigade on the North-West Frontier in India and who knew my father. His below-average height and diffident manner belied a born leader who quickly became well known and loved throughout the desert army. I was privileged to serve under him and in fairly close contact throughout what was to be the first successful land battle of the war in which British troops were involved.

Throughout those hot summer months of 1940 I don't remember being unduly concerned about what was happening at home; the miracle of Dunkirk, the London blitz, the Battle of Britain and the very real threat of invasion were noted, no more, unless of course you had family involvement, which I had not. It was as though we were fighting in another world. I will not attempt to describe the desert battles which took place during the next eight months between our forces — 'Wavell's 30,000' as they came to be called (the equivalent of two divisions), and Graziani's huge army which so outnumbered us.

We worked virtually non-stop in our dugout among the sand dunes, plotting every Italian movement and building up a pretty complete picture of the enemy who faced us. Relaxation was a swim in the clear waters of the Mediterranean most evenings. Fresh water was always scarce so the sea was not only refreshing but kept us clean.

On September 13th the Italians began their long-awaited advance into Egypt. Our covering troops withdrew as planned and Graziani halted just east of Sidi Barrani sixty miles across the frontier, where he was to remain for the next three months. Rome Radio announced that 'the shops are open in Sidi Barrani and the trams are running again'. Our casualties had been very light but the Italians lost 3,000 men and their lines of communication were considerably extended.

About this time Colonel (as he then was) John Harding began regularly to visit us in the Desert. He had handed over command of the 1st Somersets in India after barely a year, been promoted and posted to the Middle East. To begin with he acted as a senior liaison officer between Cairo and General O'Connor. He was also able to give me first-hand news of my father. After a month or so of these visits General O'Connor was so struck by Harding's obvious ability that he arranged for him to become his Colonel GS (or Chief of Staff). It was this key appointment which started Harding on a career which was to bring him a peerage and the rank of Field Marshal.

Meanwhile we in the Intelligence branch were very busy providing every scrap of information that we could about Italian strengths, tanks, guns, supplies, morale and dispositions. Our main sources were prisoners (who of course were officially only allowed to give their name, rank and number), air reconnaissance including photography, the Bedouin of the desert, agents and other secret sources. Information flowed in but it all had to be checked for reliability and usefulness.

We knew that General Wavell was planning a major winter offensive to drive the Italians out of Egypt and secure the Canal Zone base but details were available only to the most senior commanders.

A new British tank suddenly appeared in the desert, having been shipped out from the United Kingdom round the Cape. It was officially called an 'I' or Infantry tank, was heavily armoured (front armour was two inch) and travelled at little more than walking pace. We knew them as 'Matildas'. Because they were rare and much heavier than any possessed by the Italians, elaborate precautions were taken to conceal them. Each tank, and we only had about fifty, was hidden in a camouflaged hide until the last possible moment.

At the end of November a major training exercise was launched and we all left our dug-outs and practised working from vehicles. A week or so later, a second 'training exercise' was held which was to prove the real thing. We took most of our small personal possessions with us, which was just as well as we never returned. We were about to advance 400 miles in two months and capture half of Libya, quite apart from recovering the small strip of Egypt which the Italians had occupied since September and didn't seem to know what to do with.

It was a campaign that not even General Wavell in his wildest dreams could have anticipated would be so successful. In desert warfare surprise is not easy to achieve, particularly if the enemy's air force is active. But by moving forward on two consecutive nights and keeping our heads down by day, and by pretending that the second training exercise was just that, General O'Connor achieved it.

Another feature of desert warfare is that it is unusual for either side to have a continuous front line; it follows that wide enveloping movements can often be carried out, and that it may well be possible to attack the enemy from his rear. This is indeed exactly what happened on December 9th when the Italian forward troops in their perimeter camps suddenly found themselves attacked by heavy British tanks from the west, which continued to advance even when field artillery was fired at them point blank. Rommel was to give us a taste of this unpleasant medicine eighteen months later in the desperate battles behind the Gazala line. Surprise was complete; some officers were taken prisoner in their pyjamas! Several senior officers had tin trunks full of full dress uniforms including white cloaks which they intended to wear on arrival in Alexandria. The incredible uniforms, foodstuffs, wines, brandy and other luxuries found in the front line perimeter camps are graphically described in Barrie Pitt's book *Crucible of War I*.* I don't remember seeing any of these myself; we were far too busy evaluating the mass of documents and maps which also fell into our hands.

In the three days from December 9th-11th the Western Desert Force, consisting of two divisions, took 38,000 prisoners including 4 generals, 273 light or medium tanks and over 1,000 vehicles. Four Italian divisions were written off and two more very roughly handled. We were in a state of high jubilation despite having to work day and night, and experiencing a severe water shortage; there was barely enough for our own troops let alone thousands of demoralised Italians. We captured vast quantities of Chianti which seemed to have been their staple diet — but no longer. Scarcely knowing what it was, our men drank it until they could hardly stand up.

Thus ended the first phase of this amazingly successful campaign. Once the Italians were back across the 'wire', as we called the Egypt-Libya frontier, General O'Connor moved his HQ into a huge underground cistern in the forward area. We had to climb down a ladder to gain entrance, and most of the planning for the next phase was done there.

Those not on duty at night slept under the stars. It can be cold in the desert in the winter and we were issued with sleeveless leather jerkins to wear over khaki drill. It was before the days of battledress. I can remember little about Christmas except that we all drank lots of Chianti and felt very pleased with ourselves.

On January 1st, 1941 HQ Western Desert Force became HQ XIII Corps and John Harding was promoted to BGS (Brigadier General Staff). The 4th Indian Division was withdrawn from the desert to go to Eritrea and was replaced by the 6th Australian. They were to prove a very tough fighting formation.

Bardia was General O'Connor's next objective, a small port just across the frontier into Libya, with strong defences on its landward side consisting of a continuous chain of posts protected by wire, anti-tank ditches and mines. 7 Armoured Division had already cut the only escape route (to Tobruk). Surprise was not possible. It was obvious that we were going to attack; all that we could conceal was exactly when and where. The Australians were to advance when all was ready and we concentrated on providing them with every possible scrap of information. Thanks to air photography and the mass of prisoners already captured, we were able to build up a fairly accurate picture of the defences, though our estimate of the garrison strength at 23,000 was way out. The actual figure was to be 41,000 of whom we took 38,000 prisoner when the Australians attacked on January 3rd. Only twenty-five Matildas were runners by now, but it was enough and they played a key role.

*pp. 108-9, Jonathan Cape, 1980.

Our next target was Tobruk sixty miles to the west, a more important prize than Bardia because of its not inconsiderable harbour. HQ XIII Corps moved to Gambut about halfway between Bardia and Tobruk. The attack by 6th Australian Division on January 21st supported by the remaining eighteen Matildas followed much the same pattern as at Bardia; a break-in by infantry under cover of darkness to bridge the anti-tank ditch and let the tanks in followed by a general fanning-out within the perimeter. By the evening of January 22nd it was all over with the surrender of a further 27,000 prisoners. Our casualties since the campaign began on December 9th were about 1,000.

Fortunately two water distilleries and some artesian wells which between them could produce nearly 40,000 gallons of water per day were found undamaged and greatly relieved the water shortage.

Odd incidents stick in my memory. What does one do with quite a large group of Italian generals at Corps HQ? Bob Priest asked General O'Connor whether he would see them; the answer was no. I was sad in a way though of course the Corps Commander was extremely busy and probably very tired. In the end we got them away somehow to Cairo.

There were no set-piece attacks after Tobruk. XIII Corps' orders from General Wavell were to occupy Benghazi as soon as possible and destroy the remaining Italian forces in Cyrenaica.

West of Tobruk the coastline bulges northwards. This was the main area of Italian settlement, the Jebel Akhdar (green mountains) which rose to over 2,000 feet and were well cultivated. General O'Connor directed 7th Armoured Division first to secure Mechili (south of the bulge) and then to cut the main coast road south of Benghazi; the Australians were to take Derna on the coast, and then advance on Benghazi via Barce. Corps HQ moved from Gambut to Bomba west of Tobruk, and then to Mechili. In a brilliant forced march over unreconnoitred ground, forward elements of 7th Armoured cut the only road at Beda Fomm on February 5th and faced thousands of Italian troops trying to escape southwards. Though there was some desperate fighting during the following forty-eight hours victory was complete by February 7th. The final tally in two months of operations was 130,000 prisoners, 400 tanks and over 1,000 guns. Our total casualties were 500 killed and 1,373 wounded.

Two quotes sum up the campaign: Anthony Eden, then Foreign Secretary, telegraphed to Churchill 'If I may debase a golden phrase; never has so much been surrendered by so many to so few',* and in his excellent book *Against Great Odds* Brigadier Barclay wrote 'One can search the annals of war from the earliest times and not find a greater

*The Second World War, Vol III, p. 13

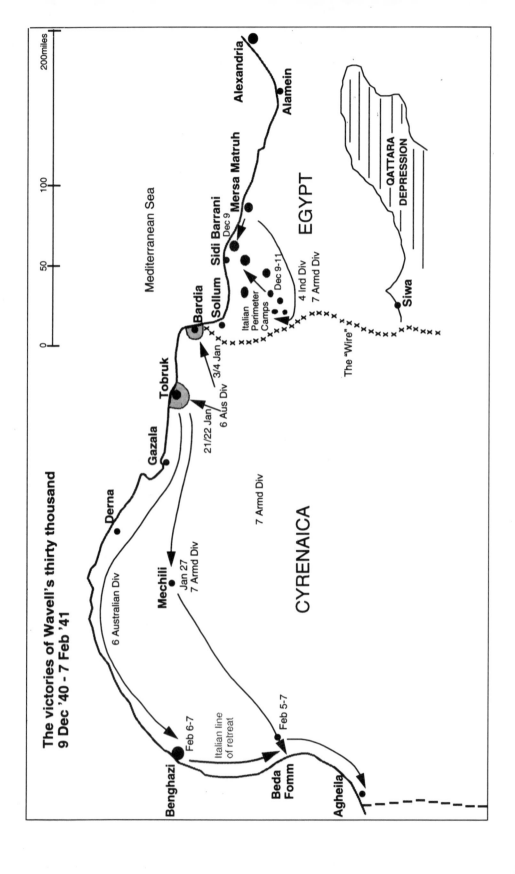

The victories of Wavell's thirty thousand
9 Dec '40 - 7 Feb '41

200miles   100   50   0

Mediterranean Sea

Alexandria
Alamein
Mersa Matruh
Sidi Barrani   Dec 9
Sollum
Bardia
Tobruk
Gazala
Derna
Benghazi

EGYPT
QATTARA DEPRESSION
Siwa

Italian Perimeter Camps
Dec 9-11
4 Ind Div
7 Armd Div
The "Wire"

3/4 Jan
21/22 Jan
6 Aus Div

6 Australian Div

Mechili
Jan 27
7 Armd Div

7 Armd Div

CYRENAICA

Feb 6-7

Italian line of retreat

Feb 5-7

Beda Fomm

Agheila

victory than this.'* How lucky I was to have participated so early in the War in such historic events. At my humble level, the strategic aspects of the campaign went unnoticed, but to put these jottings in perspective we need to remember that General Wavell was under tremendous pressure initially to send troops to Greece after Italy delivered an ultimatum in October 1940, and later to counter the much more serious German threat. Equally, throughout the campaign General O'Connor's plans were often liable to dislocation by the withdrawal of troops or equipment for Greece, or by the threat to do so. Once Benghazi had fallen, the bulk of the RAF was withdrawn and 7th Armoured Division was relieved by part of the inexperienced 2nd Armoured Division recently arrived from the United Kingdom, and 6th Australian Division (destined for Greece) was replaced by the less well-trained 9th Australian Division.**

Historians and others have argued endlessly during the last fifty years over whether the British Government was right to embark on what were to be disastrous campaigns in Greece and later Crete, at the expense of calling a halt at Benghazi. On February 7th, though 7 Armoured was stretched to the limit (and most of its equipment worn out), it could and would have gone on, and indeed there was little serious opposition before Tripoli. But there were advance parties of Germans already in North Africa and Rommel himself arrived in Tripoli on February 12th, five days after Beda Fomm. Perhaps the fates were on our side even though it was to be two years before Eighth Army finally entered Tripoli.

Corps HQ moved to Barce, which I remember as a pleasant little Italian settlement up the escarpment from Benghazi. There was some welcome greenery around and it was fresh and cool. The pressure was off and we could relax. I cannot have been at Barce more than a few weeks but it was long enough to 'acquire' an Italian motorbike on which I roared about the dirt roads in the Jebel Akhdar. It was a powerful beast. I had never ridden one before — and never have since.

General O'Connor (by now Sir Richard), the hero of the campaign, left us for a well-earned rest and was relieved by Lieutenant General Philip Neame, VC who had been commanding in Palestine. I agitated to be posted nearer the 'sharp end' so quickly returned to the Canal Zone to join 1st Battalion, the Durham Light Infantry. This was in March, by which time the German build-up in Tripoli was proceeding apace. Rommel attacked and drove back the forward elements of 2nd Armoured Division at Agheila on March 31st.

*Against Great Odds, Brig C. N. Barclay, p. 70
**9th Australian Division subsequently proved to be one of the best (if not the best) fighting division in Eighth Army.

CHAPTER 4

At the Sharp End

1 DLI was then part of 22 Guards Brigade which in turn was part of the 6th Division, earmarked for operations in the Dodecanese to forestall the German Air Force. However, within days of my joining 1 DLI the situation in Cyrenaica had deteriorated to such an extent that we were ordered to return to the Western Desert and hold a defensive position on the frontier. In barely a fortnight Rommel had overrun most of Cyrenaica, surrounding Tobruk which was occupied just in time by 9th Australian Division, and was now almost in Bardia. It was an unbelievable reversal of fortunes. With hindsight, General Wavell, assuming the desert flank of Egypt would be secure, was too greatly preoccupied with sending troops to Greece; nobody realised that we were facing probably the most brilliant German field commander of the War, and at a time when practically all our battle-experienced troops had been replaced by men whose knees were barely brown. Worse still, General O'Connor had been sent back to Cyrenaica to advise his successor, General Neame, and in the general confusion of withdrawal both were captured driving together in a staff car on April 6th, a week after Rommel's first thrust. Wavell later proposed that O'Connor should be exchanged for any six Italian generals but Whitehall turned the idea down.

Harding nearly suffered the same fate. Fortunately he took a different route back, drove straight into Tobruk, and played a leading role in organising the defence of a town that we had captured only two months earlier.

I found myself 2nd in Command of A Company in 1 DLI. My company commander Major P.H.M. May, known as 'Crackers', was a natural leader, fearless and very popular with the Geordies. I was lucky. Our first action on arrival at the Libyan frontier was quite dramatic, and I quote from the regimental history:

'A' Company had been sent off on that afternoon with orders to hold Bardia with one troop of light tanks, one section of carriers and an anti-tank gun which was actually pulled off the column before it even reached the town. 'Crackers' May had protested that when Bardia was captured the latter had over 30,000 men there — but in vain! Off the Company went

24

to do what it could to protect the two large pumping stations with good water which were Bardia's main claim to fame. During the early part of the night of the 11th firing grew nearer and louder and the sound of traffic by-passing the Italians' town increased. About 10 p.m. the telephone went dead. There was no wireless in those days; but not long afterwards a dispatch rider turned up with a message saying, 'Believe you are surrounded. Blow everything. Good luck'. Fortunately the Sappers who were there had the pumping stations and port prepared for demolition, and about two hours later, after a series of shattering explosions, the Company was able to pull out and drive post-haste in the bright moonlight back to Sollum.*

My recollection of this incident was quite simply that our job was to destroy the pumping stations and get out. I cannot believe that one rifle company could seriously have been expected to hold Bardia. If the regimental history is correct it shows only too clearly how the German threat was underestimated in those early days.

The battalion then occupied the top and bottom of Halfaya Pass (known as 'Hellfire'), one of the very few routes down the escarpment south of Sollum. A Company was dug in at the top of the pass and I remember hearing the clank-clank of tracked vehicles through the heat-haze and dust, but we were never actually attacked, only shelled. It was during this relative lull that I was detailed to take out a fighting patrol of about twenty men by night to ambush any movement on a well-used desert track and capture a prisoner. We reached our objective without difficulty, perhaps a mile or so forward of the so-called front line, and awaited developments. I had the only anti-tank weapon issued to rifle companies in those early days, a .5 Boys Rifle, one LMG and the rest of us were armed with rifles. After an hour or two I heard the noise of vehicles approaching from right to left. As they got nearer they sounded very like tracks, and as they came abreast of us I was still convinced that they were light tanks or half-tracks. Consequently I told the men to hold their fire as I thought that we could not take on any form of armour. Too late I realised in the half-light that they were motor-cycle combinations, a curious mode of transport favoured by the Germans in those days. So we returned empty-handed.

I felt that I had made a proper nonsense of my first chance of action and volunteered to go out again the next night determined to do better. This was agreed but never materialised as we were ordered to withdraw that day to avoid being cut off.

A week or two later the battalion was ordered forward again to take

*The D.L.I. at War, David Rissik, p.54.

part in a brigade operation. The battalion objective was Fort Capuzzo, a former frontier post now occupied by the Germans. The terrain was flat, open desert and we moved up by night in three-ton lorries. At dawn we deployed in desert formation, three companies up led by thirteen tanks with the CO, Eustace Arderne, and myself in his pick-up in the middle. He had ordered me to accompany him as I was supposed to know the desert, having been with XIII Corps during the attack on Bardia only three months earlier. It was rather like a fleet at sea. As we had no wireless, the CO waved different coloured flags to represent 'Advance' or 'Halt' or 'Attack' and to keep in touch with the tanks he actually drove up alongside the squadron leader's tank and shouted at him. Unhappily the fog of war descended. We saw some tanks on our objective, assumed them to be ours and motored forward in full view of what were German tanks. Fortunately they had made the same mistake and thought at first that we were their own troops withdrawing from Hellfire pass. But they reacted quickly and our three companies suffered the nightmare of being caught by tanks in open country in soft-skinned vehicles. Though the men tumbled out of their three-tonners like lightening and went straight into the attack, they inevitably suffered heavy casualties. We had no anti-tank guns, only the useless anti-tank rifle, and no communications except runner. As evening drew on, the rifle companies withdrew — what was left of them — and surprisingly the Germans withdrew too. We spent an unhappy and tense night grieving over our losses and preparing for a German counter-attack at dawn. Fortunately it never came and we were withdrawn to lick our wounds. The battalion lost 11 officers and 185 men in an action which is one of the regiment's battle honours. On our night move to the Sidi Barrani area I found myself at the wheel of a three-ton lorry full of very tired soldiers with a sergeant in the passenger seat to keep me awake. I can only assume that there was a shortage of fit drivers, otherwise why me? I felt a certain sense of achievement at the end of an exhausting night.

Our next task was a very different one. A Company was ordered to guard a remote airstrip about fifty miles south of Mersa Matruh where Wellington bombers refuelled on their way from the Canal Zone to attack shipping and other targets in the Benghazi area. It was very peaceful. The war seemed thousands of miles away except when the bombers glided in most evenings with their deadly cargoes, and took off again westwards an hour or so later with full tanks.

It was in this remote spot that we heard on June 21st on the radio that Hitler had launched Barbarossa, the attack on Russia. My feelings were mixed. I was glad that the pressure must ease on poor old Britain, still fighting alone, but anxious for Russia. Would they survive the blitzkrieg which had overrun Western Europe, and from which we had only been saved by the sea?

Our rest did not last long; orders suddenly came to return to the Canal Zone and on to Palestine to fight the Vichy French in Syria. The regimental history says that we moved in cattle trucks. I don't remember this. Perhaps the officers had third-class carriages. Palestine, 'the land flowing with milk and honey' was nice after the desert, but we only passed through. On July 1st, just ten days after that dramatic broadcast about Barbarossa which we had heard hundreds of miles away in the Western Desert, we took over from an Australian battalion in the village of Merdjayoun facing Vichy French to the north. Alongside us were French Foreign Legion and Senegalese, a proper mixed bag. Hardly had we arrived than the French withdrew and we saw no action except some shelling. I was suddenly detailed to take a large fighting patrol, at least thirty men, across the Litani river to our west and establish a forward base-cum-observation post overlooking the French rear. We had quite an exciting time wading across the river with all our kit and established what I thought was an excellent position to observe and stand our ground if necessary. Our only communication was helio lamp and my signaller managed to contact battalion HQ about two miles away. Our message was acknowledged but followed almost immediately by another saying that this particular little war was over, all forward troops were to stand fast for forty-eight hours and we were to rejoin the battalion at once. So that ended my second 'fighting' patrol.

The battalion then moved up to the foothills astride the Beirut-Damascus road and was ordered to build a camp. Relaxation included climbing Mount Hermon, 9,000 feet high, which thirty-eight of us, led by the CO, achieved on July 23rd. Finally we moved north once more and occupied a former French barracks in Aleppo. It almost seemed like peacetime soldiering, but not for long.

In September I was suddenly told that I was to return to the Western Desert and become GSO 2 Intelligence XIII Corps. Bob Priest had been promoted and was with the recently-formed Eighth Army HQ, and I was to take his place. This meant that I would be a major after barely a year. Quick promotion like this is common in war; it is important to be alive, to have some experience and be in the right place at the right time. And so after only six months with the DLI it was back to the staff.

CHAPTER 5

Forwards and Backwards in the Desert War

THE summer of 1941 had been disastrous in the Middle East for Britain and her Allies. It had been necessary to evacuate Greece in April; it was a miracle that over 50,000 British, Australian and New Zealand troops were taken off but our losses were still over 11,000. Then came Crete in May. 16,500 men were evacuated to Egypt, casualties totalled 13,000 and over 5,000 had to be left behind. The Royal Navy lost three cruisers and six destroyers, together with another nine damaged; several capital ships were damaged and had to leave Alexandria for repair elsewhere.

I remember that before the DLI left for Syria a large number of officers was assembled at Mersa Matruh to hear General Freyberg tell of the Crete affair where he had been in command. A VC and DSO from the first war, he was a born leader and widely respected by all, particularly his beloved Kiwis. He told us of the very heavy losses suffered by the Germans, perhaps 15,000 in all, together with 170 troop-carrying aircraft lost or damaged. In retrospect perhaps the most significant fact of all was that throughout the remainder of the War the Germans never again used airborne forces in any strength. But General Freyberg's overall message was: never under-estimate the fighting qualities of the German, be he soldier, sailor or airman.

In the Western Desert, operation 'Battleaxe' in mid-June involving some 25,000 men had the aim of driving Rommel from the frontier area and relieving Tobruk. It failed and stalemate set in. At this juncture Churchill decided to change the high command and appointed General Sir Claude Auchinleck C-in-C India to relieve Wavell. We were sad about this though the reasoning was understandable; Wavell had carried enormous responsibility for an ever-increasing theatre of operations since the beginning of the War. Though successful in Abyssinia, Iraq, Syria and in the first winter campaign in the Desert, things had not gone well since Rommel's appearance, and there had been the unsuccessful campaigns in Greece and Crete. Wavell was popular and held in very high esteem by us all, but he never really hit it off with Churchill. Bernard Fergusson in his superb little book, *Portrait of a Soldier*, described him 'as an example of integrity and of the soldierly virtues which is unlikely ever to be surpassed', and as 'the greatest figure in the Army . . . I believe he is a potential Marlborough, and that if the chance ever comes his way he will be one of the great commanders of history.'* The chance did come his way and he was undoubtedly one of the great commanders of the War, but he was unlucky whereas Montgomery, the other famous man under whom I was privileged to serve, was almost always lucky. But I am digressing.

Auchinleck was under heavy pressure from Churchill to launch another offensive in the Western Desert and to relieve Tobruk whose garrison had now been surrounded (except from the sea) for five months. At great risk a convoy carrying over 300 tanks had been sent through the Mediterranean instead of round the Cape, thereby saving forty days. However Auchinleck was adamant that he would not be ready until November, and it was on the 18th that Operation 'Crusader' was finally launched, our second major winter campaign. O'Connor had attacked from nearly the same base line on December 9th, 1940.

By this time I had been back in the desert over two months, building up a new team of Intelligence officers and assessing enemy strengths, both German and Italian, in the very changed situation that faced us. David Hunt was G3, the post that I had held the previous winter. He was twenty-eight, a double first from Wadham College Oxford and Fellow of Magdalen, who had been through the Greek campaign. There were four Intelligence officers (IOs); Alban Coventry who had been with us the previous winter, Derek Cotton, Mark Allen (another Oxford graduate) and Donald Prater. All spoke German and/or Italian. I had a high-powered team. David and Mark both became ambassadors in later life, and of course David became better-known as a winner of the BBC television programme *Mastermind* and later *Supermind* (winner of the first ten *Masterminds*). He is kind enough to refer to me in his own account of his wartime career, *A Don at War*: 'The G2 was a regular officer Major Freddie De Butts. If I was pleased with my new appointment I was even more pleased with my new chief; a man of outstanding common sense, hard working and quick to grasp a point, he was an excellent example of the advantage which accrued to Intelligence in the Middle East in general from the fact that the bulk of those engaged in it were people with active experience of proper soldiering.'**

The newly-named Eighth Army consisted of two corps: XIII which was mainly infantry, XXX Corps which was mainly armoured, and the

*pp. 12, 47.
**A Don at War, David Hunt, p. 68. William Kimber, 1966

70th Infantry Division in beleaguered Tobruk; perhaps 60,000 men in all commanded by Lieutenant General Alan Cunningham, brother of Andrew Cunningham, the C-in-C Mediterranean and one of the most distinguished sailors of the war. In XIII Corps our commander was Lieutenant General Godwin-Austen, a shrewd and energetic man who refused to be rattled and possessed a ready wit. Both generals' war experience was limited to fighting the Italians. Harding was still BGS XIII Corps and was to play a key role in the battle that followed.

Opposing us were Panzergruppe Afrika consisting of the Deutsche Afrika Korps (DAK) of two panzer divisions under General Cruewell, and a motorised division, all under Rommel, and two Italian Corps; the XXI conducting the siege of Tobruk and the XX which included an armoured division. Overall command was vested in an Italian, General Bastico.

Tank strengths, always a critical factor in the desert war, were about 750 British and 550 German and Italian. However, these figures are misleading since we were soon to discover that the German armour was superior to ours in almost every aspect: mechanical reliability, armour and gunnery, quite apart from the skill and dash with which it was used. We did have considerable superiority in the air.

I shall not attempt to describe the to-ings and fro-ings of operation Crusader. They are all in the history books. The British aim was to clear the frontier zone, relieve Tobruk and destroy Rommel's army. XXX Corps was to take on the German armour and XIII Corps, having recaptured the frontier forts, was to advance towards Tobruk and link up with the garrison who would break out to meet them.

During the first five days extremely fierce tank battles raged to the south-east of Tobruk resulting in heavy losses on both sides, but the advantage lay with Rommel who then staged his famous raid on the frontier — 'the dash to the wire' as it came to be called — with his remaining tanks causing considerable havoc and alarm in our rear. Meanwhile XIII Corps, led by the New Zealand division under its redoubtable commander General Freyberg, was advancing slowly but steadily towards Tobruk. Our heavy tank losses in those first few days, coupled with the alarm caused by Rommel's raid, caused the Army Commander General Cunningham to advise the C-in-C General Auchinleck that we should withdraw and regroup. Auchinleck decided immediately to replace Cunningham and put his Chief of Staff Neil Ritchie* in command. It was a bold and extremely critical decision to have to make in the heat of battle. Churchill and lesser mortals have

---

*Then only a major-general.

since argued that he should have taken over personal command himself. I rather agree.

As a result of Rommel's raid (from which he was forced to withdraw) the battlefield between Tobruk and the frontier was strewn with tanks and vehicles from both armies moving in every direction. XXX Corps HQ was right in the track of Rommel's advance and was dispersed to the four winds when the German column drove right through the middle of it. It was an extraordinary situation which could only occur in open desert where there was no front line. There can be very few occasions in war when a Corps HQ is advancing following a divisional axis, knowing that a strong enemy armoured force is *behind* it. This was exactly what happened to XIII Corps during those critical days in late November. We would pass columns of vehicles including tanks at night not knowing who they were, and not caring to investigate too closely. David Hunt who was with me at the time describes the scene well.* At least one officer from Corps HQ was captured simply driving out to see who was who. At one time I was sitting on our thunderbox when an unidentified column drove past, almost certainly German.

Fortunately we in XIII Corps had a commander, and particularly a BGS John Harding, who kept their heads 'when all about them were losing theirs', and in front of us were General Freyberg and his Kiwis. When it became apparent that there were some German columns behind us, Godwin-Austen made his much-quoted remark: 'Godwin plus his objective and minus his L of C** is much better than Godwin minus his objective and plus his L of C.' Later, when we had actually driven into Tobruk through the narrow corridor between extensive minefields, he signalled Army HQ 'Press may now be informed that Tobruk is as relieved as I am'.

By December 10th Rommel was in full retreat and the nine-month siege of Tobruk was over. One of the main aims of Crusader had been to relieve Tobruk and this had certainly been achieved. The equally important one of destroying Rommel's armour was only half-accomplished. Official figures for enemy tank losses are 300 but perhaps a third of these were Italian. Our losses were about the same.

To our delight XIII Corps was ordered to pursue Rommel as far as resources would allow whilst XXX Corps tidied up the frontier area. It was December 1940 all over again, and so was the sequel though we were oblivious to this threat at the time.

*A Don at War, pp. 83-4.
**Lines of Communication, i.e. supply line.

As we bumped over the desert chasing an elusive enemy, momentous events which shook the world were happening thousands of miles away in the Pacific. The Japanese attack on Pearl Harbour took place on December 7th just as the Tobruk garrison was breaking out, and the United States was catapulted into the war. Ninety-four
ships of the US Navy were in Pearl Harbour at the time. Seven out of eight battleships were sunk and 2,000 American seamen lost their lives in an air attack lasting two hours. The following day Japanese forces landed on the Malayan Peninsula and two days later the *Repulse* and *Prince of Wales* were sunk by air attack 100 miles north of Singapore.

We were so preoccupied with our war in the desert that these naval disasters went almost unnoticed. It had been the same eighteen months earlier at the time of Dunkirk. We had no newspapers, only the radio which was rather unreliable, and I think the really bad news was covered up as far as possible.

David and I celebrated Christmas bumping along in our office truck on a desert track well south of the bulge of Cyrenaica. Corps HQ was eventually set up in Antelat.

Churchill calls Volume IV of his *Second World War* 'The Hinge of Fate' and it deals entirely with the year 1942. 'In it,' he says 'we turn from almost uninterrupted disaster to almost unbroken success'. In Libya as we sat facing Rommel at the end of a 500 mile L of C, we were cheerful but in a rather delicately poised condition. Unlike the previous winter at Beda Fomm, we were unable to cut off the retreating German forces. Rommel withdrew to Agheila, and stood firm. With hindsight we clearly underestimated his ability to re-group and counter-attack if an opportunity presented itself. He had been considerably reinforced with new troops and equipment, particularly tanks, and his L of C to the port of Tripoli was shorter whereas ours to the Delta was much longer.

We did not expect an attack, and indeed were about to attack ourselves when on January 25th Rommel launched what was called a reconnaissance in force which quickly developed into a much deeper thrust. By the end of January XIII Corps had been forced to give up Benghazi and the bulge of Cyrenaica and dig in with some desperation on the Gazala line covering Tobruk. Looking back now, and remembering what happened the previous winter, it must seem incredible to students of military history that we were caught unawares for the second time at this same fatal corner against the same enemy. Reading Auchinleck's telegrams to Churchill* as late as January 15th,

Second World War, Vol IV, ch II.

six days before Rommel attacked, it seemed that everything was all right.

I played no part in the 'Second Benghazi Handicap' as it came to be called, as to my intense disappointment I suddenly went down with chicken-pox — of all things — caught I suspect from a Bedouin, and was evacuated by field ambulance some 200 miles back to Tobruk where a tented hospital had been set up near the sea. I have seldom felt more frustrated. News from the front was sketchy but it was clear that a major British withdrawal was taking place.

I eventually rejoined Corps HQ behind the Gazala line at Acroma, forty miles to the west of Tobruk. Here the front stabilised and there was to be a lull which lasted four months.

Godwin-Austen was relieved as Corps Commander by 'Strafer' Gott, the most respected and popular senior officer in the Eighth Army. He was then commanding 7th Armoured Division and had been in every action in the Desert War since it began in June 1940. His name was legend. He had received the nickname Strafer in 1915 from the German prayer *Gott strafe England*. In 1939 he was commanding the 1st Battalion of his regiment, the 60th Rifles (Kings Royal Rifle Corps) in Egypt. Within months he was promoted Brigadier to command the Support Group of 7th Armoured Division, and by the time Crusader was launched he was commanding 7th Armoured Division. Promotion from Lieutenant Colonel to Lieutenant General took only two years. I was privileged to serve directly under him until his tragic death in action in August, but more of this later.

During the four-month lull both sides were busy preparing for the next offensive and at the same time protecting themselves with minefields. 'The confrontation of the two armies, in bare desert, without the complicating factors of civilians or property, has a classical military quality not unlike the battles of ancient Greece and Rome.' This quote from Nigel Hamilton's biography of Monty* refers to the period immediately before the Battle of Alamein. It equally applies to the lull before Rommel's attack at Gazala five months earlier. In the Intelligence branch of Corps HQ our main concern was to predict Rommel's next move, and in particular his tank strength.

It was on a few days' leave in the fleshpots that I was invited by a naval friend to go on board HMS *Queen Elizabeth*, the C-in-C Mediterranean's flagship in Alexandria harbour. Secretly I was told that she was sitting on the bottom! On December 19th, 1941 six bedraggled-looking Italians had been found sitting on buoys in the harbour.**

*Vol I, p. 715

Refusing to say what their mission had been, Admiral Cunningham ordered them to be distributed among the larger warships under their armoured decks, and to be watched closely. Sure enough, within hours they became anxious about the time; lower decks were immediately cleared just before explosive charges went off under the QE and the *Valiant*, seriously damaging both battleships. When I went on board the QE four months later the C-in-C's flag was being flown and to the uninitiated she looked ready for sea. Brasses were highly polished and protocol strictly observed. I believe German Intelligence never discovered what really happened that December morning. We have to thank our Egyptian friends as Alexandria and Cairo were crawling with agents paid by the Axis. Both ships were eventually patched up and sailed to the United States via the Cape, where they were made fully operational once more.

Spring in the North African desert can be full of colour at times. I can remember the ground being covered with yellow flowers after rain. But I can also remember the sandstorms and the difficulty we had in marking maps and even writing when our office was a canvas lean-to against a three-ton lorry, and papers were permanently covered with fine sand. Whereas my particular form of relaxation may have been to read the latest thriller, David Hunt would be happily engrossed in Homer's *Odyssey* in the original Greek! On one occasion we must have shown a light after dark as a stick of bombs fell across the HQ and one man was seriously wounded. He was carried into the armoured command vehicle (ACV) where Harding, the BGS, was working. I recall that such was the latter's concentration that he scarcely looked up. He was a man of great charm and kindness, but he saw at once that the wounded man was being cared for, and then continued with his work.

He was also a perfectionist and preferred to do things himself which were really the duty of subordinates because he reckoned that he could do them better. An example was the evening 'sitrep' (situation report) which we were required to send to Army HQ. This would normally be drafted by a Grade II staff officer and cleared by the BGS before despatch. Harding preferred to write them himself and I can remember that there would often be two staff officers standing at his side with maps, pencils, rubbers, etc., only volunteering information when asked. Such was his charm of manner that they never appeared to resent having their work done for them.

**p.33. They had entered the harbour sitting astride two-men 'pigs' — seven metre-long torpedoes with controls for the crew. The leader of this very daring raid, Luigi Durand de la Penne, became an admiral after the war, died in 1992 aged 77, and was honoured by an obituary in *The Times*.

I remember that in the evenings we all used to tune in to Radio Belgrade to listen to that haunting song, *Lili Marlene*, which was beamed at the DAK (in German of course.) The words did not matter. It was the girl's voice and the tune which appealed to us just as much as it must have to Rommel's men. I believe it was voted the most popular song of World War II and is often played by bands and orchestras today.*

It was during the spring and summer of 1942 that we first really got to know some of the big names among war correspondents; men like Richard Dimbleby and Alan Moorehead were then making their mark. They tended to come to the Intelligence office to be briefed and it was a pleasure to discuss the latest developments with men whom one could trust to report only what would be harmless if it fell into enemy hands, but which would nevertheless be avidly read by people at home. It should be remembered that for eighteen months the Desert War was the only front on which British troops were engaged outside the UK. The Malayan disaster culminating in the fall of Singapore on February 15th seemed to come and go in a flash.

We in the Intelligence section were more than just staff officers. On one occasion Donald Prater and another officer drove a jeep round the southern flank of the German/Italian line and managed to get as far as an airfield south of Benghazi 200 miles behind the front, where they were able to pick up valuable information on aircraft strengths and enemy movements generally. Sadly, on their return they were blown up in our own minefield. Donald was badly wounded but lived to tell the tale.

It became apparent by early May that Rommel was about to attack. Auchinleck was also under intense pressure from Churchill to attack and take some of the heat off Malta, which was almost at starvation point. We anticipated that Rommel would carry out a wide encircling movement on the open desert flank (to the south), together with a holding attack on the main front, which was exactly what he did on May 26th. As in Crusader six months earlier, confusion reigned from the start. HQ 7th Armoured Division was overrun on the first day, and back at Corps HQ at El Adem, sixty miles from Rommel's start line, we were actually shelled by German artillery that first morning. The main British front stretching forty miles south from the coast at Gazala to Bir Hacheim was held by two infantry divisions and the Free French in strong defensive positions. Behind were the two armoured divisions and a series of defended 'boxes' covering the approaches to Tobruk.

*The full German text is reproduced at Appendix 1.

Despite the speed of his initial right hook and the confusion it caused, Rommel had not appreciated the depth of our reserves and his timetable to have captured Tobruk in four days had to be revised. Ever quick to improvise, he set about punching a hole in our long front to shorten his supply route before Ritchie, Eighth Army Commander, could mount the counter-attack that he was planning. This eventually came ten days after Rommel's initial attack, and failed. It was the turning point of the battle and withdrawal became inevitable. XIII Corps HQ moved into the Tobruk perimeter and I remember briefing the 2nd South African Division intelligence staff on enemy strengths as we saw them. I had the feeling that they were not terribly interested. A second siege was not on the agenda.

I remember an amusing anecdote from the desperate tank battles behind the Gazala line. In action we normally spoke 'in clear' on the R/T to save time, but being as guarded as possible, particularly when referring to units or formations. General Herbert Lumsden, a former 12th Lancer and now the flamboyant commander of the 1st Armoured Division, had won the Grand Military Gold Cup at Sandown shortly before the war. His division was always referred to as the 'Gold Cup Winner' in the hope that it would confuse the enemy. It certainly did, as we heard later from prisoners.

By June 14th another major British withdrawal was in full swing. XIII Corps was ordered back to the Egyptian frontier and we hurriedly pulled out of Tobruk. The move back was not unlike our advance over the same ground behind the New Zealanders only six months earlier; columns of vehicles moving at night throwing up enormous dust clouds in a following wind, engines overheating and trucks being turned into the wind to cool off whenever there was a halt. Brigadier Bobbie Erskine*, now BGS (John Harding had been promoted Major General and gone back to GHQ), would stand up in his car on the centre line waving a flag and directing operations.

On June 20th during a brief halt after we had crossed the Egyptian frontier, we intercepted a German message in plain language which read 'I agree to the unconditional surrender of the garrison'. David Hunt passed the message to me; it meant of course that Rommel agreed to our unconditional surrender of Tobruk. I had the unenviable task of taking it straight to Strafer Gott the Corps Commander, who had with him both General Norrie commanding XXX Corps and General Ritchie, the

*Later General Sir George Erskine, GCB, KBE, DSO

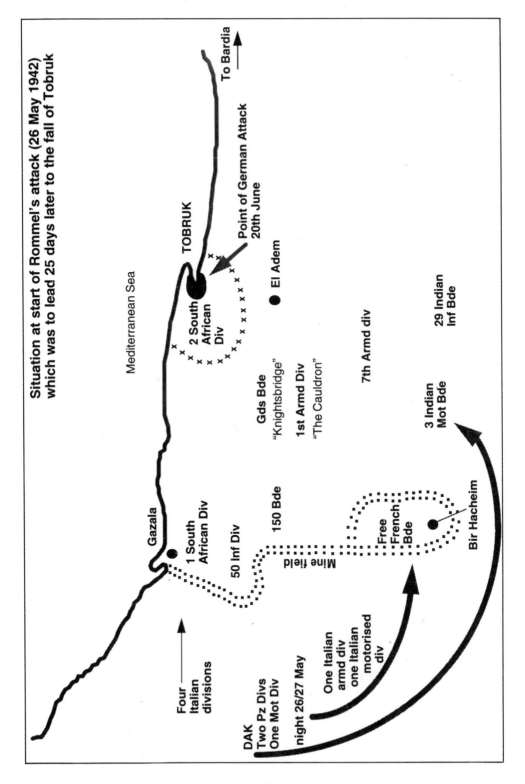

Situation at start of Rommel's attack (26 May 1942)
which was to lead 25 days later to the fall of Tobruk

To Bardia

Mediterranean Sea

TOBRUK

Point of German Attack
20th June

El Adem

2 South
African
Div

Gds Bde
"Knightsbridge"

1st Armd Div
"The Cauldron"

7th Armd div

29 Indian
Inf Bde

3 Indian
Mot Bde

Gazala

1 South
African Div

50 Inf Div

150 Bde

Mine field

Free
French
Bde

Bir Hacheim

Four
Italian
divisions

DAK
Two Pz Divs
One Mot Div

night 26/27 May

One Italian
armd div
one Italian
motorised
div

Army Commander. It was the first news they had of this disaster, and a moment that I shall never forget. Few young officers of those days could have equalled this experience as a bearer of bad news. The generals remained calm; however predictable, it must have been a bitter blow.

Historians have argued over the years why Tobruk survived a seven-month siege in 1941 but was lost in two days in 1942. Rommel attacked at the weakest point of the perimeter but it was held by two of the best brigades in the Eighth Army, 11 Indian Infantry Brigade (with whom I had travelled from India nearly three years before) and 201 Guards Brigade.

Rommel was on the crest of a wave; his men's morale was extremely high. As far as we were concerned the possibility of an attack on Tobruk had seemed inconceivable when our position at Gazala was first attacked three weeks earlier. One might say that the two sides were on a different wave length.

On June 25th Auchinleck relieved Ritchie of his command and took over himself, a move which Churchill had been urging him to make ever since Rommel first attacked in January. He rightly decided that Mersa Matruh, the only Egyptian town of any importance between the frontier and Alexandria, could not be held and that the whole army should withdraw to Alamein where the open desert flank was barred by the impassable Qattara Depression. The front would be thirty-five miles long and the L of C to Alexandria a mere fifty miles.

The Eighth Army was exhausted and demoralised when it reached Alamein. We had been defeated in battle twice by Rommel in five months and been forced to withdraw over 550 miles.

The leadership that Auchinleck displayed at this extremely critical time probably made this his finest hour, though within a month Churchill was to dismiss him. There are photographs of Auchinleck, a tall very good-looking man standing arms akimbo on that long straight switchback coast road, metaphorically saying to Rommel 'thou shalt not pass'. I am reminded of the famous picture of the King of the Belgians defying the Kaiser in 1914, though in his case defeat was inevitable. I remember we were told as we drove ever eastwards that a very strong, well-prepared position awaited us at Alamein. However when we finally arrived at the end of June the alleged defences were far from obvious. We dug in desperately; fresh troops were rushed forward from Palestine and the Delta, and the line held. As Arthur Bryant so aptly puts it in *The Turn of the Tide*: 'Auchinleck and his men — fighting in the British Army's spiritual home, the last ditch — held the Nile Delta'. Rommel's army was also exhausted and at the end of an exceptionally long L of C. His main base, Tripoli, was 1,000 miles to the west. Nevertheless we were looking over our shoulder. Where did we go from here? One day, Strafer Gott sent for me and said in the strictest confidence 'I hear that you have driven up the Nile to Upper Egypt. What is the road like and what about bridges?' He was referring of course to my visit to Luxor with the Emerys two and a half years earlier, and the possibility of abandoning Egypt and withdrawal to the Sudan.

Strafer, like 'the Auk' (as Auchinleck was called), was imperturbable though desperately tired. He was served by two exceptional young staff officers of the highest calibre; Paul Hobbs, Royal Horse Artillery, and Pat Hobart, Royal Tank Regiment. Paul had been one of my heroes at Wellington when I was a small boy; sadly, he was killed in Tunisia in 1943 in almost the last action of the North African campaign. Pat became a Major General after the war but was tragically killed with his wife in a car accident in 1986. Together they looked after Strafer, knowing how vital his leadership was at this critical time. I remember that he loved reading *Country Life* when there was a spare moment and somehow copies appeared from nowhere. Paul and Pat would be laughing and joking with the Corps Commander and anticipating his every need.

An enormous fillip to morale were Churchill's two visits to the desert in August. His first was on August 5th when in his boiler suit and topee he drove around with the Auk in order to see as many troops as possible, and in particular to meet Strafer Gott. In Volume IV, *The Hinge of Fate* Churchill describes how as they drove together in Gott's staff car he looked into his clear blue eyes and asked him: was he tired?* Yes, said Gott, he was tired and would greatly enjoy some leave but would of course accept any further responsibilities entrusted to him. On his return to Cairo that evening Churchill decided on major changes in the high command of which the two of most concern to us were Alexander to replace Auchinleck as C-in-C and Gott to command Eighth Army.

Two days later, Strafer took off in a large Bombay transport aircraft with some twenty other passengers to fly to Cairo for a few days' break, and to be told of his new command. That morning he had held a most important conference to decide how the battle should be fought if, as was expected, Rommel should make a final attempt to break through. German fighters had been around that day and they met the Bombay within ten minutes of take-off; 'a chance in a thousand' as Bobby Erskine put it in a subsequent letter to Mrs Gott. The aircraft was shot down and caught fire. There were only three survivors. Strafer

*Vol IV, p. 414.

was not one of them. It was a shattering blow to us all. Again I quote from Erskine's letter: 'Your grief will be so widely shared that I don't suppose there is a single officer or man out here who will not feel that he has lost a personal friend and a great and gallant leader'.* He was only forty-four, ten years younger than the man who was to succeed him.

Churchill made the immediate decision on the advice of the Chief of the Imperial General Staff, to send for Montgomery** and on August 12th flew to Moscow to confer with Stalin. By the 17th he was back in Cairo and on the 19th paid his second visit to the desert, this time with Monty as his host.

The incredible uplift in morale that took place throughout the Eighth Army when Monty arrived has been described many times by historians. I was there and can only say that it was absolutely true. Few of us knew anything about him, especially those like me who had been overseas since before the War. His amazing self-confidence and inexhaustible energy went before him on his rounds. Officers and men would be gathered together wherever it was reasonably safe and given Monty's famous pep talk: 'There will be no withdrawal from Alamein. We shall fight where we stand. I shall knock Rommel for six,' and so on. It may sound corny today but in 1942 we lapped it up. It was a tonic that we badly needed.

I do not wish to enter the ring and argue the relative qualities of the Auk and Monty. I served under both throughout the Desert War and admired them both, but I have no doubt whatever that Monty was in a different league. In his biography of Auchinleck, *The Lonely Soldier*, Philip Warner quotes me as saying; 'Auchinleck was no match for Rommel at tank warfare, and furthermore could not pick the right subordinates to help him'. I have no reason to alter those views; perhaps the most serious mistake the Auk nearly made when choosing staff was to select his Chief of Staff Lieutenant General Corbett to command Eighth Army, an appointment that was immediately cancelled by Churchill on his first visit in August. Corbett had had no desert warfare experience at all and had not held a field command in the War.

I have often wondered what the course of events would have been if Strafer had not been killed and had commanded the Eighth Army. It

---

*A moving tribute was published privately in 1984 by the Royal Greenjackets: *Strafer Gott 1897-1942*, ed. Dick Vernon.
**It is interesting to note that Monty, who had commanded 3rd Division in the BEF and conducted a brilliant withdrawal to Dunkirk, had always been Brooke's choice before Gott was killed (*Turn of the Tide*, p.440).

was almost as if divine providence intervened and made the decision for us. Could he have endured the strain of a further nine months before the North African campaign was finally over? Monty, it seems, would have commanded the British First Army under Eisenhower when 'Torch' (the landings in Algeria) was launched in November. He and Gott would have met at Tunis! There is no point in speculating further.

Our new commander in XIII Corps was another relatively unknown man from home, Brian Horrocks. Philip Warner in his biography of Horrocks *The General who Led from the Front* quotes my impression of our new Corps Commander's arrival:

He appeared as one of Monty's lieutenants about a fortnight later to take over XIII Corps, the oldest established corps in the desert army. I well remember his first day. The entire staff were immediately assembled and he gave us a taste of what became the famous Horrocks oratory. Enormous confidence, a dynamic and forceful delivery and great charm of manner. The message was personal from Churchill . . . We are going to win — important reinforcements and vast quantities of war material are arriving — You've done a great job. . . Monty has got Rommel taped.

We lapped it up and I for one went away feeling a lot better.

That evening in the Mess he told a story about World War One which I can remember today as clearly as if he had just spoken. It was about his treatment as a wounded p.o.w. in a German hospital. I went to bed hating the Germans which was exactly what Horrocks intended.

Alam Halfa was Horrock's battle as much as Monty's. The strategy may have been Monty's but the man who directed the battle was Horrocks. We were lucky that the Intelligence appreciation was spot on, and to a large extent Rommel played into our hands.*

On August 31st, within ten days, Rommel launched what was to prove his last attempt to break through to the Delta. The Battle of Alam Halfa, as it came to be called, was to many historians the turning point of the Desert War. The German attack came in the south against XIII Corps exactly as I and others had predicted. Our forward screen withdrew and the German armour penetrated our minefield and swung north. A faked map showing good going for tanks northwards and soft sand to the east was allowed to fall into enemy hands. We heard later that this piece of deception played its part. Rommel swung north towards the Alam Halfa ridge where our own tanks were waiting, hull-down, in extremely strong positions. For two days the battle raged before Rommel was forced to withdraw under heavy air attack. Our own tanks had scarcely moved from their prepared positions, and every

*pp. 116, 123. Collins, 1960. Readers may remember Horrocks' television presentations some twenty years ago of famous battles.

attempt to lure them out failed. From the British point of view it was a set-piece battle which had been carefully rehearsed; everybody knew exactly what was expected of them, and the enemy obligingly reacted as we intended him to. The DAK lost over 100 tanks and were never again to launch a major offensive in North Africa.

The elation felt at Corps HQ and of course throughout the Eighth Army was indescribable. Monty and Horrocks, these funny white-kneed new generals who had been in England and never seen a shot fired since Dunkirk, had gone around telling us hardened desert warriors what was going to happen next and how the battle was to be fought, and seemed to have been right. Rommel had been given a real bloody nose. Horrocks himself, whose battle it was, gives a simple and clear account in Chapter IX of his autobiography, *A Full Life*, where he makes some kind references to me. I doubt if any battle was more successful or critical than Alam Halfa. If Rommel had broken through we would have lost Egypt, the Suez Canal and vital oil supplies. The stakes could scarcely have been higher.

In his recently published and extremely well researched biography of Rommel, *Knight's Cross*,* David Fraser writes that as early as July 1st Rommel knew that time was running against him. His probing attacks against our thin red line throughout July were held in what some call the First Battle of Alamein. Rommel wrote on August 2nd (three days before our first visit from Churchill) that 'these weeks had been the severest fighting yet seen in Africa'.

Of Alam Halfa Fraser writes that the devastating attacks by the Royal Air Force, as soon as the move forward by the DAK was detected, nearly decided Rommel to call off the battle on the first morning (August 31st). Fraser goes further, and says that before and during Alam Halfa Rommel was uncertain. He was worried not only about British air superiority but also about his supply situation and his own health. 'Rommel', says Fraser, 'did not really believe in what he was doing'.

I do not remember at my level sensing any of these uncharacteristic worries; we had certainly been given a terrific boost by Monty's appearance, followed closely by his lieutenant Horrocks, but the Rommel magic was still there and feared. Nor do I recall discovering that he went on six weeks sick leave to Germany a few days after Alam Halfa and was not to return until October 25th, two days after we attacked at Alamein, to find that his deputy Stumme had died on the battlefield of a heart attack the previous day.

*Harper Collins, 1993

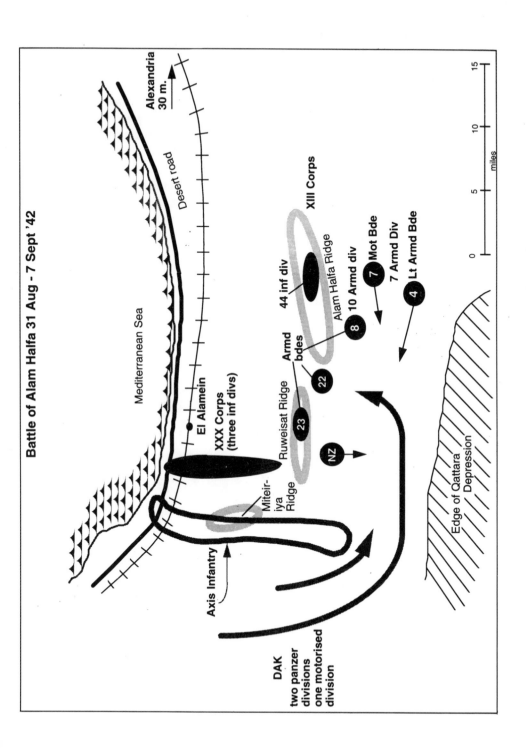

Battle of Alam Halfa 31 Aug - 7 Sept '42

After the sand had settled, the two armies glared at each other and dug in. Minefields were deepened and every known device to deceive the other side was put into action.

In September, just as I was beginning to know Brian Horrocks better and appreciate his infectious enthusiasm and confidence, I was told that I had been selected to attend the next Middle East Staff Course at Haifa beginning in November, and would be relieved almost straightaway. As a regular officer I was naturally pleased to be going to the Staff College without having to take the rather nerve-wracking peacetime exam. Curiously enough, my father had a similar experience in 1920 when he was selected on his war record to attend the first peace-time course at the Quetta Staff College in India.

I also attended but remember little about it since I was only four at the time.

CHAPTER 6

The Mysteries of Staff Work

FOUR months at Haifa was to be my only break from the desert, other than the Syrian affair in 1941, until the closing stages of the campaign in Tunisia in the spring of 1943.

The 'school' was located on Mount Carmel in the Telsch Hotel, a former German establishment built shortly before the war. Accommodation was good and the break from 'bully and biscuits' and sleeping under the stars was welcome.* A glance at the course photograph reveals that our average age was late twenties; many of us had come straight from the desert. One of the members of my first syndicate was Toby Low.** He tended to dominate discussions, perhaps unsurprisingly since he had been called to the Bar in 1939 when only twenty-five, and had already won a DSO in Greece. Tony Hunter and Robin Hastings were two brilliant young Greenjackets who 'knew it all' and must have been difficult to teach, except that they were so nice and modest. Robin used to sit at the back at all lectures and sleep, but somehow he was always awake if a question was directed at him. He became a famous steeplechaser after the War.

The only lecture that sticks in my memory was by Colonel Victor Turner who had just won a VC commanding the 2nd Battalion Rifle Brigade at Alamein. They had been attacked by over fifty tanks in an action lasting all day on October 27th and had knocked out at least thirty-four with their new six-pounder anti-tank guns before withdrawing after dark in good order†. Turner had manned one of the last guns

---

*For those who are not familiar with the term, the Army Staff College is an establishment designed to train middle-ranking officers of any arm to command battalions or equivalent, and hold staff appointments at second or first grade level. The original Staff College at Camberley, Surrey is still a much-respected army forcing house and has been reproduced with appropriate adjustments by the Royal Navy and RAF, and both the public and private sector of government and industry.
**Later Lord Aldington, KCMG, CBE, DSO
†'A month later the wrecks of 34 tanks or self-propelled guns were counted on the battlefield and no one has ever been able to establish how many of both had been towed away.' Barrie Pitt, *The Crucible of War: Year of Alamein*, p.366

in action himself and been seriously wounded in the head. Historically this battle has been hailed as the fiercest and certainly the most famous in the twelve-day Battle of Alamein. Turner's head wound was still evident when he talked to us, and he was a trifle vague about detail; but it was an inspiring talk and we listened agog, even Robin Hastings (who was also in the Rifle Brigade).

Fifty years later, when my wife and I were staying in Hobart with my Australian cousin Merris Winter, we met Bob Davies, a former Bishop of Tasmania, who had been with the 9th Australian Division at Alamein. He showed us the house which had been Monty's home for twelve years as a boy when his father too had been Bishop, and kindly gave me a copy of 'The Soldier's Prayer' (reproduced at Appendix 2) which was found in a slit trench at Alamein and eventually reached Monty who read it out at a chaplains' gathering after the battle.

The pressure was light and one could enjoy oneself. At Christmas I went skiing at the Cedars of Lebanon with some American students who had acquired a jeep. I have a photograph which shows us being the first vehicle to drive up the only road after a heavy snowfall. Little did we know as we celebrated the New Year at Haifa that, as Churchill put it, from 1943 onwards, the Allies would turn to almost unbroken success. Haifa was bombed on one occasion after dark but no one took any notice. I expect that we were in one of the night-clubs.

In February I was very flattered to be told that I had been awarded the MBE. Though not in any way comparable to the MC, which is awarded for gallantry, it meant that I could 'put up' a ribbon on my battle-dress. I was pleased as Punch. Coincidentally, at about the same time I heard that my father had been awarded the CB for his services commanding the Kohat Brigade on the North-West Frontier of India, a gong rarely awarded below the rank of Major-General.

By February we were all beginning to get rather restless about our next jobs. Sure enough, it was back to the desert for me. I received a letter from Bill Williams,* Monty's Chief of Intelligence, saying that 'he had got the Army Commander [Monty] to ask for you as soon as your course is finished to come up to be GSO 2 Intelligence Army . . . Brigadier Freddie [de Guingand] welcomed the idea with open arms'. Commissioned into the Kings Dragoon Guards (KDGs), Bill had been at Merton College, Oxford, where he won a First in History and held a Research Fellowship. In 1941 he was commanding an armoured car troop at Agheila just as Rommel was about to launch his first push.

*Later Brigadier Sir Edgar Williams, CB, DSO, Warden of Rhodes House, Oxford.

Bill's eyesight was not good, and after the front stabilised his CO arranged for him to be posted to GHQ where his very considerable talents could be more effectively used. By February 1943 he was one of Monty's 'First Eleven' (what one might call the 'think tank'.) The Desert War had moved apace since I left Alamein in September 1942. Most importantly the 'fatal corner'* had been passed! Tripoli had fallen in January and the Eighth Army was now nudging up to the Mareth Line.

On my way to the 'Front' I visited John Harding in hospital on the Canal. He had been very badly wounded in January when, as GOC 7th Armoured Division, he was standing on top of a tank in order to get a better view of the way forward to Tripoli. In his biography *Harding of Petherton* Mike Carver (then his GSO 1) tells how a special airstrip was made in one night to enable an aircraft to evacuate Harding whom the doctors said would not survive a journey by ambulance over the atrocious going.

When I saw him about a month later he was his usual charming self, impatient to be back in action.

*This phrase, aptly used by Churchill, refers of course to Agheila in Libya which both O'Connor and Ritchie reached in the winters of 1940-'41 and 1941-'42, only to be counter-attacked and driven back by Rommel.

CHAPTER 7

Victory in North Africa and on to Sicily

WHEN I had left the desert in September it was only a short fifty-mile drive into the Delta. Now the front was over 1,400 miles to the west, and actually in Tunisia! Eighth Army HQ was at Medenine preparing to attack the Mareth Line, a strong defensive position built by the French before the War to prevent an Italian invasion from Libya!

As number two to Bill Williams I was less in the know than I had been when in charge of the Intelligence branch at Corps HQ. On the other hand, I did occasionally have to brief Monty if Bill was not available. Normally one would find him in his caravan sitting surrounded by maps and the famous picture of Rommel on the wall. He was almost always relaxed and friendly and totally unpompous. But one needed to have one's wits about one; it was fatal to hazard a guess. Much better to admit that one didn't know.

The Battle of Mareth, which began on March 20th, was the most important action in which the Eighth Army was involved after Alamein until the final capitulation of the Axis forces in May. From a purely military point of view it was significant on two other counts; firstly for revealing Monty's ability to change his battle plan from a frontal attack to a wide left hook at very short notice, and secondly for the first use in the campaign of massive low level air strikes — as the Germans had employed so many times in the early days against us — to ensure success of the left hook against strong enemy defences. In his book *Operation Victory*, published in 1949 and almost the first authoritative account of the Desert War, Freddie de Guingand, Monty's Chief of Staff, describes how this 'blitz' air strike was planned.* I was present at the discussion with Air Vice Marshal Harry Broadhurst, who had commanded the Desert Air Force from the beginning. At the time I just sat and listened — only afterwards did I realise the significance of this new tactic. It was immensely successful; the German front broke open and the strong Mareth Line turned. Thirty squadrons of aircraft were used and only eight pilots lost.

Army HQ then moved to Gabes and we were ordered to plan the

Operation Victory, pp. 256-7

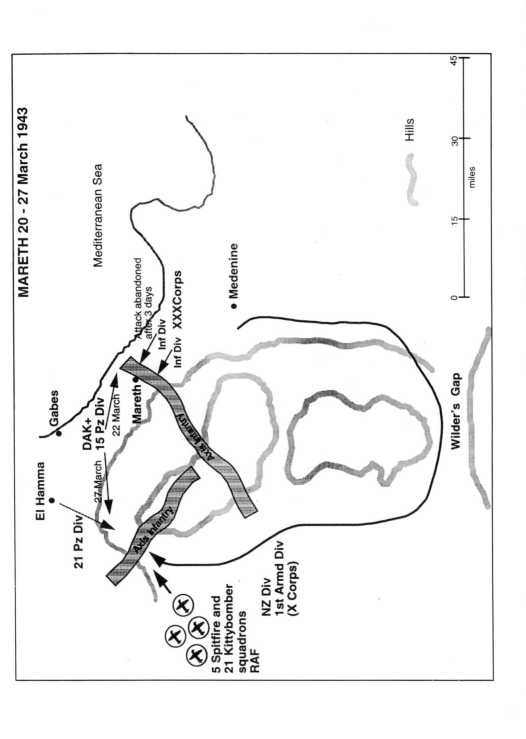

MARETH 20 - 27 March 1943

Mediterranean Sea

Gabes

El Hamma

21 Pz Div

27 March

DAK+
15 Pz Div

22 March

Mareth

Attack abandoned
after 3 days

Inf Div

Inf Div XXXCorps

Medenine

Left Hook

Axis Infantry

5 Spitfire and
21 Kittybomber
squadrons
RAF

NZ Div
1st Armd Div
(X Corps)

Wilder's Gap

Hills

0   15   30   45

miles

next battle at Wadi Akarit, where the enemy was holding a front only fifteen miles wide between the sea and impassable marshland. A frontal attack at night with no moon was made on April 6th and was successful, though resistance was tough and our casualties relatively heavy. In a letter to my father in India dated April 9th I wrote: 'the Akarit position collapsed in a day, 9,500 prisoners, almost all Italians unfortunately . . . I think this chapter of the war ought to be closed by the end of May if not earlier.'

We were now out in the Tunisian plain and immediately after Akarit were able to link up with the Anglo-American forces which had landed in Algeria early in November 1942 and had been fighting their way towards Tunis ever since. There was inevitable rivalry between the Eighth Army and the First Army. We regarded the latter as straight-laced amateurs whose knees were scarcely brown. They probably looked on us as conceited, scruffy and lucky, all of which was true. Back in February the American II Corps on the right of the First Army had been attacked by about 150 German tanks at Kasserine and suffered heavy casualties. It was their first action and many lessons were learned.

Sfax was captured on April 10th and Sousse two days later. There was now only one natural defensive position between the Eighth Army and Tunis, at Enfidaville.

General Alexander, who was now Army Group Commander in charge of the final attack on Tunis from the west and the south, decided that the thrust should come from the west. On April 30th three Eighth Army divisions were switched to First Army and we maintained a holding position at Enfidaville. By May 13th it was all over. Over a quarter of a million prisoners were taken, together with a mass of equipment. North Africa was cleared of the Axis forces.

Referring again to the letter to my father, I also wrote that 18 Army Group (Alexander's new HQ) had asked for me as a GSO 1 Intelligence but I was not allowed to go anyhow until 'this show' was over. If I had gone I might have been a Lieutenant Colonel at twenty-seven. However, career-wise it does not help to specialise as I shall point out later; so perhaps it was fortunate that I was not available.

The Allies* had decided back in 1942 that as soon as North Africa was cleared Sicily should be the next target, as a springboard to landing on the mainland of Europe. Planning staffs had been working on oper-ation 'Husky', as it was called, from January 1943. D Day was set for early July; the North African campaign did not finally end until May 13th so there was not much time.

Eighth Army, consisting of two Corps (XIII and XXX) and a total

*In effect, this meant Roosevelt and Churchill and their Service advisers.

of seven divisions, was to land in the south-east corner of the island and secure the port of Syracuse as early as possible, whilst the US Seventh Army landed on the south coast and initially captured certain vital airfields. In its early stages the plan had been far less concentrated with simultaneous landings on the east, south and west coasts. Once the North African campaign was over and Alex and Monty could give their undivided attention to the next move, major changes in the plan were made, resulting in a much more concentrated attack.

Early in May I returned to Cairo as part of a large Eighth Army planning staff. We were located in a group of buildings known as 'George', which was heavily guarded since nobody (except us!) was supposed to know what we were up to. (Years later when I was Defence Attaché in Cairo I tried to find George but failed. The buildings may have been demolished.) It was exciting work. The invasion plan was complicated because our troops would set sail from ports as far apart as Tunis, Tripoli, Haifa and Malta. The 1st Canadian Division was sailing direct from England.

My concern was the German and Italian garrisons, and in particular the extent to which they were being reinforced from Italy. We devised an elaborate deception plan which operated like this: the Allies were obviously going to invade somewhere in southern Europe; the most likely points were Sardinia, Sicily or Greece. Soldiers' guides to Sardinia and Greece were therefore printed in large quantities, and considerably fewer of Sicily; these were left in public places normally frequented by troops in Cairo and Alexandria. 'Careless talk' was almost deliberately concentrated on these two targets. One serious breach of security occurred when a fairly senior staff officer who had just attended an important and highly secret conference went to bed in his hotel leaving all his notes in the pocket of his bush shirt, hung on the back of a chair. The next morning an Egyptian servant removed the shirt and sent it to the dhobi (laundry.) A few days later the dhobi returned the notes to the army authorities. As far as we knew, the information was never leaked to the enemy, but it was an anxious moment. The unfortunate officer was disciplined.

Monty paid a brief visit to England in May after the end of the North African campaign, and found himself a national hero. On his return to Cairo John Poston,* one of his ADCs, regaled us with stories of the time that they had in London. They stayed at Claridges, the Royal box was put at Monty's disposal when he went to see *Arsenic and*

*John Poston was a very colourful 11th Hussar who served Monty as ADC and later as one of the élite band of LOs right through from Alamein to the finale in Germany only to be killed in action on April 21st, 1945.

Old Lace and he was cheered wherever he went. John told us that one evening he invited a lady friend up to his room and she eventually stayed the night. At about 6 a.m. there was a discreet tap on the door and, after a suitable pause, a hotel servant announced that when the young lady was ready she would be escorted out. Claridges was then and still is a very respectable hotel. Nobody but a member of Monty's staff could have got away with that! We were suitably impressed.

Towards the end of June the planning was over and action was once more at hand. We were to sail to Malta in two warships: senior staff in HMS *Orion* and juniors in HMS *Abdiel*, a 35-knot minelayer. Security was very tight as we embarked at Alex for Sardinia, or might it be Greece? In *Abdiel* we were packed like sardines and slept in rows on the upper deck. About halfway to Malta, the Captain was ordered to search a square of sea for the crew of a crashed bomber who were thought to be drifting on a raft. We slowed right down and were lucky enough to find them. As we all crowded the rail to watch this dramatic rescue a German Junkers 88 came at us out of the sun at mast-head height. *Abdiel*'s guns opened up at once, and I remember the shells hitting the sea very close to the ship since they were actually firing below horizontal. At the same time, we went to thirty-five knots from stationary and steered south away from Malta, with the unfortunate bomber crew dangling over the side in their raft and being hauled on board. We were at Actions Stations for a long time as it was felt very likely that the lone bomber would give our position to the Luftwaffe and heavy air attack was to be expected. Miraculously nothing happened. After steering towards the African coast until it grew dark we stole into the Grand Harbour at Malta the next morning. *Orion*'s voyage with all the top brass on board had apparently been uneventful.

Eighth Army HQ spent about two weeks in Malta. We had an underground operations room in Valetta close to the harbour, where I spent a good deal of time with the 'Ops' staff keeping the various wall charts up to date. Toby Low was on the Army staff then and I have a photo of us busy marking up maps.

It was extremely hot and occasionally there was time for a bathe out at St Pauls Bay. I remember visiting Mosta church and seeing the hole in the famous dome through which an unexploded bomb had penetrated and merely left a largish dent in the nave. The Maltese regarded the incident as a miracle and worshipped at the spot.

In Volume V of *The Second World War* Churchill describes the capture of Sicily as 'an undertaking of the first magnitude. In the initial assault nearly 3,000 ships and landing craft took part, carrying between them 160,000 men, 14,000 vehicles, 600 tanks and 1,200 guns . . . the greatest amphibious operation so far attempted in history'.* The enemy garrison consisted of two German divisions (one of them armoured), four Italian infantry divisions and six Italian coast defence divisions of low quality. In the air, superiority of more than two to one. July 10th was chosen as D Day. The weather, which had been fine, worsened considerably on the 9th and that night there was a heavy swell and a Force 6 wind. However, by this time the invasion fleet was well on its way, and there was no turning back. In the event, the Italian coast defence troops had decided that invasion was unlikely that night, and had gone to bed! So we achieved tactical surprise. The campaign lasted thirty-eight days. The land battle went well initially but later there was tough resistance from German paratroops who had been flown in from mainland Italy. We used airborne forces for the first time to secure two vital bridges but neither operation was completely successful; aircraft pilots were inexperienced, the weather was bad and the flak heavy. Holding the Plain of Catania was the key to the defence of the island, and it was here that German resistance was strongest.**

Army HQ moved to the Syracuse area on about D plus 3, but not for long as we were too close to the port and suffered a continuous hail of our own anti-aircraft shrapnel and 'overs' from the enemy. For most of the campaign our HQ was in an olive grove at Lentini, inland from Augusta. It was quieter there but extremely hot. One incident lives in my memory. A German prisoner was brought in, probably a straggler. One of our German-speaking Intelligence Officers was interrogating him when he suddenly broke away and almost disappeared amongst the olive trees. I snatched a rifle from somebody and shot him dead at a range of about 100 yards. I am not a good shot particularly with a rifle in the standing position. It was a fluke. I was both shaken and somewhat elated at the time.

I have already mentioned the heat. It was July and the many thousands of vehicles which were jammed onto every track or road in the south-east corner of the island created clouds of dust. At night a phenomenon new to us desert rats appeared — mosquitoes, and they were malarial. We were all ordered to take yellow anti-malaria pills called mepacrine. The troops didn't like them at all, firstly because they made your face look yellow, and secondly and perhaps more importantly, because it was alleged to make you impotent. It is not easy to prove the latter when you are operating in an enemy-held island. I heard it said after the campaign that the Eighth Army had almost as many casualties from malaria as in battle.

*p.52. Volume V, pp. 24, 32
**There is a parallel here with the German defence of Caen in Normandy almost exactly a year later.

CHAPTER 8

'Crawling up the Leg of Italy Like a Harvest Bug'

VERY shortly after 'the last German soldier was flung out of Sicily', as Alexander put it in a cable to Churchill on August 17th, 1943,* I saw Monty and asked to be posted nearer the 'sharp end'. He was sympathetic and within days I was told to go at once to HQ 15 Infantry Brigade and take over as Brigade Major. 15 Infantry Brigade was part of the 5th Infantry Division which had joined Eighth Army for the invasion of Sicily. Its divisional sign was a Y for Yorkshire and virtually all the units were from Yorkshire. The division had had a pretty dull time since Dunkirk; after a long spell in England, it was sent to India via Madagascar, missed the Burma campaign, and in 1943 was sent to Palestine to prepare for 'Husky'**. It was a tightly-knit division; the men had been together a long time but lacked battle experience. Monty was not impressed with their performance in Sicily, and decided to remove a good many of the senior officers, including the Divisional Commander, the Commander of 15 Infantry Brigade and his Brigade Major. This is where I came in. The only snag was that whilst I had been told verbally to pack my bags and go, the unfortunate Ian Murray whom I was relieving did not know that he was to leave. The Brigade was dispersed in the plain between Mount Etna and Catania so it didn't take me long to get there. When I arrived Ian was very philosophical and said that I had better see the Brigadier (a Highlander called George Rawstorne) at once. He too was very polite and said 'As a matter of fact, I am off too, but don't tell anybody yet.' It was a fairly unusual way to start what turned out to be probably the most responsible and enjoyable six months of the War for me. BM is generally considered to be the best Grade 2 staff job in the Army. You are the mouthpiece of the Brigade Commander, and issue his orders to all the units in the brigade. Apart from the three infantry battalions, in our case the Kings Own Yorkshire Light Infantry, the Green Howards and the York and Lancaster Regiment, there was a field regiment Royal Artillery, a field

*The Second World War, Vol V, Closing the Ring, p. 38.
**Codename for the Invasion of Sicily.

54

company Royal Engineers and various supporting arms, in all perhaps 4,000 men. The new Brigade Commander, Brigadier 'Tubby' Martin, a former Northumberland Fusilier, was a desert rat who wasn't too interested in staff procedures, knew that I had recently qualified at the Staff College, and told me to get on with it. He was a bit deaf and possessed a fiery temper, but also had lots of charm and was great fun when in a good mood. As he had just been promoted he was in excellent form (most of the time).

Within a week of my joining, Monty arrived to give his by now famous 'pep talk' to the troops about what was going to happen next. The entire brigade was assembled in a hollow square and Monty addressed us standing up in his car. We were to be one of the first brigades to sail across the Straits of Messina, and invade the mainland of Europe — the toe of Italy.

Monty spoke very simply in his own special way; short staccato sentences, lots of repetition and a few jokes. It was language which every soldier could understand. He told us that very shortly we would cross the Straits of Messina, and that there would be very little opposition. The men who had had a pretty tough time during the Sicily landing found this somewhat difficult to believe, but Monty was so confident that they gave him a great cheer when he left. He was probably only with us for about half an hour. I heard Monty address officers' gatherings on several occasions but only this once to a complete infantry brigade about to go into battle. I doubt whether any general in history has done it better, or with more effect.*

Events were moving apace in Italy. Mussolini was arrested and deposed on July 25th, and it was apparent that the Italians had no more stomach for the War. Army morale was at rock bottom, but there were a lot of German troops deployed throughout the country, and every indication that they were certainly not going to withdraw.

On September 3rd we did sail across the Straits of Messina in landing craft. We were prepared for the worst but there was very little opposition, and the whole Brigade was ashore in Reggio on the first day. Progress up the 'toe' of Italy was bound to be slow; never was a country more suited to delaying action. The main coast road, which was the 5th Division axis, hugged steep cliffs which jutted into the sea, and there were innumerable small rivers over which the only bridges had been destroyed. Our sappers were kept extremely busy. Fortunately

*In his autobiography *Sword and Wig* (Quiller Press, 1993) Robin Dunn describes a similar performance by Monty addressing an entire brigade, this time in Scotland in the spring of 1944 shortly before D Day. 'It was most impressive and had a lasting effect on us all'. pp 52-3. See also Appendix 3.

large quantities of Bailey bridging had been stockpiled in the Messina area and was towed across the Straits as a high priority.

As soon as the coast road was open for a few miles Monty suddenly appeared standing up in his staff car. Our men were marching in file on each side of the road and gave him a rousing cheer. Cigarettes were thrown to them in large quantities by his ADC; I think they were called 'Vs', and as a fag were considered poorer quality even than Woodbines, but this didn't matter to the many would-be chain-smokers amongst us. Monty had said that there would be virtually no opposition; he was proved right, and we now had the utmost confidence in his generalship.

Meantime as anticipated, Italy capitulated on September 8th, only five days after we landed. Hitler, far from writing off Italy (as he should have done) and concentrating on defending Fortress Europe against the invasion which must eventually come from England, was sending more divisions south of the Alps. At the same time the US Fifth Army under General Mark Clark, consisting of the VI US Corps and X British Corps, was landing in the Gulf of Salerno, south of Naples. The troops had heard of the Italian surrender as they approached the beaches and, as Churchill put it; 'the news came as a shock to men keyed up for battle, and had an unfortunate psychological effect. Many thought that on the morrow their task would be a walk-over.'* The landing was far from a walk-over and it was largely due to General Alexander's personal leadership that the bridgehead held during the first critical days.

It was obviously important that the Eighth Army, of which we were the spearhead, should link up as soon as possible with the Fifth US Army, who were fighting for their lives at Salerno against very determined German opposition. The 5th Division did manage to join up with some American troops about two weeks after we had landed, by which time the situation at Salerno was under control. We advanced rather laboriously up the 'toe'** through places like Catanzaro, Cosenza, Lagonegro and Potenza. It was autumn, my first in Europe for six years; the apples were ripening in a countryside covered with orchards and the Italian peasants were glad to see us. My job was exciting, I had a lot of responsibility and we were advancing, albeit slowly. For accommodation Brigade HQ was usually billeted with local people who did not seem to mind. Tubby Martin and I stayed with one particularly friendly family near Potenza for about a week.

---

*The Second World War, Vol V, p.124.
**In The Turn of the Tide, p.671, Arthur Bryant relates that Churchill applauded the American decision to land at Salerno and asked: 'Why crawl up the leg like a harvest bug from the ankle upwards? Let us rather strike at the knee.'

On one occasion our leading battalion was held up, and the best route forward appeared to be through a railway tunnel! The CO spoke to me on a field telephone late at night and said that he did not agree with the latest orders that I had issued (on behalf of the Brigadier). I woke up Tubby. He listened carefully, got up, paced up and down the room in order to work himself into a fury and then snatched the telephone from me and told the CO to obey orders. This relatively trivial incident is an example of how orders are normally issued by the chief staff officer on behalf of his commander. If they are queried, he will in all probability have to refer to his boss. At a very much higher level, there was the famous incident at the height of the battle of Alamein when Freddie de Guingand summoned two corps commanders back to Army Tactical HQ in the middle of the night, and woke up Monty who listened to what they had to say, and then told them that his orders stood, and they were to get on with the battle.

By the middle of September a further landing (V Corps) had taken place at Taranto inside the 'heel' of Italy. We were directed to the Foggia airfields whilst V Corps secured Bari. Some 74,000 British prisoners of war were believed to be in Italy, many of them caught in Rommel's capture of Tobruk in June 1942, including the Cameron Highlanders with whom I had sailed from India in August 1939. In return we had 'at least a quarter of a million Italians captured by Wavell . . . and parked around the world'.* Any form of deal became impossible when the Germans took over northern Italy, and in late September moved as many British POWs as possible to camps in Germany. However, at least 10,000 escaped into the hills before the Germans arrived. Quite a number eventually came through our brigade when we were in the Campobasso area, about halfway between Naples and the Adriatic coast. One day I was sitting in my makeshift office when an orderly came in and said that there were two very scruffy looking men outside who claimed that they were British brigadiers. Should he show them in? I said yes and wondered whether I ought to stand up and salute.

It was immediately obvious that they were genuine, and I made them as comfortable as possible before sending them on to Divisional HQ. One later became GOC London District.** Hugh Mainwaring† who had been GSO 1 at Eighth Army HQ, and was unfortunately captured after Alamein when recceing (reconnoitring) a new Tactical HQ well

*The Second World War, Vol V, p.55.
**Maj. Gen. Sir George Johnson, KCVO, CB, CBE, DSO, DL
†Later Brig. H. Mainwaring, CB, CBE, DSO, Lord Lieutenant of Flintshire and Clwyd, died 1976.

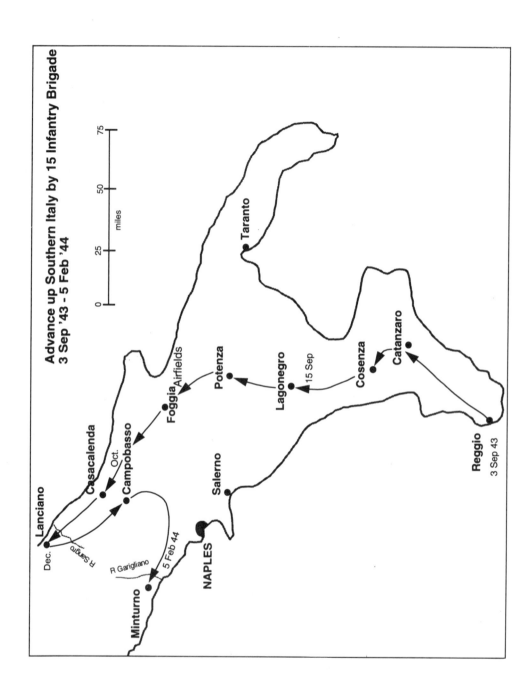

Advance up Southern Italy by 15 Infantry Brigade
3 Sep '43 - 5 Feb '44

forward, was another distinguished officer who came through our lines. But the person I was most pleased to see was my old friend Ronnie Borradaile, who walked in with David Blair, later of Ryder Cup fame. Both had been with the Camerons in Tobruk. Their POW camp was at Chieti, opposite Rome on the other side of the Appennines. Ronnie told me that the Italians removed all sentries on September 8th, but nobody left camp because the Senior British Officer (SBO) had orders via a secret wireless net that all POWs were to stay put as they would shortly be led to safety and shipped away from the small port of Pescara. However, a German parachute battalion suddenly appeared before the move to the coast had been organised and all POWs were ordered to be ready at 8 a.m. the next morning to go to Germany by train. Ronnie and David were at the time working on a tunnel (one of two in the process of completion). Early that morning they went down into their tunnel and were able to hide until the camp was clear. They then walked south and came through our lines at Casacalenda on October 21st, about a month later.*

Eighth Army's advance up Italy from Foggia to the Sangro, a distance of about 120 miles in October, November and December is not a very exciting tale. The weather was worsening, and by the time we reached the Sangro the whole area was a sea of mud. German resistance was stiffening all the time as reinforcements were moved south.

One incident remains clearly in my memory. Brigade HQ was somewhere near Lanciano. The Brigade staff were gathered in a room of a farmhouse in the evening of December 29th having a Christmas drink when German artillery opened up and the building was bracketed (i.e. one shell went over and the next one was short). We should have dispersed; I suppose there wasn't time. The next shell was a direct hit, and a young liaison officer, Ralph Rivers-Bodilly who was standing next to me, went straight over. A large piece of shrapnel had hit him in the back. He died instantly.** There were some other casualties but they were relatively minor. We were all shaken and saddened at the loss of a young officer.

Much has been written about that first winter in Italy. The campaign had started so well down in the toe. Rome by Christmas had been a sober assessment based on the German intention, known from Ultra, to withdraw north of Rome and defend nothing south of the later Gothic Line. In October, however, Kesselring persuaded Hitler to change his

*Nine months later he and Audrey, Simone and I were to marry on the same day and in 1994 we celebrated our Golden Weddings.
**He was in the Duke of Cornwall's Light Infantry and is buried in the Sangro River War Cemetery.

mind and make a stand south of Rome. The Germans made full use of many natural defensive positions, usually on river lines. Now we seemed to be bogged down, and not only by the weather.

Several veteran Eighth Army divisions were withdrawn and sent home to take part in the 'Second Front' about which we constantly heard rumours. It appeared that Italy was to become a secondary theatre. Thoughts such as these did not bother us unduly at the time. We wanted to get on but seemed to have run out of steam. On top of everything, Monty was suddenly recalled to command the 21st Army Group for the invasion of northern Europe. His departure on December 31st was a very serious loss to the Eighth Army which he had led so brilliantly from the dark days at Alamein in August 1942, sixteen months earlier. I have as a most treasured possession an autographed copy of his book, *Alamein to the Sangro*. It is not particularly well written, and was ghosted for him by David Belchem, but it is an important part of World War II literature.

By the end of the year the 5th Division had been in action almost without a break since the Sicily landing on July 10th. There was an excellent spirit in the division despite our slow progress. We had some outstanding senior officers, particularly Brigadier Lorne Campbell who had won the VC at Wadi Akarit in Tunisia and was commanding 13 Infantry Brigade. He was a Territorial whose peacetime occupation was in the wine trade — champagne I think. The other two Brigade Majors both made names for themselves after the war.*

Shortly after Christmas — not a very festive occasion in the mud, cold and rain — 5 Division along with two other divisions was switched to the Naples front and became part of the Fifth US Army. We in 15 Infantry Brigade moved up to the River Garigliano which flows into the Gulf of Gaeta about thirty-five miles north of Naples, and found ourselves once more in the front line. The objective was Rome, still eighty miles to the north, and the main allied effort was to be concentrated west of the Appennines.

We were centred on Minturno, a few miles across the Lower Garigliano. The position was not a strong one and the one Bailey bridge over the river, our lifeline, was constantly shelled. On January 22nd the

---

*Richard Sharples became Monty's Military Assistant when he was CIGS, then went into politics and was appointed Governor of Bermuda. He was tragically murdered in 1973.

Ronnie Colville, whose father was Governor of Bombay when I was serving there in 1947, succeeded his father as Lord Clydesmuir in 1954 and is now Lord Lieutenant of Lanarkshire and Captain General of the Queen's Bodyguard for Scotland.

Anzio landing took place. It was designed to turn the deep defensive lines* which the Germans had set up covering Rome, and centred on Cassino. In fact our link-up with the VIth US Corps at Anzio was not to take place until late May.

Soon after we arrived on the Garigliano I remember meeting General Alexander, the Army Group Commander (Fifth US and Eighth British), who was touring the front in an armoured car. He popped his head out of the turret, asked who I was and immediately said that he remembered my father in India. Little touches like this can endear senior commanders to much younger officers and men. Alex was immensely popular wherever he went.**

One day in mid-January I was sitting in the Brigade office when an unknown, rather alert-looking Lieutenant Colonel walked in and said 'My name is John Whitfield. I am your new Brigade Commander'. It was rather like a re-run of the two escaped brigadiers affair except that on this occasion I did not hold the trump card (that is, I could hardly tell him to wait outside while I checked up). Up I got and saluted and took him along to meet Tubby, who I think had been told that he was to go but was probably keeping quiet until his relief actually arrived. I was sorry that the change was to take place as I had enjoyed working under Tubby, and we had developed a good understanding. The trouble was his deafness. It had reached a point where he would take me along to attend the Divisional Commander's 'O' Groups† so that he could be quite sure that he had heard correctly what the brigade was to do next!

John Whitfield, who like Tubby had come straight from commanding a battalion, was a very different person. Extremely energetic and precise, he led from the front in a big way, and appeared to enjoy being shot at or shelled. He also thought that I should accompany him. Though I had always tried to visit the three battalions as often as possible, I had not expected to find myself standing in exposed positions with the brigadier in the front line as a normal routine. On several occasions we were shelled and I would dive for the nearest ditch. John Whitfield just waited for me to rejoin him. I began to think that I was getting tired and jumpy and perhaps needed a change even though I had only been BM for six months. It was almost as though the Almighty agreed with me because very early in February I was suddenly told that I was to go home to the Staff College at Camberley as an instructor. I

*Known as the Gustav line.
**He and his wife had sailed out to India in 1934 in the same ship as my parents, Alex to command the Nowshera Brigade and my father to be GSO I Peshawar District.
†The military term for a commander giving out his orders.

was to leave at once. This was a plum job and meant promotion, although when it actually came to going I was sad because my six months with 15th Infantry Brigade had been happy ones and intensely interesting. Six months in war is actually quite a long time; John Whitfield, for example, was promoted Major-General and was commanding 56 (London) Division by the autumn, and had won a bar to his DSO.

CHAPTER 9

England in War Time

SO after six continuous years overseas, I was at last to go home. I could hardly believe it. The journey was fairly tortuous. Back to Naples by jeep, Naples to Algiers by Dakota, then on to Casablanca and finally a long night flight to Scotland in an American transport. We flew right out into the Atlantic to avoid German night fighters and then turned east towards Scotland. As it grew light I saw the Irish coast; it looked wonderfully green and tidy after the desert and even Italy: almost a fairy land. We landed at Prestwick and were given breakfast in a canteen, waited upon by fresh-faced Scottish girls. To my unaccustomed eyes each one looked prettier than the last. I took a walk into Ayr in the afternoon and drank in the marvellous scenery of the Firth of Clyde and Arran.

That night I was booked on the sleeper to London and arrived in the middle of an air raid. During the early months of 1944 there was a minor blitz on London. Some damage was done but nobody seemed to bother unduly. I was required to report at Camberley during the first week of March. I flew into Prestwick on February 8th, in order to spend those precious three weeks' leave at home; but I didn't have a home. My parents were still in India where my father was commanding his brigade on the North-West Frontier. Unusually however, I had three grandmothers! My mother's mother lived in Norfolk, my step-mother's mother lived alone in Oxford and my father's mother lived with a daughter in Devon. I had not of course been able to let any of them know that I was back; I turned to Katie Beauchamp in Oxford. She had always been very kind and hospitable when I was at Oriel. Having recovered from the initial shock of hearing my voice on the telephone, she immediately invited me to stay in her comfortable Victorian house in north Oxford. I based myself there and travelled round calling on my two other grandmothers and various relatives. I remember being asked to speak about the Italian campaign to a Home Guard gathering in Oxford, where the audience gave me a marvellous reception, as though I were a war hero, which I did not feel I was.

The most important task I set myself during this short break was to look up any of my girl friends of six years ago who were not already married. My first port of call was Great Gaddesden in Hertfordshire, where 'Simone' Halsey lived with her parents in their large family mansion looking down on the Gade Valley. Simone had joined the FANY* in 1938 and transferred to the ATS when it was first formed a year later. She drove ambulances and staff cars and had been through some of the worst bombed parts of London. After four years away from home she had the option of signing on again as a member of the ATS or becoming a farm worker, and in 1942 exchanged an ambulance for a tractor on her father's estate.

We arranged to meet in London at Grosvenor House. I wore battledress Eighth Army style, that is, with a sweater sticking out a foot below the blouse, and two medal ribbons, the MBE and the recently awarded Africa star with an 8 in the centre. According to his biographer** Monty had arrived at Claridges a year earlier similarly dressed (though with rather more medal ribbons!). We had a delightful evening together and arranged to meet again.

I duly reported at Camberley on March 1st correctly dressed as a Lieutenant Colonel, though the rank was only 'local', i.e. unpaid. On the first evening I met another new DS (Directing Staff) at the Cambridge Hotel just outside the Staff College gates. The conversation came round to rowing. Yes, said Harold,† he had rowed a bit at Cambridge. I eventually discovered that he had rowed in the winning Cambridge crew three years running, for Leander in the Grand at Henley, and was a member of the British crew at the Olympic Games in 1932! I spent a weekend at his house a month or so later, and found that the drawing-room had been especially extended so that all the oars he had won could be correctly hung. I think he had about twelve: college, university, Leander and Olympic.

My tour of duty was to cover two short war courses each lasting four months. There were about 200 officers on each course, the majority British army; there were also a few RAF and Royal Marines and some Canadians, Australians, and New Zealanders. 140 were accommodated at the Staff College itself, and the remaining sixty at an imposing pseudo-gothic mansion called Minley Manor just below the Hartford

---

*The First Aid Nursing Yeomanry which dated back to the Boer War, and was an entirely voluntary organisation. The ATS (Auxiliary Territorial Service) became the main army corps for young women as war became imminent and covered every military duty for which they were considered suitable.
**Monty, Vol II, Nigel Hamilton, p. 275.
†H.R.N. Rickett, Queen's Regiment.

Bridge Flats four miles west of Camberley. I was lucky enough to be sent to Minley. Students were divided into syndicates of six, and I found that I would teach four syndicates for a month each during the course. The syllabus was almost identical to that which we had been taught at Haifa. The only differences were that the war was now sixteen months on, the North African campaign was over, the only active theatre apart from Burma was Italy, and obviously the Second Front was about to open. Most of us DS had served in the Middle East, and our job was to convey to students the latest thinking on tactics and staff procedures.

Having come straight from being a BM in an active theatre, the first course was relatively easy for me. Many of the students hoped to be given similar jobs to mine when they left. All I had to say was 'This is how we did it', and there wasn't much argument. However, the pressure of work was considerable; apart from compulsory PT for about half an hour every day we were hard at it for five and a half days a week. I used to spend long hours in the DS library at Minley, a lovely room with superb views over formal gardens, correcting students' written work. We were given a DS solution to each exercise known as 'the pink' because it was typed on pink paper. It was of course possible merely to say to a student 'I'm afraid that your solution is wrong. I attach a copy of the pink'. But one wouldn't have lasted long. Standards were extremely high, and even our corrections were checked by more senior staff.

Harold Rickett's routine was incredible. After supper he would work in the library on corrections for an hour or two, then lie down on his bed fully clothed with his alarm set for about 3 a.m. when he would get up, have a shower and work until breakfast before taking his syndicate all day. He did this regularly week after week. His corrections were extremely detailed and of enormous value to students. Whenever he was around, I felt (unsurprisingly) rather inadequate. The only edge I had was active service experience. Harold had been stuck in England since Dunkirk.

By April I was engaged to Simone Halsey and spent every spare moment at Gaddesden. I had a complicated journey through London starting with a bike ride to Fleet station — very few of us had cars. On one occasion I attended a party given by the 11th Hussars who were in camp at Ashridge, only a few miles from Gaddesden. It had been arranged that another DS who happened to be an 11th Hussar himself, and had a car, would collect me at Gaddesden later that evening and drive me back to Minley. Unfortunately he went to sleep in his car and when he woke up could not remember where Gaddesden was. He claims to have called at a large house nearby where he was sent packing by a nurse wearing a mask since he had inadvertently arrived at a converted maternity hospital. After that he abandoned his search for me and drove unsteadily back to Minley. Meantime I slept on a sofa for a while, then borrowed a bike, rode ten miles to Watford and caught the first tube to Waterloo at 6 a.m. I managed to face my syndicate at 9 a.m. but it was a close shave, and I doubt whether they learnt much that day.

Tension rose during May as D Day approached. There must have been several officers on the course who knew the outline plan, and possibly some who knew the date was to be early June. I never knew, nor did anybody let on that they knew. Perhaps nobody did know! This was an example of good security.

When D Day finally came on June 6th we were made only too aware of the sheer size of the operation by watching the air armada going overhead. Churchill wrote that the Allies flew 14,600 sorties during the first twenty-four hours.* From midnight onwards three airborne divisions were dropped slightly inland to seize bridgeheads and assist the seaborne assault on the beaches.

One Monday morning in mid-June there was an empty chair in my syndicate. Later in the day we heard that John Gilliatt (Irish Guards) had been killed along with some 200 others when a flying bomb, or 'doodle-bug' as they came to be called, landed on the Guards Chapel only a stone's throw from Buckingham Palace and totally destroyed the building in the middle of a special service.

The course ended on July 6th and most of the students were immediately posted to staff appointments in 21 Army Group.

John Rockingham, a Canadian Lieutenant Colonel who had been in one of my syndicates, went straight to the 3rd Canadian Division as a CO and was soon commanding a brigade! In November he wrote to me: 'Once one has been taught the principles by the Staff College it seems to be just common sense and the will to win . . . we have had just about every type of fighting so far except mountain warfare (no mountains in north-west Europe) and withdrawal . . . I moved the Brigade after Falaise about fifty-five miles in one day . . . '

My first course ended on July 6th and I married Simone Halsey on July 8th in the lovely village church at Great Gaddesden where her family had worshipped for 400 years (as memorials and tombstones bear witness), and where her father Sir Walter Halsey was patron of the living. Her grandfather had been MP for South-West Herts for twenty-five years, was a Privy Councillor and created a Baronet. Her uncle, Admiral Sir Lionel Halsey, had been Comptroller to Edward Prince of

*The Second World War, Vol VI, p.3.

Wales for twenty years, and her brother Tom was Captain of the *King George V*, one of our newest battleships. Earlier in the war he was a Captain (D) during the Dunkirk evacuation. I was marrying into a very distinguished Hertfordshire family. My father was overdue for retirement and he and my stepmother just managed to get home in time. It was only a month after D day and the flying bombs were active, but the church was pretty full. We travelled up to Scotland that night on the sleeper and had a blissful fortnight at Appin in Argyll.

My second course started on August 3rd. There wasn't much time to find somewhere to live; fortunately we were offered a farmhouse on the Sandhurst road which we shared with two other families. We called it Toad Hall. At weekends we bicycled to Windsor and caught a bus to Berkhamsted (for Gaddesden). Meanwhile I was finding the second course a good deal more difficult, partly because Italy was 'old hat'. Normandy was the only front that mattered and I was out of date.

I watched the air armada flying overhead on September 17th on its way to Arnhem, little realising how crucial to the successful conduct of the campaign this massive airborne operation was meant to be. Had we been able to secure the bridge over the Neder Rijn at Arnhem the way could have been open into the German plain north of the Ruhr and the Siegfried line.

After the breakout from Normandy Monty had been locked in controversy with Eisenhower over the future strategy of the campaign in north-west Europe. He was all for a single thrust north of the Ruhr directed at Berlin, whereas Eisenhower wanted an advance on a broad front. I was not involved at all at this stage but have always felt that Monty was right and the risks were worth taking. De Guingand takes the opposite view, saying in *Operation Victory* that this was the only major issue throughout the war over which he did not agree with his chief, Monty.*

At Camberley the course ended on November 30th with a brilliant talk by the CIGS General Sir Alan Brooke** on the state of the war. Speaking without notes and using a wall map of the world, he told us what was happening on every front clearly and quite simply. It was masterly.† 'Brookie', as he was affectionately known in the army, was second only to Churchill in bearing the full burden of the conduct of the war. Unlike Monty he had few enemies but, like Monty, was very widely respected.

*pp 410-11
**Later F.M. Viscount Alanbrooke, KG, GCB, OM, GCVO, DSO
† 'Sir Ian Jacob was equally impressed by Brookie's talks on global strategy given without notes and holding his audience enthralled.' Arthur Bryant, *Turn of the Tide*, p. 551

CHAPTER 10

Victory in Europe

MY next posting was to the staff pool of 21 Army Group and I was to report in Brussels on December 15th. We had a few precious days packing up at Toad Hall and spent the last weekend at the Bay Tree at Burford, a delightful Cotswold pub.

Simone returned to her tractor at Gaddesden. Missing our first Christmas together, especially after my long spell abroad, was a considerable wrench, and for the first time in years I felt thoroughly homesick as I boarded the blacked-out ferry at Folkstone. On arrival in Brussels there was a major flap on as Rundstedt had just launched his famous offensive in the Ardennes. There was no job for me; I was told to wait until someone was sacked or killed. Monty's Tactical HQ was at Zonhoven just north of Hasselt in Flemish Belgium, about fifty miles east of Brussels and only fifteen from the front line on the Maas. An old Desert Rat friend, Joe Ewart, was up there as Monty's intelligence staff officer, Bill Williams being back with the main HQ outside Brussels. I managed to contact him and told him I was at a loose end; he invited me to stay for Christmas. I hitched a lift and found myself a spectator during one of the most critical weeks of the entire campaign.

By mid-December the Allies had closed right up to the Siegfried Line and in some cases breached it, for example at Aachen. Further south in the rolling uplands of the Ardennes the American First Army held a frontage of seventy-five miles with four divisions, none of them very experienced. Presumably the US Army Group Commander Omar Bradley thought that there was no threat at this point, even though it was through the French Ardennes that Moltke had successfully attacked in 1870; much more recently Hitler in 1940 had directed a major thrust through the Belgian Ardennes which overwhelmed the Maginot Line and was aimed at both Paris and the Channel Ports.

It was at this point that Rundstedt launched his counter-offensive on December 16th with twenty-eight divisions, ten of them SS or Panzer. It was thought at first that his attack was only in divisional strength. Joe Ewart, listening carefully to the 'phantom' net (the Allies' forward wireless communications), was the first to realise from identification of

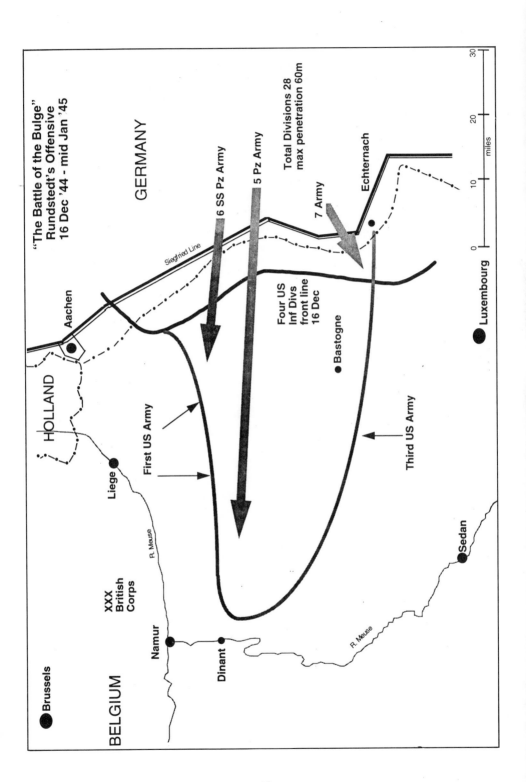

"The Battle of the Bulge"
Rundstedt's Offensive
16 Dec '44 - mid Jan '45

GERMANY

6 SS Pz Army

5 Pz Army

Total Divisions 28
max penetration 60m

7 Army

Echternach

Aachen

Siegfried Line

HOLLAND

Four US
Inf Divs
front line
16 Dec

Bastogne

First US Army

Liege

Third US Army

Luxembourg

R. Meuse

XXX
British
Corps

Namur

Dinant

R. Meuse

Sedan

Brussels

BELGIUM

69

prisoners that Rundstedt was using two Panzer armies. The weather was appalling: sub-zero temperatures and fog, which virtually grounded the Allied air forces for the first critical days. German paratroops in American uniforms were infiltrated deep behind our lines causing considerable alarm and despondency as far back as Rheims and Paris.

It quickly became clear to us — but not quite so clear to the Americans — that Rundstedt's aim was to cross the Meuse and then drive north to Brussels and Antwerp, thereby cutting off the whole of 21 Army Group; this would be almost a re-run of 1940. Three divisions of the US First Army were virtually written off in as many days as the tanks of the 5th and 6th Panzer Armies thrust ever westwards towards the Meuse. There was a temporary collapse of American communications and some divisional HQs were abandoned.

Up in Zonhoven, Monty's only effective way of discovering exactly what was going on some fifty miles to the south was by sending out his hand-picked liaison officers to selected US corps, divisions and sometimes even brigade HQ with orders to see the commanders; they were to weigh up the situation and report back without fail by that evening. Each carried a letter of authority signed by Monty. On a later visit to the front Churchill told Monty that his system resembled that of Marlborough and 'the conduct of battles in the eighteenth century when the commander-in-chief acted through his lieutenant-generals... posted at different points on the front, who knew his whole mind and were concerned with the execution of his plan'.* Like Monty's LOs they did not command troops. They were also described by Brookie in his diary as 'the modern form of the general and his gallopers'**. It was a dangerous job requiring considerable tact and the ability to assess a situation quickly and correctly. They were all majors who had had a lot of battle experience in north west Europe and/or North Africa. They included Dick Harden, DSO, OBE, MC, later a Unionist MP for Co. Armagh; Carol Mather, MC, later Sir Carol Mather, MP for Esher and Comptroller of HM Household; John Poston, MC and Charles Sweeney, MC. The last two were both killed in action. I used to talk to them in the evenings after they had been de-briefed, and some of the stories they had to tell were pretty hairy. I remember Carol Mather telling us about the US First Army HQ which he had just visited and found totally abandoned, Christmas decorations and all. Having digested the information that they brought back, Monty would telephone to de Guingand at Main HQ 21 Army Group outside Brussels with his orders for the following day.

*Churchill, Vol. VI p.364.
**Triumph in the West, p.438.

1. My father *c.* 1937

2. My mother *c.* 1915

1

3. Simone, 1944

4. Author at Camberley, 1944

5. Author at Wellington aged 15; winner, Little Kingsley

6. Oxford Torpids, 1936, Oriel II bumping Hertford I in first minute. Author at 3

7. Italian General Gallina, captured in
December 1940, had commanded the
Libyan Group of Divisions

8. David Hunt in the Desert, 1942

3

9. Iraq Army manoeuvres, 1956. The Director of Military Intelligence on a
mule

10. Some of my team in the ACV HQ XIII Corps, 1942

11. Eighth Army Underground HQ, Malta, July 1943. Author marking maps with Toby Low and Andy Anderson

4

12. Transport coming ashore in Sicily, July 1943

Tactical HQ at Zonhoven was quite small and Monty was well guarded. Several tanks and armoured cars were sited in the immediate vicinity. I certainly had no impression of any alarm though there was in Brussels where secret documents were being destroyed. It was almost reminiscent of Cairo in the black days of July 1942 when Rommel was only fifty miles from Alex. Monty found time to attend Holy Communion in the tiny village church on Christmas Day (as did several of us) and there were festivities of a sort; by this time the situation was under control. Rundstedt's tanks were within three miles of the Meuse at Dinant but got no further, partly through lack of fuel. Fortunately the weather improved and our air forces got busy.

On December 20th Eisenhower had been reluctantly obliged to place all American troops north of the 'bulge' (as the German penetration came to be called) under Monty's command. In effect this meant the Ninth and First US Armies totalling eighteen divisions. Historians have gloried in either praising Monty's handling of the battle at this stage, or blaming him for gloating over the American apparent inability to react quickly and effectively to a German thrust which had cut sixty to seventy miles through their front line.

Monty has also been criticised for being too cautious and slow in reacting to the German advance. Those who knew him well remember the meticulous way in which attacks and counter-attacks were planned. He refused to be rushed. American planning tended to be rather the opposite: very quick decisions and movement which did not always produce results. But Rundstedt's advance to the Meuse was stopped by heroic American troops fighting desperately with their backs to the wall. The British provided the long-stop.

Sitting on the touch line watching the huge operations map being constantly marked up and listening to the Liaison Officers' reports, it seemed obvious to me that Monty had very quickly realised where the threat lay. He had ordered all Meuse bridges between Liège and Givet to be heavily guarded, and moved four divisions into a central reserve behind the river covering Brussels. I suspect that General Hodges, the First US Army Commander, and his Corps commanders were secretly quite relieved to be given orders by Monty, who exuded confidence and 'kept his head when all about him were losing theirs'.

Before leaving the Ardennes affair — the Battle of the Bulge — it would be wrong not to mention the historic defence of Bastogne by the US 101 Airborne Division under its gallant commander Brigadier-General McAuliffe. Rushed up to the front in a ground defence role, it was ordered to hold this key road centre and high ground. Rundstedt's tanks by-passed the town in their drive towards the Meuse. Surrounded and attacked from all sides, 101 defied the enemy and when invited to surrender McAuliffe replied with the single word 'Nuts'.*

Alan Moorehead, the well-known war correspondent and Monty's first biographer, is quoted as saying that in his estimation the battle of the Ardennes was Monty's finest hour. I would not disagree with this view. The stakes were high, and there seems little doubt that Eisenhower the Supreme Commander and Bradley who commanded the US Army Group were caught off balance.

A day or two after Christmas my role as a fly on the wall at the nerve centre of an Army Group controlling thirty-four divisions came to an abrupt end. I was ordered to report to 1st Battalion the South Lancashire Regiment as 2IC (2nd in Command). The battalion was in 8 Infantry Brigade of the 3rd Division and was holding a sector of the front line on the River Maas (as the Meuse is called after it enters Holland). The contrast to my week at Zonhoven could hardly have been greater.

I had not been with a battalion since those six months with the DLI in 1941. I am not quite sure what happened to my predecessor but there was no 2IC when I arrived. My CO was a charming man from the Duke of Wellington's Regiment called 'Swazi' Waller. He was the regiment's seventh CO since D Day! The South Lancashires had been one of the few battalions that had actually landed on the Normandy beaches at H Hour** on D Day, a record of which they were very proud. However, they had paid a heavy price; over 500 casualties in six months meant that very few of the officers and men that I was to join had actually waded ashore on D Day.

We held a front of about a kilometre on the river with two companies forward. The Germans held the other bank about 200 metres away. Battalion HQ was in a house on the edge of the village of Venraij (twenty miles south of Nijmegen). The winter of 1944-'45 in north west Europe was very severe. When I arrived the dead-flat plain through which the Maas flows at this point was covered with snow, and there was hardly a pane of glass in any window that faced east. It was extremely difficult to keep warm by day or night, however many layers of clothing one wore.

By this sixth year of war the army was becoming very short of men. To be blunt, we were scraping the bottom of the barrel with regard to manpower. There was a feeling among newly drafted men that the war was nearly over and consequently a certain reluctance to 'get stuck in'.

---

*Many years later I visited the impressive American War Memorial and Museum at Bastogne, and saw only too clearly how vital it must have been to hold this key point.
**H Hour was the time that the first troops were to land on the beaches.

Under these circumstances, good leadership was all-important. Waller was fearless and set a splendid example; so particularly did our brigade commander Eddie Goulburn, a Grenadier guardsman.* He had only one medal ribbon, the DSO and bar, both of which he had won since D Day. He was a tall man who never wore a tin hat, and I have a clear memory of him walking calmly about in the forward area whilst many of the men were in their foxholes and not too keen to get out of them.

On New Year's Eve I was invited to go back to Brigade HQ for supper. After a very pleasant evening I got back to Battalion HQ to find that the Germans had sent a strong raiding party across the river at Wanssum which our right forward company had so far failed to dislodge. Waller had enjoyed an equally good evening, and was difficult to wake up. I talked to the company commander on the radio, then went up in a jeep to see him and spent the rest of the night listening in. I felt certain that Goulburn would be up at first light to see the situation for himself, and I was equally sure that Waller would recover quickly. He did, and after a lightning visit to the Company was ready to receive the brigadier. It had been an uneasy night and not one which I would forget in a hurry.

The next day was also one of drama as the Luftwaffe staged almost their last major attack. Messerschmidts came over our lines in waves at ground level and went on to shoot up aircraft at airfields in Holland and Belgium. Large numbers of allied aircraft were destroyed but the Luftwaffe also lost about 200, which they could ill afford.

By the middle of January the Battle of the Bulge was in effect over. It is interesting to note that American casualties were at least 75,000 in twenty-seven divisions, and German losses much more serious in both men and materials. No small battle by any standards.

Monty could now consider his next move, in fact the one that he had been planning when Rundstedt interrupted him. His aim was to close up to the Rhine by a major thrust south-east from Nijmegen between the Maas and the Rhine itself. The Battle of the Reichswald, as it came to be known, started on February 8th and was to involve our division. The weather was still very bad, a mixture of snow and fog, and the German resistance has been described as some of the fiercest of the war. Ten divisions were fighting for the first time on German soil in defence of their famous river, the Rhine. General Horrocks, who was now our Corps Commander, also describes the conditions very vividly in his autobiography and goes so far as to say that 'this was

---

*There were a disturbing number of men 'absent without leave' from most of the front line divisions, and the Military Police were busy picking them up from homes in Holland and Belgium where they were hiding.

unquestionably the grimmest battle in which I took part during the last war'.* By March 10th, after a month of fighting, organised German resistance west of the Rhine had ceased. The battle for the Reichswald was to be the last major operation on the Western front and marked the final break-up of the Wehrmacht. No sooner had it finished than I was on the move again, back to the staff. I had had too little experience at battalion level to hope for a command, so I suppose I was lucky to be promoted again to lieutenant colonel as GSO 1 (Liaison) between Second Army and the Ninth US Army.

I was to be based with the Americans at their HQ in Maastricht and was required to travel north most days to HQ Second Army, who were in some farmhouses about halfway between Roermond and Nijmegen. Before leaving Maastricht I would see the Operations staff and be briefed on their latest situation. On arrival at Second Army I would be de-briefed and then acquaint myself with the latest moves on the British front, to be passed on to the Americans. Second Army commanded all British troops in the 21st Army Group, whilst Ninth US Army (which was still under Monty's command) was the northernmost of the three American armies and consisted of two corps. The Army Commander was General Simpson, whose appearance was unusual in that he always kept a completely bald, shaven head. He was very approachable and kind whenever I met him.

It was an absorbing job as I knew what was going on at a high level; but for all that I was really only a glorified messenger boy! Perhaps the most interesting aspect of the job was to compare the two Army HQs. At Maastricht, the Americans had taken over several large buildings on the edge of the town. There was a huge self-service canteen where officers of all ranks up to eagle colonel** queued up for meals. Second Army provided me with a caravan, staff car, driver and batman. Though not told so in as many words, I was clearly expected to behave as the Americans imagined British officers normally did. So I used to invite American staff officers to join me for a whisky in the evenings, making full use of my batman. This went down rather well.

The other aspect of American life which amused us was that officers wore tin hats and boots most of the time, wherever they might be, and were expected to shave in cold water. It was even rumoured that this was the custom in major HQs much further back such as Rheims and Paris. Our attitude was that 'any fool can be uncomfortable'; staff at Army HQ would be as relaxed as possible. At Second Army there were about three small officers' messes supplied with newspapers and glossy

*A Full Life, pp 251-55.
**Equivalent of UK full colonel.

magazines from home, where you could get away from it all for a bit. Dress was very casual, modelled of course on Monty's. I can hardly remember wearing a tin hat throughout the war, and I wasn't exactly confined to base.

The crossing of the Rhine north of the Ruhr was to begin on the night of March 23rd-24th, only a fortnight after the end of the Reichswald battle. To cross a fast-flowing river 500 yards wide, the greatest natural barrier since the D Day landings, and opposed by German troops fighting to defend their homeland, was bound to be a major undertaking. However, thanks to their 'do or die' policy, or to put it another way, their refusal to accept tactical defeat, Hitler's armies had fought to the death west of the Rhine, and as a result were unable effectively to oppose the massive allied onslaught when it was launched. The actual crossings by four divisions (two British and two American) north and south of Wesel had been preceded by four days of intense air interdiction during which 42,000 sorties had been flown, and the RAF's new ten-ton bomb used for the first time.

The weather was fine over the whole of that critical week. A massive air drop by two divisions, one British and one American, to secure a deep bridgehead took place after the initial crossings and was entirely successful, though there were fairly heavy casualties. Churchill, Brookie and Eisenhower were able to watch the air drop in relative safety from close to the west bank.

It was clear that the end was near; there had already been secret peace overtures on the Italian front in late March. Ninth US Army reverted to command of 12 US Army Group on April 3rd and my liaison job ended. I returned to HQ Second Army and was to stay with them as GSO 1 Liaison until the final surrender on May 7th. The BGS to whom I reported was Selwyn Lloyd, who eleven years later was to be Foreign Secretary during the Suez crisis.

The advance from the Rhine to the Elbe was swift as German resistance crumbled. Two impressions remain in my memory: surprise at finding hams galore hanging in the cellars of German farmhouses when we had been led to believe that the people were starving, and the endless stream of huge American ten-ton lorries thundering eastwards along the roads of the north German plain.

Even at Army HQ I was not aware of the arguments raging between Monty, Bradley and Eisenhower over the axes of advance. Monty had planned to go for the Elbe and enter Berlin before the Russians; moreover he had the full backing of Churchill. It seemed as though the Americans underestimated the profound psychological and political effect of the fall of Berlin to the Western Allies.* Eisenhower and his

*The Second World War, Vol V1, p.405

principal subordinate Bradley planned to clean up the Ruhr and then advance on the axis Kassel-Leipzig-Dresden, linking up with the Russians well south of Berlin. Inevitably the Americans had their way. By 1945 there were over sixty US divisions in north west Europe whereas the British had only fifteen, and this number included the Canadians. Politics and not common-sense military strategy would always win in the end. Most historians are agreed that after a Rhine crossing which proved much easier and less costly in casualties than had been anticipated, a concentrated drive north of the Ruhr aimed straight at the heart of Germany, Berlin, via Hanover could have changed the post-war map of central Europe. The Russians were held up on the Oder and the way was clear. We should also remember that the German armies were frightened of the Russians whom they regarded as savages, and as the end drew near were falling over each other to surrender to the western allies rather than face POW camps in Siberia. It seems to have been a combination of Roosevelt's failing health and the need to involve the full might of the US Army under its own leadership (as opposed to Monty's) that decided the outcome and allowed the Russians to get to Berlin first.

One is inclined to forget that three of the principal actors throughout World War II died in April, one at the moment of victory, two in defeat. Roosevelt died suddenly on April 12th. His health had been failing for some time but it was particularly sad that he should go at the supreme climax of the war. Churchill says he felt 'as if I had been struck a physical blow. My relations with this shining personality had played so large a part in the long, terrible years that we had worked together'.* Mussolini was shot on Communist instructions on April 26th and Hitler shot himself on April 30th.

The final surrender, when it came on May 7th at Luneberg Heath, was of course a momentous event. For some time it had been a question of 'when' rather than 'if'. There were naturally celebrations throughout the Army but these were not as boisterous as in London, judging by what we read in the papers.

There was still an immense amount to be done; in particular, the demobilising of that portion of the German Army which had surrendered on the 21 Army Group front. This totalled about one and three quarter million men.

Monty decided that we must use existing German HQ to do the job for us. The problem was to choose a German general to be in charge whom we could trust, and who was known to be efficient. We thought of Rommel's team from the desert days and discovered that Kramer,

*The Second World War, Vol VI, p.412

one of the most able panzer generals in the DAK, was hiding somewhere on the Elbe. Like Rommel he had been implicated in the July plot to assassinate Hitler, but had somehow escaped the attentions of the Gestapo. We tracked Kramer down and he agreed to do the job on one condition; his wife and daughter were living in the stables of their schloss near Kassel and he wanted them to be with him. I was given the unusual task of taking Kramer to Kassel and bringing back the family to Hamburg, where his HQ was to be based.

We set off on the long drive in an army staff car one morning in late May. Fortunately Kramer spoke quite good English — my German is very limited — and during the journey we refought many of the desert battles. Kramer was a snob and I particularly remember him saying that both the German and British armies sent only their élite troops to North Africa. In the case of the British, he was referring to the Guards and Cavalry. I politely pointed out that there had been a huge cross-section of our army in the desert, and he smiled.

On arrival at the family schloss that evening (Kramer of course having given the driver instructions) I found that it was occupied by an American infantry company who were all pretty merry. I entered the castle alone, introduced myself and announced that I had come on a strange mission. I had a German general in my car outside who was looking for his wife. Did they know where she was since this was the family home? The Americans thought that this was the best story they had heard in years . . . it was several drinks later that I staggered out to the car having been told to look wherever I liked. So off we went to the back courtyard and there sure enough in a first-floor room above the stables were Frau Kramer and her young daughter, plus quite a few *objets d'art* from the main house. There were about ten carpets piled one on top of the other to start with, then a rather good-looking dining-room table. The easiest course seemed to be to spend the night there, and we had a simple meal together perched up on top of all those carpets. Next day, after checking out with our American hosts, we drove back to Hamburg, the Kramer family sitting in the back and I in front with the driver.

During these early days of 'peace' I was involved in the arrest of von Ribbentrop, whom we caught hiding in his pyjamas in a back street of Hamburg. We had received a tip-off from local people who had no love for a man who had been close to Hitler. He was later to be executed as a war criminal.

By June the military machine was gradually being wound down and demobilisation was in full swing in both the British and German armies. There was no job for me at HQ Second Army (which was itself shortly to be disbanded) and I was posted to the newly-formed VIII Corps

District as GSO 1 (Intelligence). Our area of responsibility was Schleswig-Holstein; the Danish frontier was to our north, and the newly-created boundary with the Russians twenty miles to the east. Our HQ was in an impressive-looking schloss* beside a lake at Plön, about halfway between the former German naval base at Kiel and Lübeck, which was the last sizeable town reached by British troops during the race across the north German plain.

A few miles to the north of us at Flensburg on the Danish frontier Admiral Donitz, who had briefly on Hitler's death called himself head of the Third Reich, and Field Marshal Keitel, Chief of the German General Staff, were still trying to order the defeated German armies to surrender to the western allies and not to the Russians. The latter was later to face trial at Nuremberg and be executed as a war criminal.

The tempo of work had eased sufficiently to enable VIII Corps to send a hockey team to play the Danes in Copenhagen. I found myself included, though I had scarcely played since Wellington. We drove through cheering crowds and drank innumerable tiny glasses of schnapps which have to be knocked back in one. On arrival in Copenhagen (drink-driving laws were unheard of in those days) we found that we were to play the Danish national side; they had assumed that we represented Britain! Fortified with more schnapps we took the field and were soundly beaten about 12-0, but it didn't seem to matter.

Back at Plön, the work mostly involved security matters such as rounding up suspected war criminals and cells of resistance. There was time to row on the lake and even participate in a regatta in Hamburg.

During the fateful summer of 1945 the General Election in Britain was caused by the Labour Party's refusal to continue in a coalition government. The result, announced on July 26th, was defeat for the man who above all had won the war for Britain — Churchill. For us in Germany it was difficult to understand how the British electorate could have done this; it must have been incomprehensible to our allies around the world. Thinking back I am pretty certain that the average person in Britain did not realise that he was in effect disapproving of Churchill. It might be said that the electorate felt an overwhelming need for a change of government to lead the new peace-time Britain. So both Roosevelt and Churchill, the two giants among the Western Allies who together had brought about victory, disappeared from the post-war scene. Stalin alone of the triumvirate survived.

Another more earth-shattering event was the dropping of two atomic bombs on Japan on August 9th, resulting in immediate surrender.

*Later to become a boarding school for British children run by Freddie Spencer-Chapman.

PART III, 1946-1958
India, Malaya and Cyprus

CHAPTER 11

Whitehall Commuter in Uniform

IN September I was suddenly told that I was to be posted to London as a GSO 1 in the Military Intelligence Directorate of the War Office. This was my fourth job in nine months, though I could scarcely complain as it meant reunion with Simone. We had only had five and a half months of married life together and the thought of stability of a sort in post-war Britain was very exciting.

We found a semi-detached house in south Purley and moved in straight away. My office was initially underground in Montagu House Terrace, Whitehall. My branch was called M1 4/14, a 'country' section dealing with virtually the whole of Western Europe. The Director of Military Intelligence (DMI) was Freddie de Guingand, now a Major-General. I knew him well and found him very easy to work for.

We were mostly concerned with security aspects of the demobilisation of the German army, and accounting for all the leading personalities. Were they dead? If alive, where were they? A mass of German documents also needed to be examined and sorted.

One of our most interesting visitors was General Freyberg, VC, the former Commander of the NZ Division and now Chief of the General Staff in New Zealand. His government wanted evidence of the effect that the allied intervention in Greece and Crete in 1941 had had on Hitler's plans to invade Russia. Was it true that the German attack on Greece delayed Barbarossa* by six weeks, and in the end resulted in Hitler's failure to reach Moscow before the snow, in the same way that Napoleon had been caught in 1812? New Zealand's casualties in Greece and Crete had been heavy, and there was obviously national pressure demanding justification.

This is an extremely interesting question which has never been satisfactorily answered. Churchill is quoted as saying: 'Our intervention in Greece ... delayed the German invasion of Russia by six weeks.

---

* Codename for the German attack on Russia.

Vital weeks. So it was worth it'.* I remember Joe Ewart telling me that
he interrogated General von Thoma, Commander of the the DAK
under Rommel at Alamein, who was captured as the German front
crumbled on November 4th, 1942. During the interrogation von Thoma
handed over his field glasses and said 'I have looked at Moscow through
these glasses'. (He might have added 'longingly'.) I believe Freyberg
went away satisfied, which was what mattered at the time.

A new book entitled *Crete: The Battle and the Resistance* by Antony
Beevor** argues that 'Barbarossa was not delayed by the redeployment
of formations after the invasion of Greece, but by the remarkably slow
distribution of mechanical transport, much of it captured from the
French the previous year, to units destined to lead the advance into
Russia . . . the notion that the battle of Greece and Crete delayed
Barbarossa with fatal effect was nothing more than wishful consolation'.

Early in 1946 we moved into the main War Office building and I
had a pleasant office to myself, complete with a coal fire, looking over
Whitehall. It must seem odd today but in 1946, though the war in
Europe had been over for six months, we were ordered still to wear
uniform. I commuted to Charing Cross from South Croydon whilst we
were still in Purley and, when we managed to find a tiny furnished flat
above a shop in Lower Grosvenor Place, walked across St James' Park.
It was a posh address but the accommodation hinged round one large
first-floor room looking onto Buckingham Palace Mews, a small
bedroom at the back, and a kitchen and bathroom on the second floor.
The rent was three pounds a week. During the summer Simone and I
often had a sandwich lunch together in the Park. I can remember several
times seeing Attlee, then Prime Minster, also walking in the Park.

Every morning at nine thirty, the 'country section colonels' as we
were called, would brief the DMI on world events in our area of
responsibility. The daily newspapers were often quicker with the news
than official telegrams, and I remember feeling that it was rather a waste
of time because there was not a lot that I could tell the DMI that he
didn't know already. This particularly applied when General Templer†
took over from de Guingand in the middle of 1946.

Templer was on his way up the ladder to the top and was a tiger for
detail. He knew the situation in Germany far better than I did; his
previous post was that of Monty's Military Government Director. He
was a slightly alarming person to work for but his bark was worse than
his bite. I was to serve under him seven years later in Malaya when he

Wavell - Soldier and Scholar, John Connell, p.330.
**John Murray, 1991
†Later Field Marshal Sir Gerald Templer KG, GCB, GCMG, KBE, DSO

was kindness itself.

In the immediate post-war years, the War Office was still the Army's nerve centre. An integrated Ministry of Defence had not yet been created and NATO was not formed until 1949. Monty took over from Brookie as CIGS in June, and I attended a pep talk to middle-ranking staff. He entered the room behind a small, rather insignificant looking man who was the Secretary of State for War; Jim Lawson, a Geordie from Durham. It brought home to me the realisation that professional soldiers are ultimately responsible to Parliament through their Secretary of State. Perhaps this is just as well because there were times in the early post-war years when Monty was reluctant to bow to anybody. Churchill was out of office, Brooke had retired — who else had his knowledge and experience of soldiering, or of defence matters as a whole?

I paid one visit to my 'parish' which involved staying with the British Military Attachés in Lisbon and Madrid, and I was required to brief a young man called Christopher Soames*, a captain in the Coldstream Guards, who was subsequently posted to Paris as Assistant MA. The following year he was to marry Churchill's daughter Mary, and twelve years later would be Secretary of State for War himself.

The other incident that remains in my memory was an unusual meeting in my local, the Bunch of Grapes on the corner of Buckingham Palace Road and Lower Grosvenor Place. I was chatting to a youngish man who seemed rather deferential. I eventually asked; 'What do you do?' He replied, 'I am the King's valet'. Though he didn't say so I sensed that he was willing me not to probe further, which I didn't. He told me that he had accompanied the King when he visited the Eighth Army after the capture of Tripoli, so we were able to reminisce about that occasion.

By the end of 1946 I knew that my elevated position in the War Office must end. I was thirty, and should return to 'regimental soldiering' if I was going to get anywhere. Sure enough I was posted back to my regiment, the Somerset Light Infantry, initially as 2nd in Command of the 2nd Battalion in Greece; but this was changed at the last minute to the 1st Battalion in India. Simone and I were spending Christmas with my parents, who had by now settled in Ireland, when the telegram came: 'For Greece read India'. From a family point of view this was a better posting as I could be 'accompanied' whereas the situation in Greece did not allow families.

---

* Later the Rt. Hon. Lord Soames, GCMG, GCVO, CH, CBE, PC.

CHAPTER 12

Ultimus in Indis

I SAILED from Southampton early in January 1947 on the troopship *Brittanic*, a converted passenger liner. It felt strange, returning to India almost exactly nine years after I had first gone out as a green young subaltern to join the same battalion. Five and a half years of war in the desert, Italy and north-west Europe, the Staff College, and marriage had obviously matured me but I was still very ignorant of regimental soldiering above the company level.

On arrival at Deolali, some ninety miles north-east of Bombay up on the Deccan plateau, I was met at the railway station by the CO, Charles Howard, who said 'I am off to another job and you are to assume temporary command until the new CO, John Platt arrives. He is at present with the British Joint Staff Mission in Washington and it may be several months before he can be released. So make sure you are correctly dressed [as a Lieutenant Colonel] before I introduce you to the officers!' It was an exciting but alarming start. Charles Howard was an extremely experienced regimental officer who knew the battalion backwards; he was alleged to know the name of every soldier. He knew me slightly from Poona in 1938-'39 and assumed that because I had had a fairly successful war I must know a good deal about how to command a battalion — which of course I didn't, particularly in a peacetime situation. However, it is well known that there is no better way to learn a job than to be thrown in at the deep end and told to get on with it.

I had a good team, particularly amongst the younger officers who were in their early twenties, none of whom I knew.* The battalion had spent most of the war in Burma, a campaign I was thankful to have missed. If I had not been given that unusual posting as Field Cashier to Force Heron in 1939 I should almost certainly have spent the war on the Burma front.

It seemed very fitting that I should find myself serving with one of the last British units to leave India, considering my family connections

---

*The Adjutant was Peter Bush who later became a major-general and Colonel of the Light Infantry.

going back nearly 100 years. It turned out to be the last, though I did not know this at the time.

As part of its plans for the post-war era the Attlee government announced in 1945 that India should be granted independence as soon as practicable. Wavell had then been Viceroy for two years and the extremely difficult task of recommending to whom HMG* handed over power fell on his shoulders.

There were two major political parties in India: the Hindu Congress, formerly led by Gandhi but now by Nehru, and the Muslim League led by Jinnah. Though Hindus outnumbered Muslims by four to one** the Muslim League was extremely powerful and Jinnah had continually insisted on dividing the sub-continent into what ultimately became India and Pakistan.

Wavell was unfortunately at loggerheads with Attlee throughout the protracted negotiations. The journal which he wrote up daily during the four years that he was Viceroy† makes sad reading. At the end of 1946 he wrote 'I have now committed myself, and very nearly committed HMG to . . . a definite date of termination of our control of India . . . I think I am right, and that this is the only way to avoid a worse disaster . . . It has been my fate for the last five or six years to have to conduct withdrawals, and to mitigate defeats, and I have had no real opportunity of a success'. On February 9th, 1947 he strongly advised HMG that a final attempt should be made to bring Congress and the League together before taking the decisive step of announcing a date for withdrawal. His advice was not accepted, and within a week HMG announced that power would be transferred to 'responsible Indian hands' by not later than June 1948, and that Mountbatten would succeed Wavell as Viceroy in March to put into effect the British government's plans.

This was the political scene when I assumed temporary command of the Somersets at Deolali. I was told that we would move to Bombay in April and be the last British unit to leave India early in 1948.

We were part of the 29th Infantry Brigade commanded by Brigadier Rupert Good, with whom I got on extremely well. A bevy of wives came out by troopship in March including Simone and Monica Good.

The winter of 1946-'47 in Britain was very severe and Simone recalls her problems in packing wooden crates and trunks of household goods on the top floor of her family home at Gaddesden Place, and then arranging for them to be collected by the LMS. The railway van could

*His Majesty's Government.
**Approximate figures were 400 million Hindus and 100 million Muslims.
†*Wavell — The Viceroy's Journal* Edited by Penderel Moon, p.402.

not get up the steep hill to Gaddesden because of snow drifts and eventually all the baggage was taken down on a farm trailer towed by a tractor. As though that was not enough, the troopship was due to sail from Glasgow and the main line over Shap was blocked for a few days. All ended well and the good ship *Cameronia* sailed with families and luggage in February.

We lived in a tiny bungalow which we called the 'cowshed' because it looked like one. We slept on the verandah under mosquito nets and were looked after by my old Hindu bearer, Krishna, who had been with me in Poona in 1938-'39. He had just turned up at Bombay when I arrived in January, and said: 'Sahib, here I am'. I wondered how he would cope with valeting a married couple but need have had no qualms. He had been bearer to the matron of a hospital during the war and knew the form. When he brought us early morning tea or woke us after an afternoon siesta, there would always be a discreet cough and a pause before he appeared through the curtains (doors would usually be open to keep the house cool).

There was little serious soldiering to be done at Deolali. We were mainly concerned with packing up, and preparing for Bombay. The battalion travelled there by train and I had decided that we would march to our barracks at Colaba Point on the sea from the main Bombay station, Victoria Terminus, known as 'VT'. It was a distance of two or three miles and it rained most of the time, but Bombay in April is quite hot and our khaki drill (KD) dried on us. A lot of Indians turned out to see what was going on and we had a very friendly reception.

Colaba Barracks was an imposing collection of buildings probably built before the first war and not at all like the average Indian cantonment. Our men liked it because they could get into the big city quite easily; they were by the sea and they knew that they were going home within the year. Simone and I were allotted a pleasant first-floor flat just outside barracks and overlooking the harbour. It had a long, very wide verandah and was well fitted out, which was just as well as we had to do a lot of entertaining including putting up Rupert Good, the Brigade Commander and Major General 'Bolo' Whistler, the extremely popular Major General British Troops India (MGBTI). Whistler had been commanding the 3rd Division in Holland when I was with the South Lancashires.

We acquired a dachshund puppy and called him Rommel (in no way disrespectful to the Field Marshal but in his memory). Simone took him everywhere in the basket of her bicycle. None of us had cars in those days. The only transport was an open army truck. We even went to smart functions at Government House in them, the ladies in their long dresses and very anxious about their hair. Simone remembers going out several evenings on her bicycle in a long dress.

John Platt, the 'proper' CO, did not finally arrive until July so I had a further very interesting three months in command. We had an IS (Internal Security) role in Bombay in the event of riots, which obviously had to be rehearsed, but otherwise training was restricted to our lines at Colaba.

Under the Viceroy each of the major Indian provinces was ruled by a British Governor. The Governor of Bombay was Sir John Colville whose son Ronnie had been a Brigade Major with me in the 5th Division in Italy. We saw a good deal of the Colvilles socially; they lived in great state at Government House. When HE dined with us one evening in the mess, 'The King' was played by our band when he entered the room. (As the king's representative, the governor was known as His Excellency, abbreviated to HE.) The highlight of my time in command was an invitation from the Colvilles to spend a weekend with them at Ganeshkind, about eighty miles from Bombay up in the hills. The Government always moved there when the monsoon broke in June and it became very sticky in Bombay. The protocol involved was unbelievable. We were told to send our bearer with the luggage by train in the morning and to be at VT ourselves for the Friday evening *Deccan Queen* to which the Governor's special coach would be attached. We were met at the station and escorted to the coach. I don't think we even needed tickets. Drinks were served on the coach during the two-hour journey. On arrival at Ganeshkind we were taken to our room and found Krishna squatting outside in the corridor waiting for us. Our suitcases had been unpacked, evening clothes (black tie and long dress) laid out and a bath run. We did not meet the Colvilles until we went down to dinner where there were several other guests. On Saturday guests breakfasted on their own. I was then invited to play golf with HE, and Simone received a written note from Her Excellency, to which she was expected to reply, inviting her to take coffee mid-morning. Later there was riding, followed by a large formal dinner party including many Indians, at which HE and Lady Colville made a state entrance. At the meal HE was always served first and walked into the room in front of the ladies. The next day we all went to church and after another ride took the train back to Bombay, travelling of course in the Governor's coach.

Pomp and ceremony such as this must seem extraordinary today, especially when one remembers that Indian Independence was to be declared only two months later on August 15th, but the Colvilles combined the dignity expected of them with great charm of manner, and we were made to feel at our ease. The sun was setting on the British Raj but it still had a red glow and we felt privileged to have been there.

John Platt arrived in July and took over command. Though we had not served together before, his younger brother Humphry had been at Wellington with me so there was a connection. We got on extremely well right from the beginning.

The new Viceroy's instructions from HMG were quite clear, independence not later than June 1948. But by June 1947, less than three months after he had assumed power, Mountbatten announced that the date would be brought forward to August 15th, 1947. He had already decided that partition into two sovereign states was inevitable. Violence was always very close to the surface, particularly in the Punjab where the worst effects of partition would fall. In Bombay, however, we were strangely insulated from the overall political scene. We took part in a moving parade on Independence Day; the Union Jack was lowered and the new flag of India raised after just under 200 years of British rule.* There was general rejoicing in the streets but no anti-British demonstrations. It was the same in Delhi where the Mountbattens were loudly cheered. It was when the details of partition became known that the killings began. In the Punjab a mass movement of migrants began, Muslims west and Hindus and Sikhs east. The number killed was officially put at a quarter of a million but may have been much higher.

We in Bombay escaped these horrors as the city was almost entirely Hindu. Many of us felt that if HMG had not been so determined to get out of India quickly, much of the bloodshed could have been avoided.

In September, after John Platt was firmly established in command, Simone and I spent a delightful fortnight's leave at Ootacamund (always known as 'Ooty'), 6,000 feet up in the Nilgiri Hills about 300 miles south-west of Madras. It was the hill station for the Madras Presidency and has been likened to Salisbury Plain with its countryside of green rolling uplands. We went by train and took both Krishna and Rommel, plus a lot of luggage as we had to be ready for anything from formal dinner parties to hunting. At the main stops Krishna would take Rommel for a trot along the platform. He would also bring us meal baskets ordered in advance at appropriate stations. The last leg to Ooty was on a cog railway which wound up through the many tea plantations covering the Nilgiri Hills. We stayed in the Ratan Tata Guest House, a comfortable establishment reserved for Government officials

*In 1757 Robert Clive won the Battle of Plessey, generally considered to be the most decisive battle in Britain's conquest of India.

and army officers on leave. Riding was the main attraction, and we were allowed to exercise the Governor's Bodyguard horses because I had known the cavalry officer who looked after them. We rode every morning quite early and hunted several times with the Ooty Hounds, when we often found ourselves galloping down steep *cudsides* (slopes) to cross *nullahs* (streams). I have never been a regular or particularly keen rider to hounds but those few days at Ooty were tremendous fun.

We were also invited to dine at Government House with Lieutenant General Sir Archie Nye, the last British Governor, who had been Brookie's VCIGS* for most of the war. Though pretty formal it was less so than Ganeshkind, partly I suspect because Ooty was tucked away in a remote corner of southern India. We returned to Bombay after an extremely enjoyable break.

We later had one weekend duck shooting and often used to sail in Bombay harbour. During our last winter in India we also hunted jackal with the Bombay and Poona Hounds at Chola. The Hunt put up a small tented camp every autumn near the kennels. We would drive out there on a Saturday evening, go to bed fairly early and be up for a 6 a.m. meet; it would be too hot to hunt much after 10 a.m. After a wash and brush up, we then sat down to a curry tiffin (lunch). The hunting was very different to Ooty: flat, brown and dusty with a few cactus hedges and many shallow wells. The main hazard was jumping a hedge and finding oneself on the lip of a well! The hunt members were mostly 'box-wallahs' (British businessmen). I remember one who regularly went to bed on Saturday evening with his hunting boots on. He would have eaten and drunk well and wanted to be ready for action.

The most unusual thing that happened to me after our leave at Ooty was John Platt's decision to appoint me Adjutant (the equivalent of Brigade Major at the battalion level) for the last five months of our time in Bombay. There was nothing much to do as 2nd in Command, but for the Adjutant a great deal of staff work and protocol connected with our final departure. I enjoyed this very much and suspect that I am one of the very few officers who can honestly claim to have been CO, 2nd in Command and Adjutant of a battalion *in that order* within a year!

Gandhi's murder by a Hindu extremist in Delhi after Independence occurred shortly before our final departure. We expected trouble in the streets but there was none.

After Christmas we began to pack up and prepare for the final ceremonial departure, which was to be on February 28th, 1948. By then nearly 50,000 British troops had been phased through the huge transit

*Vice Chief of the Imperial General Staff.

camp at Kalyan outside Bombay, *en route* home by troopship.

Ever since we had arrived in Bombay men had been going home on demob and of course were not replaced. By the New Year our strength was down to about 200 and it was not easy to ensure that we had enough really smart men left who would form the Guard of Honour to march through the Gateway of India, an imposing arch erected to mark King George V's Durbar in 1911. Fortunately we had an exceptionally good Regimental Sergeant Major (RSM) Ken Bartlett who, particularly on drill, would have compared favourably with his Guardsman counterpart, and on the day everything went extremely well. I commanded the Guard since John Platt was required to receive a silver model of the Gateway from the first Indian Governor of Bombay, Sir Maharaj Singh. The finale of the parade involved slow-marching through the Gateway and down some steps to a waiting launch with our colours 'trooped'*, and an Indian band playing 'Auld Lang Syne'. I am told that many Indians in the crowd were in tears. Simone will always remember, as she sat among the Indian officers' wives, their friendliness and lack of restraint in a very unusual situation.

The English editions of the Bombay press were kind to us the next day. Headlines included: 'Tributes paid to Battalion; Historic Ties with Country' and 'Good-bye to your great country'. Finally the *Illustrated London News* gave us its front page on March 13th. The Somerset Light Infantry had every reason to be proud of being *Ultimus in Indis*.

For Simone and me, the end of this story was rather an anticlimax. Having only served one year of the normal three-year overseas tour, I was posted to the Kings Own Yorkshire Light Infantry (KOYLI) in Malaya; so having accompanied the Colour Party out to the troopship *Empress of Australia* lying at anchor in the harbour, I had a quick glass of champagne and had to return to shore, to wait two or three days until a P & O liner the *Strathnavar* could take us to Singapore. All the same, we felt very lucky to have taken part in these historic events. My family had been so much involved in India that it seemed fitting that we should be represented in the final act.

As an epilogue to our year in India we found a home for Rommel and sent money to Krishna for several years via the Salvation Army until we heard that he no longer needed help. One might add here that the Raj has since been presented to the British public of the 1980s and '90s by the television series *The Jewel in the Crown*** and the films *A*

---

*Held in the horizontal position.
** ' "The Jewel in the Crown" is a phrase often used to describe India's position in the British Empire. No term could be less appropriate. A jewel is a small object. India is the largest and most populous territory ever to have been possessed by an imperial power.' *End of Empire*, Brian Lapping, p.17.

Passage to India and *Gandhi*, to much acclaim. However, those who know India would, I feel sure, agree with me that the depiction of the British role is in all these titles something of a caricature and frequently amounts to misrepresentation — the blimpish officials portrayed on screen, for example, bear little relation to most Indian Civil Service staff (nearly all university graduates). Perhaps the most telling tribute to the Raj is that nearly all university graduates, British tourists or businessmen who visit either India or Pakistan today are genuinely welcomed.

CHAPTER 13

The Jungle is Neutral

AFTER a very pleasant voyage lasting about eight days we arrived at Singapore and travelled on by train to Taiping in the state of Perak, 350 miles north of Singapore, where the KOYLI were stationed.

A little background information about Malaya is necessary. The country is about the size of the British Isles without Ireland and contains one of the world's three main areas of rain forest (the other two being the Amazon Basin in Brazil and the Congo Basin in West Africa). Rain is heavy throughout the year and the heat is constant. Four-fifths of the country is primeval jungle which covers the mountain range, running down the spine of Malaya and rising to 6,000 feet.

A British colony before the war, the country was invaded and taken over by the Japanese in 1942. The population was then about five million, made up of 2½ million Malays, 2 million Chinese and some 600,000 Indians (mostly Tamils from the south). Each of the nine states had an hereditary Sultan as ruler with limited powers. The Malays were essentially a rural people whereas the Chinese were the businessmen and lived in the towns. Their business of course was rubber and tin. It is not generally known that seeds of rubber trees brought from Brazil and grown in a tropical planthouse at Kew were taken to Malaya in 1877. There were no rubber trees anywhere in South-East Asia before this. Today Malaya produces about a third of the world's natural rubber. Tin was discovered at about the same time. It mostly lay near the surface in the flat plains west of the main range, having been washed off the mountains by incessant rain, and was mined by mechanical dredges. Like the rubber, Malayan tin became one of the world's richest sources.

When Japan surrendered on August 9th, 1945 a major seaborne operation was already under way to land 180,000 British and Indian troops on the west coast of Malaya at Morib. Known as 'Operation Zipper', it was too far advanced to be cancelled so the troops duly waded ashore, some of them knee-deep in mud. Waiting for them on the beach were some members of Force 136, the name given to a stay-behind organisation run by Special Operations Executive (SOE). When the Japanese invaded, the Malayan Communist Party (MCP), predominantly Chinese, took to the jungle and throughout the occupation were of considerable nuisance value to the Allies. A number of Chinese-speaking British officers were parachuted into the jungle or landed from submarines to join them. Jim Hannah, a New Zealander whom I met shortly after we arrived, told me that as a member of Force 136 he came down to the beach and watched the landings. He was suddenly accosted by a rather officious beachmaster who said to him 'What unit are you?' 'Force 136,' said Jim. The beachmaster quickly looked down his landing-table and said 'You aren't due to land until D plus 7.' Jim replied 'Sorry, but I've been here for the last three years.'

The MCP, which during the occupation changed its name to the Malayan People's Anti-Japanese Army (MPAJA), now revealed its true colours. They remained in the jungle, and very shortly after we arrived at Taiping started their campaign of murder and terror aimed at hoisting the Red Flag over Singapore. However, Malaya was almost the only former colony which had welcomed the British back after the war. We were a very useful buffer between the Malays and Chinese, rebuilding the economy and keeping the peace. HMG had tried unsuccessfully to introduce equal citizenship for all; instead, a Malayan Federation was created in February 1948 which restored the State Sultans' sovereignty and limited powers, and reserved citizenship principally for Malays.

This was the situation when we arrived in Taiping, having been told in Bombay that Malaya would be great fun — wonderful Chinese servants and a high standard of living. To my astonishment I was the eighth major to be joining the battalion (the establishment was six) so there was no proper job for me.*

I spent an enjoyable week or two up at a hill station called Maxwell's Hill, running a pre-staff college course for five or six officers who were shortly due to take the entrance exam. Then a vacancy for a rifle company occurred under rather unusual circumstances. The company commander and several men were sheltering from a tropical storm under a huge fallen tree when the trunk slipped off its base, killing a sergeant and injuring the major.

In June the balloon went up to the extent that three leading Chinese anti-Communists were shot in daylight and two British rubber planters were murdered in Perak. An emergency was declared and I had the doubtful distinction of taking out the first British company to be

*The vast expansion of the infantry during the war and the resultant crossposting between regiments was still being felt in 1948. As far as possible officers and men were posted within their geographical grouping, e.g. Wessex, Home Counties, Welsh, Lowland. In the Light Infantry, which included regiments from Durham to Cornwall, we were kept within the group.

based on a rubber plantation to protect the manager and his labour force, mostly Tamils. Morale was high, as the men quite rightly felt that there was an important job to be done.

Communist tactics appeared to be to slash rubber trees, stir up grievances among workers on estates and tin mines and, by far the most serious, to murder any British manager who presented an easy target.

Whilst we were out on our guard duties the battalion moved on to Penang Island where there was a comfortable modern barracks together with married quarters. It was comforting to know that one's wife was pretty safe — throughout the twelve year emergency there was hardly an incident on Penang Island.

Guarding rubber plantations was of course only a small part of our job. We had to go into the jungle and flush out the 'bandits' as we called them. They were later officially known as Communist terrorists (CTs). Intelligence told us that there might be up to 10,000 hidden away in the dense jungle up and down the country and they had considerable caches of arms (mostly rifles and sten guns) which we had dropped to them during the war! They were known to have 'camps' each holding about twenty, which would be well guarded.

At this critical moment a distinguished former member of Force 136, Freddie Spencer-Chapman, published a book called *The Jungle is Neutral*. He had spent two to three years with the CTs and wrote the book to tell British troops how to live in the jungle without fear. It became a bible to all of us. The jungle was a frightening place to begin with; dark with enormously tall trees reaching for the light. It has been likened to the gloom of a cathedral. There was thick undergrowth through which we sometimes had to cut our way; it was hot and sticky (though not nearly as hot as in the sun outside) and there was background noise all the time from monkeys and various birds and insects. Leeches were probably the hazard the men really hated. Whenever we halted, they smelt our blood and could be seen edging towards us on the path. They could work their way through the eyelets of boots and from there up to the more private parts of one's body. Once a leech had latched onto you the only effective way to remove it was with a lighted cigarette. We seldom met snakes or elephants though one always knew when the latter were around because the undergrowth was disturbed and leeches particularly active. There were also mosquitoes at night but they were usually non-malarial.

We got used to this somewhat alarming environment surprisingly quickly and the men were adept at improvisation in the way that they rigged up 'bashas' (jungle shelters) to sleep in, cooked rice dishes on open fires and adapted their olive green (OG) uniform to their own individual style. It was very much an individualist 'war' fought on a one-man front.

In July the Governor, Sir Edward Gent, who was ordered home for consultations was killed in a mid-air collision over London airport. In the same month I was ordered to establish my company HQ at Tapah, an important railway junction in Perak halfway between Penang and Kuala Lumpur. I kept one platoon with me and the other two were deployed up to twenty miles away. Here I worked closely with the Malayan police whose senior officers were still all British. Some had been in Japanese prison camps. Most spoke Malay and a few Chinese. We learnt a lot about the country from them and relations were generally excellent, but as a counter to the CTs they were not effective on their own.

I was given a double room in the local government rest-house and enquired straightaway whether my wife could join me there, for however brief a period. The Police Superintendent raised no objection and offered Simone a secretarial job, as Chinese staff were being threatened by the CTs and as a result laid off. We had acquired a Morris Eight in Penang and Simone immediately drove alone the 150 miles down to Tapah. Unfortunately I had to go out on patrol almost as soon as she arrived and we were unable to do justice to that nice double room. However, she thoroughly enjoyed the work, was enrolled in the Malayan Police as a sergeant and kept indexes of all known CTs in the district. Never having typed before, she brought letters that required attention back to the rest-house and wrestled with them in the evenings on my ancient portable typewriter.

In August it was announced that a Guards Brigade was to be sent to Malaya to reinforce the relatively small army garrison. As the Brigade of Guards had never been known to serve east of Suez before, this was news indeed. One of the three battalions, the Coldstream Guards, duly arrived in Tapah in September and established their HQ there. Though we were almost as green as they were, they made us feel positive veterans. In the hurry to pack up in London the Officers' Mess brought out quite a lot of silver, photograph albums, pictures and books which I imagine they must have regretted when they found themselves in tents in a very humid climate. One of the company commanders tells me that he also took a copy of Debrett's *Peerage* for luck. One day he saw a snake curled up on a chair in the Mess Tent and effectively squashed it with this tome.

As part of the deployment plan to spread army units over as wide an area as possible, I was ordered to move my company to Bidor, about ten miles south of Tapah. It became known as a bad area though I am not sure that we realised this at the time.

One day early in October I was out doing a recce in a truck with just my batman as escort. I had been told that there was a lovely deep pool of cool water on the jungle fringe, formed by a fast-flowing stream as it cascaded over rocks. It had been a popular picnic spot for the European community before the Emergency. We found it quite easily and had a refreshing swim. The water was deep enough to dive into from the rocks. Back in Bidor I told my platoon commanders, and suggested that they might include a visit on their way back from patrol. Next day Dennis Lock with about fifteen men called at this spot; he posted two sentries and told the rest that they could strip off and bathe. No sooner were they either in the pool or poised to dive into it, than CTs opened heavy fire from hidden positions within the jungle at a range of thirty yards. They could scarcely miss and the sentries were powerless; there was no target except the jungle. Four men were killed, including Dennis, and a further five injured. By the time we got there the CTs had of course disappeared, leaving nothing but empty cartridge cases. The scene in and around the pool was grim. It seems fairly certain that some CTs had been there the previous day, saw just two soldiers and said 'let's wait for a larger target.' With hindsight, we should of course have patrolled through the immediate jungle around the pool, and then posted sentries. I felt contrite and very sad.

This ambush was one of the worst throughout Malaya during that first year, and valuable lessons were learned at a cost of four lives. Our men were angry and determined to avenge the lives of their comrades.

Shortly afterwards, the Coldstream Guards with four companies took over the area which we had had to cover with just one company, and we moved further north towards Ipoh. Simone stayed on with the police at Tapah for about two months until she was relieved by reinforcements from home. A number of former Palestine policemen had volunteered to come out. Many already knew what it was like to be shot at. It was sad that Simone and I hardly ever spent a night together at Tapah Rest House but she felt far more useful there than staying in our married quarter at Penang.

At one stage we were based on a tin mine in the famous Kinta Valley, which was a considerable change from the jungle. Again the CT target would be the British manager, living in a comfortable bungalow with all mod. cons, but very vulnerable. For those interested, the method of mining was (and I suspect still is) that the area having been surveyed, a huge hole was dug, a mechanical dredge then moved into it, the hole flooded so that the dredge floated, and finally a bucket band started up. I remember that they made a rather eerie screeching noise which went on night and day.

On another occasion I went out on patrol with John Davis, probably the most well-known of the Force 136 officers who had stayed behind. He had been awarded the DSO and spoke fluent Chinese. We learnt a tremendous amount from him about the CTs, their mode of life in the jungle, their sources of food, and their tactics and philosophy.

It was their sources of food that we had to attack. In the jungle you could survive (just) on bamboo shoots and the flesh of wild pigs if you could track one down. Outside the jungle it was a different matter. There were a large number of Chinese squatter settlements on the jungle fringe, which had been created to escape the brutality of the Japanese. These 'villages' became targets for the CTs; many were terrorised in those early days into supplying the CTs with all the food that they wanted, and almost as important, information. Conversely, it became a major Government aim to win them over to our side. 'Winning the hearts and minds of the people' became General Templer's main battle cry when he became High Commissioner in 1952, as I shall describe later.

During that first winter in Malaya I was able to get back for occasional weekends at Penang. As the climate varied little, summer or winter — we were a mere four degrees north of the Equator — there was considerable competition to take a week or so off up at the Cameron Highlands, a hill station created pre-war out of primary jungle fifty miles from Tapah at a height of 6,000 feet. It was modelled on an English village, complete with pub called the Smoke House Inn. There was a nine-hole golf course, and the climate was marvellous after the sticky heat down in the coastal plain. One could book a very comfortable villa complete with staff. For those whose duties did not require them to 'jungle-bash', there were several carefully-laid paths through the jungle so that you could at least pretend that you knew what it was like. Leeches apparently found the high jungle rather chilly so one couldn't truthfully dine out on the intimate details of burning leeches off.

In my company we made several successful attacks on CT camps, usually involving a long approach march walking single file on a path — of a sort — through the jungle. If the CT base was thought to be some way in, we would probably camp ourselves for a night *en route*. It was obviously important to be extremely quiet; this was not at all easy if the jungle was thick and the path difficult to follow. We always hoped to get a clue of some sort as we approached the target; the smell of smoke, cigarette ends, possibly some noise of chopping wood and the occasional call. There would almost certainly be a sentry covering the main approach. The reader may well ask: how did we ever surprise the CTs? The answer is that we seldom did. They moved very quickly if they had the slightest inkling that danger was at hand. There were occasions when they would man their defences and fight it out but these were rare and I do not remember any that first year. Very shortly after our tragic Bidor ambush, one of my platoons was out with the Coldstream Guards when they surprised five CTs in a jungle workshop. One was shot dead; the other four escaped. Large quantities of armourers' tools, spare parts and ammunition were captured. An article about this raid later appeared in the London *Times*.

As the police gradually became stronger and more effective, CTs occasionally surrendered and could be persuaded to lead us to their former camp. The SEP (surrendered enemy personnel) would walk in front, carefully covered by our leading scout to make sure that he was not going to double-cross us. When we were close to the camp there would be a whispered conference with the SEP to make a plan of attack, and particularly to try and cut off the escape route. I went on several patrols with SEPs and was led to CT camps — but the birds had always flown.

Early in 1949 I applied for ten days' leave to go to Bangkok. I think Simone and I were the first 'tourists' to travel up there from Malaya since the Emergency began. We went by train, a distance of 800 miles. About halfway a bridge over quite a large river was still down, having been destroyed either by the Allies or the Japanese. We therefore had to change trains and cross the river in a sampan (a local boat propelled by a pole). During the inevitable wait for the other train we went for a walk along the line and met an elephant, fortunately not a wild one. The whole journey took about forty-eight hours. On arrival we stayed in a small hotel and were shown the sights by the British chaplain and his family; he had recently done a swap for a few weeks with his opposite number in Penang, where we had met him.

I have hazy memories of canals with floating markets, very ornate Buddhist temples and elaborately decorated royal barges. We wrote our names in the British Ambassador's calling book (as was the custom in those days) and were invited to lunch. Sight-seeing was hard work in the humid climate but we thoroughly enjoyed the break.

In the early summer my company was moved to Kroh in Upper Perak, close to the Thai frontier, a much sought-after location as it was about 1,000 feet above sea level, and therefore relatively cool. The area was also predominantly Malay and friendly. Our job was to patrol the most frequented routes which CTs were known to use into and out of Malaya. There was a large British-owned open-cast tin mine nine miles away at Klian Intan, the only one of its size not operated by a dredge. Its Chinese labour force was riddled with Communist sympathisers and not friendly. We needed to visit it regularly if only to prove that we were nearby.

Kroh boasted an Assistant District Officer (ADO), an official of the Malayan Civil Service (MCS) who was the Government's representative and responsible for administering the district. He turned out to be a young man from Somerset named Christopher Blake, aged twenty-nine, who had served with the Indian Army during the latter part of the war and then volunteered to join the MCS. He had actually waded ashore in Operation 'Zipper' in 1945, and had come up to Kroh in 1948 after being Private Secretary to the Governor of Singapore. We got on well together, making sure that each knew what the other was doing. Christopher had to work closely with the small Malay Police detachment (as did we) and visit the outlying *kampongs* (villages) in his area. He also had to keep in close touch with Rahman Hydraulic Ltd, the tin mine at Klian Intan, whose unpopular British manager was murdered the following year. Fortunately Christopher's boss, the District Officer of Grik, was thirty miles away and reached only by a rough road often blocked by rain, and my CO was in Penang so we were able to run our own show without much interference. Christopher tells an amusing story about a predecessor who arranged for a tree to be felled across the road when he was told that the British Resident wanted to visit. Naturally no one could be found or persuaded to move it. Communications were also uncertain. We had both telephone and radio but neither were reliable.*

Such was our isolation, but it was fun and easily the most enjoyable few months of my tour. Simone was able to visit on two occasions. Intrepid as ever, she drove up alone from Penang and stayed with a friendly couple at Klian Intan. The last nine miles from Kroh were narrow and very winding with primary jungle right up to the verge, a perfect setting for ambush, which did not escape the CTs' attention as I shall mention later. In retrospect, I can see that a lone white woman in a small civilian car was probably not considered a worthwhile target.

There weren't any particularly successful patrols from Kroh. We were so close to the Thai frontier that the CTs could slip across at any time, knowing that they were safe and we could not follow. We were able to cover the road but not the main paths through the jungle.

*Christopher's book, *A View from Within*, Mendip Publishing 1990, covers his year at Kroh in detail and makes enjoyable reading. (My only criticism is that he says that I was a Cambridge graduate whereas of course I was at the other place.)

In the late summer of 1949 we moved down to Baling in the heat of the plains just inside the state of Kedah. The jungle has a certain sameness about it wherever you are. It is only when one emerges into what was called secondary jungle or 'bluker' that it's possible to see the sky and establish one's whereabouts. I remember both a tiger and a python were brought in for our inspection (dead of course), a considerable distraction for the men. By this time we had several tame monkeys that travelled around with us, but nothing larger.

B Company was a happy unit; I had an experienced 2nd in Command, Derek Sutcliffe, who had been in action against the Japanese. There were also three very different but reliable platoon commanders: Colin Huxley, who was the first post-war Sandhurst cadet to be given a regular commission in the KOYLI, Robin Handley, Kings Shropshire Light Infantry (KSLI), a very keen and rather unorthodox man which in this sort of soldiering was no bad thing, and Sergeant Peter Firth, an excellent NCO who was later commissioned.

The men almost all came from the West Riding of Yorkshire. Company Sergeant Major 'Tojo' Crossland and Company Quartermaster Sergeant Arthur Bland, the two key figures, were very loyal Yorkshiremen who regarded an outsider like me with some suspicion to begin with. However, after a month or two we were getting on excellently. Forty-one years later, Bland called in to see us at Gaddesden and gave me a framed photo taken in Kroh. Once Yorkshiremen accept you there is no holding them!

After a month or so at Baling I was told that I had been selected to attend the RAF Staff College course at Bracknell (Berks) which started in January 1950 and lasted a year. Simone and I were to pack up and leave by troopship in a matter of weeks.

So my eighteen months commanding a company on active service was to end. It had been very valuable experience and I was sad to say goodbye to a fine bunch of men. We naturally considered ourselves to be the best company (of the four in the battalion). We had had our fair share of contact with the CTs and apart from the Bidor ambush had had no casualties.

Within a week or two of my departure, Sutcliffe, who had taken over command, was ambushed on the Klian Intan road and had a very lucky escape himself though sadly three of his men were killed. He was returning from visiting Colin Huxley's platoon at Klian Intan with three vehicles: two open Dodge trucks with one man in the back as escort and he himself in his jeep between them. The CTs must have seen this small lightly-armed convoy going up to Klian Intan and concluded correctly that it would return before dark. The ambush was sited on a long horseshoe bend and all three vehicles were inevitably caught. On the outside (higher) part of the bend the jungle had been cleared and gave good fields of fire. The inside of the bend dropped sharply and the CTs had sited a cut-off in the gully to pick off anybody who tried to escape that way. The two drivers and one of the escort were killed outright, and the other escort feigned death and even survived a *coup de grace* from an automatic which just missed his left ear. Sutcliffe escaped uphill towards one of the firing parties which appeared suicidal, but he went to ground in the *lallang* (long grass) and though the CTs searched for him, even calling out: 'We'll get you, Red Fox', (he had red hair and a red moustache) he was still there and unhurt when Colin arrived with his platoon, by which time the CTs had vanished across the Thai frontier only 300 yards away.

Hearing about it afterwards, I could picture the scene so well. It shows only too clearly how vulnerable we were and how unfriendly the jungle can be. I also reflected how easily it could have been me.

CHAPTER 14

RAF Staff College and Another War Office Job

WE sailed home from Singapore on the troopship *Dunera*. I had spent just under the statutory three years overseas. Simone was unfortunately taken quite seriously ill when we were just past Malta, and it was decided that we would both have to be put ashore at Tripoli where there was a military hospital. The *Dunera* duly hove to and we went off in a launch, Simone having been hoisted by davit on a stretcher while waving to our fellow passengers as she was high with morphia. After a week in hospital she joined me in a sea-front hotel where Rommel had stayed during the war! It was almost as though we were required to pay our last respects to that charismatic figure.

The problem then was how to get home for Christmas. No troopships were due to call and all aircraft seemed to be full. Fortunately an old friend from the Staff College was working at the local HQ and found us two seats on a York, a civilian version of the Lancaster bomber. After rather a noisy flight we landed at Blackbush on December 7th and were driven to Gaddesden. Whilst Simone rested I went up to Liverpool to recover our luggage. In those days officers accompanied by their families travelled in some style; our kit included a dining-room carpet bought in Bombay (which we still use), a teak and camphor-wood Chinese chest bought in Penang, several cabin trunks of uniform and clothes, and the usual packing cases of china, glass and personal effects, in all perhaps twenty items. A sofa and two armchairs also bought in Bombay had somehow found their way home with the Somersets' Officers Mess eighteen months earlier. Fortunately Customs were friendly and I did not have to open anything.

As we sorted ourselves out, it was just as well we did not know that three years later we would be returning once more from Singapore by troopship, would lose all our luggage, and arrive home by air only with what we stood up in; but I am anticipating events.

My parents had settled into their new home in Ireland at Coolnakilly and we were able to spend a quiet Christmas with them. My father had inherited the house from an elderly spinster cousin whose father, Captain James Whitshed De Butts, was one of Augustus' nine sons. James had three daughters, none of whom married. It was an attractive Regency house set in sixty-four acres five miles inland from the sea and about thirty miles south of Dublin. I had spent several holidays there as a boy when old cousin Eleanor was alive. Conditions were primitive; no piped water, no electricity, no telephone. Eleanor died in 1938 and the house was empty throughout the war. My parents settled there in 1946 and installed mod. cons, and Katie Beauchamp joined them shortly afterwards, having sold her north Oxford house.

Early in January 1950 we rented some rooms in Sunninghill Vicarage, Ascot, conveniently close to Bracknell. I bought another ancient Morris Eight, which was fine on the flat but didn't like hills, and we acquired another 'Rommel dog' — that is, a dachshund puppy. The RAF Staff College was the equivalent of Camberley for the Army. A few RN and Army officers were also selected to attend, and there were about eighty of us altogether. Many of the RAF students had distinguished flying records from the war and were well decorated. One such, Squadron Leader Tommy Byrne, DSO, DFC, had lost a leg but managed to play a good game of squash by standing in the middle of the court and making his opponent run round him. Another, Wing Commander Andrew Willan, DFC, had been shot down in 1940 in a Whitley bomber over Hamburg and spent the duration as a POW. His brother serving in the Greenjackets had been killed in the defence of Calais, so at one stage Andrew's parents feared that they had lost both their sons. I became friendly with Andrew and it turned out that we had both rowed at Oxford. We were able to join up with two members of the Directing Staff to form a four and row from Leander Club at Henley, the only time that I have been privileged to use this mecca of the rowing establishment. I was delighted when two years later Andrew invited me to be godfather to his daughter Andrea.

Much of the early part of the course was fairly basic. Unlike the four-month war courses, there was time to learn, and it was like being at school again. We had a lecture on how to write English. After telling us to be concise, use short words and not to waffle, the speaker said that the best examples of modern English prose were *The Times* leaders and Churchill's wartime speeches; both were written to a tight limit in terms of both words and time. I believe that advice holds good today.

We went over to Ireland for Easter and Simone announced that she was going to have a baby. The doctor said that she should take things easily, so my parents invited her to stay on at Coolnakilly until November when the baby was due. I 'lived in' at Bracknell for the rest of the course.

We naturally studied the lessons of the war in the air, and in particular the effect that heavy bombing had had on Germany's ability to continue the struggle. We considered area bombing like the 1,000 bomber raids on Cologne and Hamburg, pin-point attacks on specific targets like ball-bearing factories, and raids on railway marshalling yards, oil plants and many others. We noted that our economic intelligence had been seriously at fault in that Germany was able, even as late as 1944, to increase war production, and that it was also not until then that we could deliver a heavy attack with real precision. Finally we studied the dramatic effect of the bombing of communications, particularly railways and oil plants during the period before and after D Day.

We had lectures from members of the Air Council and several distinguished scientists. The one that remains most clearly in my memory was that given by Professor R.V. Jones, Head of Scientific Intelligence at the Air Ministry during the war, whose individual contribution to final victory must have been immense. It was he who studied the German rocket development at Peenemünde on the Baltic, and who was able to warn the War Cabinet of the timing and nature of the threat from the V1 and V2. The particular story which intrigued me most was to do with jamming. The German night fighters which went up every night to intercept Bomber Command's raids were directed onto their targets by ground controllers, whose transmissions were heavily jammed from Britain by German speakers who gave the night fighters entirely different information on height, bearing, etc. We knew that this misinformation was very effective, and that the night fighters sometimes never found the main bomber stream at all. One night, in desperation, women were substituted for all the German male controllers. Jones told us that it was anticipated that the Germans would do this, and he had German-speaking women ready and waiting to carry on the work — a brilliant piece of anticipation by any standard.

The course also included visits to bomber stations, fighter stations, army units, warships and some factories. RAF officers in the GD (General Duties) Branch — that is, pilots — have to keep their hand in at flying when not on flying duties in order to qualify for flying pay. Bracknell had an arrangement with a small RAF station at White Waltham nearby to provide aircraft. On several occasions I went up as a passenger, and when our son David was born on November 15th was able to get a quick lift to RAF Valley on Anglesey Island and then catch the night boat to Dun Loaghaire.

David's arrival in Hatch Street Nursing Home, Dublin was a matter of great family rejoicing as I was an only child and there were no other male De Butts around except in the USA.

The Korean War started in that summer of 1950 (and was to involve a complete division of Commonwealth troops). One of the special events at the end of the course was a series of addresses by very senior members of the three services. When the Army's turn came the speaker began quite normally, but after about ten minutes there was suddenly a long pause and it was obvious that something was wrong. We all became very embarrassed and he then said 'I'm very sorry but I've dried up'. The Commandant who was sitting at the back of the hall said quickly 'Ten-minute break', and we all trooped out and went to the bar. We later reassembled and the General invited questions, but he had lost his train of thought and was floundering. We heard afterwards that he had been under very heavy pressure in the War Office because of Korea, and when his MA (Military Assistant) reminded him of the Bracknell engagement and asked whether he would like some notes prepared, had said 'Quite unnecessary'. So he came without any form of aide-memoire and must have had a minor brainstorm. I have always remembered this rather sad occurrence and its lesson: always have some notes in your pocket, just in case.

The Bracknell course duly ended in mid-December and we had a very happy family Christmas at Coolnakilly, including David's christening. Among the guests was Brigadier Tubby Martin, my old Brigade Commander from Italy who was now living in retirement outside Dublin.

My next posting was to the War Office in a Grade 2 (Major) Q staff appointment. Q branch dealt with the supply and maintenance of the Army, that is, virtually all administrative matters except personnel, which are the responsibility of A branch. My previous jobs had been almost entirely on the G (General Staff) side and we were always told that it was important to have a balanced career. It was not a very exciting job but I was not concerned as our new family came first. We bought for £6,500 a four-bedroomed detached house, which we called Parson's Field, in Potten End, the village next to Gaddesden, and moved in straightaway. I commuted to Euston from Berkhamsted — steam trains in those days. Sadly, Rommel died under unusual circumstances within a week or two. He had swallowed a long darning needle which had been used by the Irish cook to sew up our Christmas turkey and had subsequently been thrown away together with some of the turkey's innards, which Rommel scavenged. The needle perforated his stomach. I saw it sticking through his ribs and pulled it out but the damage was already done.

We engaged a Norland nanny at £3 per week to look after David.

Her name was Miss London. She was middle-aged, much too efficient and treated us like children too! Her contract ended after a year and we advertised for a replacement nanny. A Scottish girl from Perth with nursery nursing training answered and after getting a good reference from her minister, we took her without interview. Her name was Marion.

In the autumn of 1951 the first Army manoeuvres since the war were staged on Salisbury Plain and involved a Corps of two divisions. It was said to be the largest deployment of regular troops in the UK in peacetime, and involved very complicated clearances with farmers and other landowners. My War Office branch was involved because we were looking at new ways of maintaining an army in the field. I spent ten very interesting days in perfect autumnal weather on the Plain.

The King died suddenly at Sandringham on February 6th, 1952. Only six days before he had seen off Princess Elizabeth and the Duke of Edinburgh on the start of what was to have been an Australian tour. He even had a day's shooting on February 5th. Simone and I were allotted seats on the Horse Guards for the State Funeral on February 15th.

Early in 1952 I was told by the Colonel of the Somersets, Lieutenant General Sir John Swayne, that he would like me to be one of the Light Infantry instructors at Sandhurst as my next posting, which was due at the end of the year. This would be an attractive job especially since, as a University candidate, I had not been commissioned from Sandhurst myself. However, no sooner had we got used to this idea than it was cancelled! The Somersets, then stationed at Wuppertal in Germany, were ordered to Malaya and would leave by troopship in October. I was required to join them as soon as possible as 2nd in Command.

CHAPTER 15

Malaya under Templer — Winning the Hearts and Minds

CAROLINE was born on June 26th and after a family christening at Gaddesden we packed up Parson's Field and went over to Ireland. I then set forth once more for a very brief visit to Germany and joined the Somersets at Wuppertal. They too were packing up and my job was simply to get to know people again as the battalion would go on block leave in September before reassembling at Bulford (Wilts) for a farewell parade. The CO, James Brind, together with the company commanders would be flying out to Malaya ahead of the battalion and I would be required to take the main body by sea, leaving Southampton in late October.

I was able to spend a week or two at Coolnakilly in late September. Families would be allowed to follow the battalion to Malaya as there was accommodation at Kuala Lumpur, which was to be our base. Since Caroline was only three months old and not an easy baby we decided that Simone would not join me until the early summer of 1953. Marion had agreed to come too and would rejoin the family in Ireland a few weeks before they sailed.

Carter Barracks, Bulford was a hutted camp and adequate for our short term needs. Early in October, after everybody had returned from embarkation leave, the CIGS Field Marshal Sir William Slim, of Burma fame, visited us. Like Wavell, he was a taciturn man who had been a very popular and successful Commander of the Fourteenth Army. Later, when Governor General of Australia, he was at a public function when a reporter came up to him and said 'A smile please, Your Excellency, for the camera.' Slim is alleged to have replied 'Young man, I am smiling.' Slim's visit was followed about a fortnight later by John Harding, now a full General, who was to take the salute at our farewell parade. Fortunately Ken Bartlett, still RSM, was able to raise the level of drill to a high standard. The weather that October was cold but dry and the parade went well. I was required to command it as the CO was inevitably involved in protocol with General Harding and other dignitaries.

There was just time before we left to attend Andrea Willan's christening in Oxford, where her father was commanding the University Air Squadron.

On October 27th, 1952 we duly sailed for Singapore in the troopship *Dilwara*. A high proportion of our men were doing their eighteen months as National Servicemen and few had ever been overseas before. Many came from the West Country, Somerset and Cornwall, but there were also a few from Yorkshire and Durham. Their training on call-up was limited to ten weeks but they would be on active service as soon as we landed. During the four-week voyage we continued with training, particularly weapon handling. Every afternoon I arranged for men to fire live ammunition at tin cans towed in the wash of the ship. This was popular with the men but very unpopular with some of the passengers (service families or civil servants) whose afternoon naps were disturbed. I had to explain that these young men would be risking their lives as soon as we disembarked, and it was my duty to give them as much practice as possible in firing their weapons.

At Aden we stopped to refuel and I planned a route march through the town. The doctors on board raised their eyebrows; it would be very hot, the men were not used to marching in this sort of climate, there might be cases of heat stroke. I considered it important that they should have at least an hour's marching and it was finally agreed that this would take place at 7 a.m. I don't think that a single man fell out. They then had a short time to look round the local bazaar before re-embarking. I heard afterwards that this was the first time for many years that a British regiment had marched through Aden. I remember being very pleased that I had stuck to my guns.

We arrived at Singapore on November 24th, were met by the CO and the rest of the advance party and went straight to a tented camp at Kota Tinggi just across the Straits into Johore. We were to be there until after Christmas, training for jungle warfare and acclimatising the men. The camp was badly equipped; it rained almost continuously and officers and NCOs had their work cut out making conditions as tolerable as possible for young conscripts who wondered what had hit them.

The reader may well ask: what had happened during the three years since I had left the KOYLI in October 1949? The simple answer is that there had been a general deterioration in the security situation; this was caused partly by the Communist victory in China and by HMG's recognition of the new regime. Two more brigades of British troops had arrived, and a Director of Operations had been appointed, Lieutenant General Sir Harold Briggs.* He immediately tackled the problem of

*Briggs had commanded a division in Burma under Slim and retired in 1948. He agreed to come back but for eighteen months at the outside.

Chinese squatters, resettling them in new villages surrounded by a wire fence patrolled by police. The Briggs Plan, as it came to be called, was a very sound measure but it had not long been in existence when we arrived. Briggs also directed that the Army would 'dominate' the jungle whilst the Police looked after security and maintained law and order in the populated areas.

Despite these eminently sensible instructions the CTs had killed over 1,000 members of the Security Forces and civilians in 1951 (their largest total in any one year), culminating in the ambush and murder of Sir Henry Gurney, the High Commissioner, in October. He and his wife were driving up the winding, jungle-lined road to Fraser's Hill, the hill station near Kuala Lumpur, in the official Rolls Royce with an escort. The usual tactics were used: a tree across the road on a steep bend. Gurney got out of the car to draw fire away from his wife and was instantly shot dead.

This tragedy coincided with the General Election in Britain and Churchill's return to office. There was an urgent need for one man to be put in charge of both the Government and the Security Forces with full powers. The choice eventually fell on General Sir Gerald Templer (my boss in the War Office in 1946) who arrived in February 1952. He was a man in the Monty mould: direct, ruthless, extremely energetic and decisive, who was prepared to ignore protocol and cut through red tape when necessary. He toured the country unceasingly, talking to everybody, breathing fire on occasion but also delighting people with his human touch. Though we did not arrive until the end of his first year in Malaya, it was clear that he had achieved a great deal in terms of restoring confidence amongst the Chinese, the Malayas and the British business community. His arrival must have been a little like that of Monty's in the desert in August 1942. Some of the old diehards were shocked by Templer's dynamic behaviour but they soon realised who was in the driving seat. The Chinese in particular, who naturally respect strength and toughness, were gradually won over.

Within a month of his arrival, the water supply at the town of Tanjong Malim in South Perak was cut and twelve killed in a subsequent ambush. No information was forthcoming so Templer suddenly appeared by helicopter, imposed a twenty-two-hour curfew and told the inhabitants, mostly Chinese, that they were a lot of bastards.* This was duly translated by his interpreter as; 'His Excellency wishes me to inform you that your fathers and mothers were not

*A View from Within, Christopher Blake, p.144. John Cloake, Templer's official biographer, claims in Templer, Tiger of Malaya, (p.272) that the incident occurred at Kulai, near Johore.

married'. After a pause, Templer added 'And I can be a bastard too'.

This was interpreted as; 'His Excellency wishes to add that his father and mother were not married either'. On another occasion when visiting a police station Templer saw an elderly prisoner and asked 'What's he in for?' — 'Rape', was the answer, to which Templer replied, 'Gawd, there's hope for me yet'.*

Templer's direct manner may not have found favour with all, but there is no doubt that the personal appearance of the High Commissioner immaculately dressed as he always was, even in that heat, had a considerable effect on those Chinese who had been used to getting away with murder (literally). Meanwhile tremendous efforts were being made to re-train the police. Mainly Malay, their morale had been poor, and it was vital that they gain the confidence of the people.

Such was the scene that Christmas of 1952 as we prepared to move to Kuala Lumpur (known as KL), the Federal capital and seat of Government. Our area of responsibility was to be the southern half of the State of Selangor; the four rifle companies would be spread out, covering as many key points as possible. Battalion HQ was in a hutted camp on the edge of KL very near a tin-mine dredge, which squeaked away day and night.

The 2nd in Command's job in an operational battalion is not an enviable one. He has to be ready to take over as CO at very short notice if for any reason the boss becomes a casualty. He therefore needs to be fully up to date with the 'war' situation. However, his main role is likely to be administrative at base and will also include supervising the training of new drafts. James Brind was very kind, knowing that I wanted to be out visiting companies as often as possible, and he excused me many of the rather tedious chores. I suppose the real snag about being number two is that one has no proper responsibility.

South of KL and right up to the border with the next State, Negri Sembilan, was a large area of swamp jungle, about 300 square miles altogether. A platoon of CTs were known to be based there, supplied with food, medicines and clothing from sympathisers living on the jungle fringe. B and C Companies were immediately sent in and after some intensive patrolling made several important contacts and killed nine CTs, virtually clearing the whole of the north swamp. This was a splendid start for the battalion and very good for morale. However, to - put this initial success in its true perspective C Company then 'jungle-bashed' for four months without a single contact.

*Templer, *Tiger of Malaya*, p.231.

Swamp jungle was particularly unpleasant. Later on I was to spend a few weeks commanding A Company at Sepang, whilst Ron Norman the company commander was away on a course, and sampled the swamp myself. One could wade all day in thick liquid, knee-deep or higher. Progress was desperately slow and measured in hundreds of yards per hour. The CTs built their camps on log platforms resting on the boles of trees. It was even more difficult to move silently than in primary jungle; we would almost certainly be heard sloshing through the swamp. It has been said that a week in the jungle makes an Englishman look like a slug from under a stone. I don't think that this is a particularly apt description. His olive-green uniform will certainly be almost black from sweat, he will look as though he hasn't shaved for a week (which he hasn't), his eyes may be bloodshot from fatigue, his jungle boots will be torn and worn,* but he may well be smiling. Why? Because the patrol is over.

One of the most rewarding aspects of serving with British troops in the jungle was the way most of them reacted to their situation. Two-thirds of the battalion were national servicemen, and we were dealing with a complete cross-section of British youth. They were thousands of miles from home in a very unfriendly environment but there was a job to be done, and provided that they were well-led, they would drive themselves to the limit. I remember somebody saying to me on the troopship 'These young men are going out boys; they will come home men'. That was true. Without being unkind to our regular content, the average NSM was of superior calibre, and he was doing a worthwhile job for a limited time.

It was while I was looking after A Company that we were told that Templer would be visiting a particularly 'bad' Chinese settlement near Sepang on a certain day; we would be required to surround it before dawn to ensure that everybody was at home. This was not difficult with well-trained troops and we awaited the High Commissioner's arrival with great interest. On the dot of 8 a.m. his helicopter landed on the *padang* (equivalent of village green) and he stepped out, immaculately dressed as usual in olive-green uniform, and walked over to the village elders who were lined up in readiness. He glared at them and then through an interpreter said he had clear evidence that they had been supplying the CTs with food and information about movement of the Security Forces. If they did not co-operate with Government and obey the regulations he would burn down their village. They had exactly one month to mend their ways. This harangue lasted about ten minutes. He

---

*One sergeant wore out fifty-eight pairs in three years.

then turned on his heel and was away. It was an impressive performance. This village did mend its ways and was not burnt down. The Chinese are tough people, and recognise a strong leader. There is no doubt that Templer's ruthless methods were effective.

One tragic accident occurred during that first year. Special Branch received information that CTs were to collect food from a house in a notorious squatter area on the edge of KL. So important was this information that Lance Searle, Head of Special Branch in Selangor and a fluent Chinese speaker, decided to go himself. His plan was to position an ambush party by night out of sight of the house and the other side of a road which ran close by on a slight embankment. David Goddard, one of our best and most experienced platoon commanders, was in charge of the ambush and after siting his men crawled through a large drain pipe under the road from which he could cover the house. After about half an hour he saw in the semi-darkness four armed men appear from behind the house and immediately opened fire at what he assumed to be CTs. Tragically the four were Searle himself who was killed, John Mackie our Intelligence Officer who was badly shot up in the leg as a result of which he had to be invalided out of the Army, and two of our men who had not been used in the ambush party. One was wounded.

Apparently Searle had decided to have a look round behind the house thinking that he would be out of sight of the ambush party. Before he died he was able to tell Goddard that he was in no way to blame. A subsequent inquiry also apportioned no blame.

Early in 1953 I went down to Singapore by train to collect a new Austin Ten which I had ordered tax-free at home; it was arriving by courtesy of the Royal Navy on the flight deck of an aircraft carrier. This was no fiddle; it was officially permitted and cost the princely sum of £5. The only problem was being allotted space on the carrier as it was a very popular method of acquiring a new car if you were serving overseas. I stayed a night or two with Christopher Blake and his wife Jane. Christopher had a Treasury appointment in the Government and they were about to go home on leave. We reminisced about Kroh and I agreed to employ their excellent Chinese servants when Simone arrived. This was happily to be quite soon in May, and I went down by train to meet her and the family. The Malayan State Railway is excellent in many ways, with comfortable coaches and a good restaurant car which specialises in fried rice and hot curries. However, there were snags. It was very slow, the 250 miles from KL to Singapore taking twelve hours — a distance which today's intercity trains in the UK cover in a quarter of the time — and there was always the chance of an ambush. The railway was single track and there were lots of bridges, but by 1953 the risk was slight.

We were allotted a comfortable bungalow quarter on the eastern edge of KL, just off the Ampang road. It was only a few miles from the jungle fringe and CTs had been seen around, but there were no incidents during the ten months that we lived there. Our neighbours included the Brinds and the CO of the Royal West Kents — so had the CTs struck they might have reaped a rich reward.

While the house was being got ready we stayed for a fortnight in an officers' hostel, and it was here that we listened to the BBC World Service telling us about the Queen's Coronation on June 2nd, and the dramatic news that John Hunt's expedition had climbed Everest.

Life for families in KL was very restricted. Unlike the early days in 1948-'49 wives were not allowed to drive outside the city precincts. Those with older children did voluntary work. When the Brigade Commander's wife rather condescendingly said to Simone 'And what do you do?' she replied naughtily 'I employ a nanny and play with my children,' (end of conversation). I would like to pay a tribute here to Elizabeth Brind. She was the perfect CO's wife. Always available, never interfering unless she felt that she could help, kind and full of fun. It was largely due to her that the regimental wives, of whom there were about thirty, were happy in that restricted atmosphere. Only once were we able to take the children to a beach near Port Swettenham, and even then a military escort was required.

Marion, then twenty-one, was in great demand among the large number of young men about. I recall a Sergeants' Mess dance where she was the belle of the ball.

The highlight for me throughout my time as 2nd in Command was a sudden summons to Kings House (Residence of the High Commissioner) late one afternoon when Brind was on local leave. Templer informed me that Vice-President Nixon, who was paying a lightning visit to South-East Asia, wanted to meet a British patrol just after they had emerged from the jungle. He could start at first light the next morning but had to be back for another engagement by 9.30 a.m. The Somersets were the obvious unit to choose. Would I let Templer know as soon as possible where the RV (rendezvous) was to be? Security was paramount. I hurried back to battalion HQ and did some quick thinking. D Company at Kajang, about fifteen miles south of KL, was the most suitable to visit. I spoke to Tom Lock, the company commander, on the telephone and discussed possibilities in as guarded a manner as possible. Fortunately there was a patrol due out the next morning commanded by a very able National Service Officer, Oliver

Eley (whose family owned Eley Cartridges). Even more fortunately, he had asked permission to come up on the radio at 5 a.m. (instead of the usual 7 a.m.) so with luck we should be able to give him an inkling of what to expect and fix a time for the meeting.

So I decided that this was the place to take Nixon and informed Kings House. There were risks, of which the most critical was whether the radio link would work at 5 a.m. Atmospheric conditions in Malaya were notoriously unreliable. To be on the safe side, Brigade HQ laid on some side-shows for Nixon which included dog-handlers and an experimental wireless set. Needless to say, I was down at Ulu Langat before dawn the next day. Oliver did come up on the radio at 5 a.m. and we were able to fix the RV for 8 a.m. But the most extraordinary part of this story is that shortly before Nixon was due, an important CT chose to walk out of the jungle and surrender to the local Home Guard! He looked the part: emaciated countenance, ragged khaki uniform, and eyes like those of a hunted rat. The VIP party led by Nixon, Templer and the Brigade Commander appeared on the dot of 8.0, as did Oliver and his patrol. It then transpired that acting on information they had found a CT camp, attacked it and succeeded in killing two men. The one who surrendered had escaped, wandered alone for several days, and finally given up.

Nixon and his aides didn't know what to believe. Was this a British trick? How could such a coincidence possibly occur in real life? Well, it had. We were very lucky. Much of the credit went to Oliver and his men, and Nixon went away a happy man convinced that the incident was genuine, as Templer would never have allowed a hoax, which was also quite true.*

The VIP whom we were all delighted to see was John Harding, now a Field Marshal and CIGS. He spent a whole day with the battalion and dined with the officers in the evening. Having already been C-in-C Far East Land Forces for two years he knew all about jungle operations and happily did not expect a tame CT to be produced for his inspection!

Very shortly after Christmas 1953 I was selected to attend the Joint Services Staff College (JSSC) course at Latimer in May 1954. This was a much sought-after posting for officers in my age group (I was thirty-seven) and I was very pleased.

The Somersets were to remain in Selangor until the end of 1954 and spent the last nine months of their three-year tour in Pahang (on the east side of the main mountain range). Only seven men were killed in

---

*A more detailed account appears on pp 206-211 of Brigadier M.C.A. Henniker's book, *Red Shadow over Malaya*, Blackwood, 1955.

action throughout this time as against fifty four CTs killed and seven captured. This is a very fine record when the difficulties of operating in dense jungle are appreciated.

So my second tour in Malaya ended. By early 1954 we were winning, thanks largely to Templer's leadership. The Army was well on the way towards dominating the jungle, Police confidence was restored, food control was working and the CTs were clearly under constraint. One-sixth of the Chinese population was living in new villages.

Templer was to leave Malaya in June 1954 to take over as CIGS from John Harding. In two and a half years he had been on 122 tours. The Chinese leaders wanted to know why this strong man who had achieved so much was leaving. A tribute from the Secretary of State, Oliver Lyttleton, read; 'You have put Malaya, HMG and myself so deeply in your debt that it is difficult to gauge and describe the extent of it'.*

In his recently published memoirs, General 'Monkey' Blacker, who was Templer's Military Assistant when he was CIGS, writes: 'the post-war years had seen all too few great men but Field Marshal Sir Gerald Templer had without question been one of them'.** Readers will detect that I am an admirer of Templer in the same way that I am a Monty fan. This is quite true and I am proud to be.

One final comment: is there any useful lesson to be learned from the differences between the Malayan scene after Independence (which came three years later in 1957) and that in India exactly ten years earlier in 1947?

We left India in a hurry to sort out their own almost insoluble problems centred on religion, over-population, a very low standard of living and a very weak economy. In contrast we left Malaya with a booming economy based on high prices for rubber and tin, and a free enterprise community in which Muslim, Malays and Buddhist Chinese lived peaceably together. The Constitution guarantees religious freedom.

We left KL in March 1954, without Marion as she stayed on with another family. She was later to marry a young man in Potten End whom she had first met when we were at Parson's Field.

*Templer, Tiger of Malaya, p.324
**Monkey Business, p.14, Quiller Press, 1993.

CHAPTER 16

Abandon Ship!

WE were to have sailed in the *Georgic*, which was fast but rather austere for families, and were pleased to be switched at the last moment to the *Empire Windrush*, which was said to be slow but comfortable. All troopships whose names were prefixed *Empire* were war prizes. The *Windrush* (14,600 tons) was formerly the German liner *Monte Rosa* built by Blohm and Voss in Hamburg in 1930, and had been employed pre-war on the 'Strength through Joy'* scheme between Germany and South America.

We left Singapore on March 5th. In the Red Sea one of the engines temporarily failed and we lost five or six hours, missing the evening canal convoy at Suez. A Dutch luxury liner which had left Singapore a week after us sailed by in the Bitter Lakes.

The evening of Saturday, March 27th, was the date set for the ship's farewell dinner and dance for families, perhaps a little premature as we were not due at Southampton until the following Friday. It was a quiet evening for us as Caroline, aged twenty months, had a tummy upset, and we retired early.

The next morning a steward knocked on our door at 6 a.m. and said that one of the engines was on fire and the Captain wanted all passengers on deck. We got dressed as quickly as possible; I looked out of the porthole and saw that we were stationary in a calm sea. There was a slight smell of smoke. Simone stuffed the children's night-clothes and Caroline's bottle of medicine into the pockets of her thick coat and had already put all her jewellery in her bag. I put on battle dress without a shirt, which for some reason I couldn't find, and tennis shoes. Our cabin was on D deck so we had to go up two levels to B deck where passengers were assembling. There was no panic on the staircase; we might almost have been going up to dinner or to practise boat stations.

However, up on B deck it was quickly apparent that things were

*KdF (*Kraft durch Freude*) was an organisation which covered all leisure pursuits in Germany, including holidays abroad.

serious. The middle portion of the ship was enveloped in smoke, and lifeboats were already being swung out. We hadn't had time to put on life jackets in the cabin so did this on deck. It was interesting that David, aged three and a half, who had always strongly objected to having a life jacket put over his head during regular weekly boat drills, did not demur on this occasion.

About three lifeboats were lowered to deck level very quickly and almost before I realised what was happening I was handing Simone and the children into one. There was no panic and very little noise. The agonising farewell between husbands and wives depicted in fiction did not take place. We hardly said goodbye! It was simply taken for granted that women and children went first. I had already seen the smoke of several ships steering straight for us so was fairly certain that they would be safe, and sure enough they were picked up after about three quarters of an hour in the lifeboat by a small Norwegian freighter. The only anxious moment was transferring the children from the lifeboat to the ship. There was no companion-way and each child was handed by the seaman in charge of the lifeboat to a Norwegian seaman on the deck of the freighter at the precise moment that the lifeboat was on the crest of a wave. Simone then had to climb up a rope ladder. There was only one accident when, in another lifeboat, a man carrying a child fell into the sea between freighter and lifeboat, but both were miraculously rescued with no ill effects.

On the *Windrush*, lifeboats were still being lowered. At the time of the explosion in the engine room there had been a power failure throughout the ship, which may have been fortunate as no alarm bells rang and everybody was amazingly calm. However, it meant that lifeboats housed on A deck which were normally lowered by power had to be cut loose and fell into the sea from about fifty feet. This was one of the more dramatic moments especially as one lifeboat was unfortunately impaled on the bow of another. The lower lifeboat was eventually rowed away full of men with the damaged empty lifeboat still hooked on. Another lifeboat crashed into the sea with a man in it but he was thrown clear and picked up.

There seemed to be no immediate urgency to get away though the order 'Abandon ship' had been given. So I paid a very quick visit to our cabin, an eerie experience in a doomed ship with nobody about below B deck. There was a little smoke, but surprisingly no heat; it seems that senior officers accommodated on A deck came off worst because the fire went straight up the funnel and spread downwards from there.

There in the cabin were some of our possessions — and we had to abandon the lot. What could I take that might be useful, or have particular sentimental value? I crammed a beret on my head (as opposed to my much smarter peaked cap), put my fountain pen and reading glasses in my pocket and, much the most important, Simone's wedding present to me, an inscribed gold cigarette case. Then I suddenly saw a carton of 500 No. 3 Players which I had bought only the previous day to take home. With feverish hands I tore it open and crammed one tin of fifty into my bulging pocket, then dashed back upstairs. There were still a lot of men about, and all the lifeboats were in the sea pulling away towards rescue ships which were standing by, or waiting for those of us still on board. There appeared to be three methods of leaving the ship: climbing down a rope ladder (the most popular and one had to queue), going down a knotted rope, or jumping. I hate queuing and don't like jumping from heights so swung out onto a rope at the bottom of which I saw a raft. There were nice large knots on the rope about every ten feet so I was able to rest at intervals and look around. When I reached the last knot I saw that the raft had floated away so I gently lowered myself into the sea, and swam away from the ship towards the nearest lifeboat.

There was always the sneaking fear that the ship might capsize (though there was no list at all at this stage) and I wanted to get as far away as possible in case I was sucked under. I don't remember whether the water was cold; I was too busy looking after myself. Quite soon I was being helped into a lifeboat which was already pretty full of men. Others were sitting on rafts or anything that floated, such as the long wooden benches normally holding life jackets which had been thrown overboard. Our dress was very varied; some men were in uniform, others in pyjamas. Those who had been in the sea were beginning to feel pretty cold by now and various good Samaritans were taking off their coats to wrap round the less fortunate. I remember distributing my cigarettes, which went down well. Being in a sealed tin they were dry. I suppose somebody must have had a lighter.

When we finally pulled away from the stricken ship there must have been about eighty of us in our lifeboat. We were by no means the last. One naval officer, finding no rope ladder or rope, rammed his peaked cap firmly on his head, did a perfect dive overboard and came up with his cap still on to the cheers of those who saw him. Others went down the ropes too fast and suffered badly blistered hands.

Those of us not rowing stared at the old *Windrush*, now burning furiously. It was difficult to believe that this was happening to us, and that it was not just a film or a bad dream. To add to the unreality of the scene the ship's siren suddenly started up and appeared to be jammed on, long after the last man had left. Carrying across the water it sounded like a cry for help, but the poor old ship was past helping now.

We made for a P & O cargo ship, the *Socotra* of 7,700 tons, and were soon being welcomed on board. The ship's company were most hospitable; we were all given steaming hot cups of coffee and later soup, and were invited to wrap ourselves in blankets whilst our clothes dried.

I suppose it was about 8 a.m. by the time we boarded the *Socotra* and about 10.0 before we finally sailed for Algiers, thirty-five miles away. All this time more survivors were still being taken on board. A Shackleton from Gib had arrived on the scene and was circling the *Windrush*. There was nothing any of us could do except stare at the burning ship, now about half a mile away, and at the sea dotted with empty lifeboats which had discharged their cargoes, rafts and various bits of wreckage. It was an amazing sight which remains imprinted on my memory nearly forty years later.

I believe that the *Socotra* eventually took about 500 of us. It was certainly pretty crowded. Fortunately the sun was up and we were able to dry out quite quickly. There was a lot of comparing notes: what did you save? Quite a few had cameras and were able to sell film to reporters when we went ashore at Algiers, but it was mostly wallets, photographs and identity cards which were laid out on deck to dry. One naval officer told me that this was the fifth or sixth time that he had had to abandon ship and he had never been able to save anything. His uniform, now dry, looked so smart that I felt the gold braid must have been especially treated to resist salt water!

When we finally sailed away from the scene of desolation we had on board all the VIPs, a Major General and a Brigadier who had embarked at Port Said, the Master, a fine looking old sea dog for whom one felt great sympathy as he watched his ship being destroyed, and the Officer Commanding Troops, a Lieutenant Colonel who had held great responsibility and could feel proud that there was no loss of life among his flock (though he did not know this yet).

I thought of all our kit on board: eight packing cases in the hold, three in the baggage room, and some fourteen smaller pieces in our cabin. We had with us practically all our silver, glass, linen and pictures, clothes, my shot gun, typewriter and sewing machine. Many of these articles were irreplaceable. As we steamed away it seemed possible that something might be saved as fire still engulfed only the upper decks and there was no apparent list. All our 'not wanted on voyage' baggage was in the holds below the water line.

A few facts are of interest; there were 1,268 servicemen on board, 978 Army, 150 Royal Navy and 140 RAF, together with 160 women and children, practically all wives and families of servicemen on board. The fire started in the engine room where an officer and three crew members who tried to fight the blaze were overcome and died. They were the only casualties. At the official enquiry several months later, it was stated that the explosion in the engine room occurred at 6.15 a.m., and the Master gave the order to abandon ship at 6.45, which shows how rapidly the fire must have got out of control. If those timings are correct it was even more surprising that there was no panic and everybody remained calm. It was of course extremely fortunate that there was only a surface swell and it was daylight.

The *Windrush* was eventually taken in tow by the destroyer HMS *Saintes* but, sadly, sank on the way to Gibraltar.

The last troopship to sink in peacetime had been the *Birkenhead* in 1852. It was on that occasion that the order 'Women and children first' became an indispensable part of British sea-faring tradition.

To return to our reception in Algiers; being a Sunday, most of the town seemed to be on the quayside to meet us. The families had been taken to a holiday camp at Ben Aknoun which had been specially opened. I was whisked away in a French army lorry to a transit camp where we had our first proper food at about 2.30 p.m. We husbands were then sent a further five miles inland to rejoin our families at the holiday camp. They were having their first meal of the day when we arrived. The French authorities had made a very big effort to look after us; accommodating and feeding over a hundred families on a Sunday in late March at a moment's notice involved a lot of organisation. Welfare workers of all sorts turned up with clothing, and even special milk for babies. Drinking water was a slight problem and I remember that Caroline had her first taste of French wine.

After the meal we were allotted a chalet which we shared with a wife and four children who were on their way home from Hong Kong. It was cold and husbands were given axes and told to go into the woods and chop firewood. We slept rather fitfully that night in our clothes.

On Monday morning we were given postcards which could be sent home free by air mail. I borrowed a French army car and some money and went into Algiers to buy Caroline some shoes as in our hurried exit we had forgotten to put any on her. Though we were given a few more essentials, our total possessions amounted to a tiny Red Cross bundle when we were driven down to the docks to board HMS *Triumph*, a light fleet carrier which had been converted to a cadet training ship. It was a stirring sight to see the ship's company lining the flight deck and the White Ensign silhouetted against a brilliant blue sky. On her way from the West Indies to Gib., she had been having a sailing race with her dinghies when suddenly ordered to proceed to Algiers at full speed to pick us all up.

The Navy did everything possible to make us comfortable; the main hangar had been converted into four dormitories with canvas rigging and camp beds provided for all women and older children. Officers were extremely well looked after. I was met on the quarterdeck by a naval officer who said 'My cabin is at your disposal. Make yourself at home'. When I saw how cramped Simone and the children were, sleeping in serried ranks, and listened to the vibration — *Triumph* went full ahead at twenty-five knots and the 'dormitories' were just above the propeller shafts — I realised how lucky I was. That evening I stood low down at the stern looking at the mountainous wash that was being thrown up, and wondered where the poor old *Windrush* was.

The twenty-two-hour trip to Gib. was uneventful, though the naval chaplain did baptize three babies. Presumably the mothers felt that their troubles might not yet be over and it was as well to be on the safe side.

At Gib. we were greeted by large crowds. The band of the Duke of Wellington's Regiment played us in with 'A Life on the Ocean Wave', and Countess Mountbatten, who had launched *Triumph* in 1944 and who happened to be visiting St John's Ambulance Brigade personnel (of which she was Superintendent-in-Chief), was also there.

'Operation Windrush' went into top gear. After essential documentation and issue of money we were sent off to our 'hosts'. All service families in Gib. had offered beds. We were billeted on the Deputy Fortress Commander and his wife, Brigadier and Mrs Lucas. They could not have been kinder. That afternoon we went to the NAAFI where Gib. families had brought any clothes and toys which they could spare, and were giving them away. I also visited the officers' shop which had been specially opened, and bought a shirt and a holdall — the French had given me a blue shirt which looked very peculiar under my battle dress. The MO gave us some dope to make Caroline sleep as she was still very nervy and upset — not surprising really!

The people of Gib. were marvellous too. There were free taxi rides, free telegrams home, free milk, toys and sweets, free cinema tickets and free *Gibraltar Chronicles* (from which I am quoting!)

The Brigadier had an extremely kind and thoughtful batman. Simone had occasion to go down to the kitchen during the night to mix a hot drink for Caroline; he heard her, got up and asked if he could help. The next morning as we were leaving I tried to give him a tip but he wouldn't take anything.

The RAF had arranged a massive airlift to take us all home. Some twenty aircraft, mostly Hastings, were used and we left that day with minimal formalities. Caroline was still pretty upset and I remember that I carried her up and down the gangway for most of the six-hour flight as that seemed to be the only way to keep her quiet. We finally landed at Blackbush and were driven to Gaddesden.

So ended four days of high drama on which we have dined out many times, though David and Caroline were too young to remember it all. Looking back it all seems rather an exciting adventure — there were practically no moments of real danger. It was of course extremely unsettling for young children and Caroline took several weeks to get over it. Had the ship caught fire at night or in a rough sea or had the shipwreck occurred east of Suez in shark-infested waters, it might have been a major disaster. If it had to happen, it was in the best possible place at the best possible time. My lasting regret is the loss of all our possessions, many of which we have never been able to replace.

CHAPTER 17

Latimer

WE spent most of our two or three weeks' leave making out lists of the possessions that we had lost. The War Office made ex gratia payments and we also of course put in insurance claims. It was a difficult task; I think we were awarded about £1,000 in the end.

We moved into Parson's Field almost straightaway as it had been let as a WD (War Dept) quarter. This meant that we had service tenants who paid a relatively low rent to the War Office (who in turn paid us) but who could be relied upon to look after the property, and to move out at short notice.

In May I went to the Joint Services Staff College, driving the ten miles across country every day from Parson's Field. The College had been set up after the war to train middle-ranking officers of all three services in joint planning and working at joint service headquarters. Officers selected would normally have already qualified at their own service staff college. There were about thirty Army, twenty RN and fifteen RAF, together with one or two Americans, Australians, New Zealanders, Canadians, Indians, Pakistanis and some civilians.

The course lasted six months and was held at Latimer House near Chesham, the former seat of Lord Chesham, a lovely nineteenth-century house overlooking the Chess valley. It had been used during the war to house captured German generals.* There was a fine walled garden and the head gardener told me how some of the generals had arrived still in tropical kit, and Saville Row tailors were brought in to fit them out. He was quick to point out, however, that they also dug the garden under his supervision.

The tempo at JSSC was steady and there were only occasional points of high pressure. All the exercises were of course joint and we army officers would often be playing the part of sailors or airmen. We had lectures from the top brass of the three services, politicians and other public figures. Templer, just back from Malaya and about to become CIGS, was one of the star performers, as was John Hunt from the

---

*Mostly those captured in Tunisia at the end of the North African campaign.

Everest expedition. My first syndicate DS was Peter Moore, DSO, MC, one of the heroes of Alamein, who as a sapper major played a leading role in clearing lanes through the vast German minefields. Earlier he had shot his way out of trouble with a revolver and wrestled with an armed antagonist in the dark. Like so many particularly brave men he was friendly, quiet and unassuming.

We also visited service establishments. I went to sea in a submarine and flew on a low-level mission lying flat in the nose of a Canberra, which was very exciting especially as it was the morning after a guest night. I managed to win the course squash knock-out competition and played some village cricket. It was a very pleasant break in lovely English country surroundings after Malaya.

The course ended early in November and I was told that my next posting was to instruct as a Lieutenant Colonel at a NATO training establishment which had recently been set up at Estoril in Portugal. Despite the superficial attractions of this job I felt that it was not my forte and rather hesitantly said so. It is generally considered a bit risky to argue your posting and this was the only time that I ever did, but it worked. I was told almost immediately that I was to go to Cyprus as GSO 1 (Operations) GHQ Middle East Land Forces, a new job created as a result of the move from the Canal Zone to Cyprus. It sounded exciting and I was very pleased. It meant that I would once more become a Lieutenant Colonel after six years as a Major. Simone and the children could follow me to Nicosia (where GHQ was located) as soon as I found a suitable house.

PART IV, 1955-1973
Command and Diplomatic Posts in the Middle East and at Home

CHAPTER 18

Cyprus and Suez — a Packet of Trouble from Makarios and Nasser

I WAS required to take over my new job immediately after Christmas and flew out to Nicosia on January 3rd, 1955. So began an almost uninterrupted association with the Arab world which was to last eighteen years.

Cyprus had only a very indirect connection with the Arab world, but GHQ Middle East Land Forces was now located there, and our sphere of interest covered the whole of the Arabian Peninsula from Aden in the south to Jordon and Iraq in the north, the Gulf Shaikhdoms, Israel, Syria, Lebanon, Iran and Libya. The winding up of British garrisons in the Canal Zone and Libya was also our responsibility. It was a huge area to cover. The only part that I knew well was the Western Desert, now of no importance, a little about what was now the state of Israel, (created in 1948) and Syria, from my time with the DLI in 1941 and at Haifa Staff College in 1942-'43. But first, how secure was our new base in Cyprus, and was it to be an improvement on Fayid? (GHQ's previous location on the Suez Canal.)

Here it is necessary to put the clock back briefly. The British connection started with Richard Coeur-de-Lion who led the Third Crusade in 1191 and spent a short time on the island. We then jump 700 years to Disraeli, who did a surprising deal with the Ottoman Turks in 1878, persuading them that their best protection against the Russians was to cede Cyprus to Britain. After the collapse of the Ottoman Empire in World War I, Cyprus as a British Crown Colony (declared in 1925) now faced a new and more sinister problem. Greece had gained power at the expense of Turkey, and the Pan-Hellenic movement of Greek Orthodox Christians was seeking to resume control of the eastern Mediterranean. This of course included Cyprus, three-quarters of whose population spoke Greek and called themselves Greek Cypriots. The other quarter spoke Turkish and called themselves Turkish Cypriots. The claim for *enosis* (union with Greece) was further complicated by Cyprus's geographical position: over 500 miles from the Greek mainland and only forty miles from the southern coast of Turkey (which is clearly visible on a fine day).

Between the wars the *enosis* movement smouldered, erupting with sufficient force in 1931 to cause Government House to be burnt down. However, until 1939 all was quiet and the island was not involved in World War II, though it is noteworthy that 14,000 Cypriots volunteered to serve in the British Army.

In 1945 Attlee's Labour government seriously considered granting *enosis* but, apart from internal constitutional progress, nothing happened and events elsewhere in Palestine and Egypt made Cyprus suddenly more important. British sovereignty over the island was not to be questioned. While HMG was taking a tough stand, at the same time two prominent Greek Cypriot figures appeared on the scene. In 1952 Archbishop Makarios, then only thirty-nine and formerly Bishop of Kition, demanded union with Greece and recruited Colonel George Grivas, a former Greek Army officer born in Cyprus and known to be harsh and cruel in his methods, who was to lead a secret army later known as EOKA (the Greek initials of the words 'National Organisation of Cypriot Fighters') that would put pressure on the British. And so, whilst on the international stage the UN voted in 1954 not to consider the Cyprus question and consequently the British position appeared secure, the underground activities of Grivas aided and abetted by Makarios (who provided funds from the Orthodox Church) were proceeding apace. Turkish Cypriots naturally hoped that we would take a tough line as in no way did they wish to become part of Greece.

This was in outline the position in January 1955. Looking back, it almost seems as though we were destined to be there as the British Empire was crumbling away; India in 1947, Malaya in 1948 (though independence was not declared until 1957) and now Cyprus in 1955. I don't remember being particularly briefed on the security situation in the island, and can only assume that in GHQ it was not considered to be serious.

Our offices were in Wolseley Barracks (named after a former Governor). Operations and Plans were combined under a Brigadier; I was Ops, and the GSO 1 responsible for Plans was part of a Joint Planning Staff including a sailor and an airman. Above us was the Chief of Staff, a major-general who was directly responsible to the C-in-C, General Sir Charles Keightley.

Our main concern during those early days in 1955 was working out Britain's role in the defensive treaty which had just been signed between

Turkey, Iran, Iraq, Pakistan and Britain to counter a possible Russian threat. It became known as the Baghdad Pact, and was intended to fill the gap between NATO and SEATO (South East Asia Treaty Organisation), 'a Middle East NATO' as Eden called it. The USA had unfortunately only agreed to 'observer' status.

Our planning did not go further than the defence of the three main passes through the Zagros mountains which form part of the frontier between Iran and Iraq. These are from north to south; the Ruwanduz, Penjwin and Paitak. How quickly could we get British troops to the passes, and in what strength? Considering that Iraq was only 120 miles from the Russian frontier and the nearest British army units were in Cyprus, and some as far away as Tripolitania, our planning was all rather airy-fairy. The only British troops in Iraq were the RAF at Habbaniya. It is worth remembering that in 1955, King Faisal II, grandson of Amir Faisal with whom Lawrence fought in the Arab Revolt of 1917-8, was ruler of Iraq at the age of twenty-one. Educated at Harrow and Sandhurst, he was not surprisingly pro-British, as was his army which we trained and equipped.

At Easter I went on a most interesting 'swan' round parts of our huge parish with Lieutenant Colonel 'Bala' Bredin, Head of MO4* War Office, Dick Vernon my opposite number in Plans, and several others. Dick and I had been at school together and in the Western Desert.

We began our travels in Jordan where we were well looked after by the Arab Legion, then still commanded by the legendary Glubb Pasha, considered by many observers to be the uncrowned king of Jordan. Glubb was then fifty-eight; after a conventional career in the British Army he had retired as a captain in 1926, and had served in the Trans-Jordan Defence Force (later the Arab Legion) ever since. A man of considerable charm who spoke fluent Arabic, he was widely respected throughout Jordan. Under his leadership the Arab Legion (Jordan's Army) was easily the most efficient and battleworthy Arab force in the Middle East, and one that even the Israelis watched closely. A number of very good British officers were seconded as COs to serve under Glubb.

We visited the West Bank of the Jordan and stood on the high ground looking at the Mediterranean nine miles away across the narrow waist of Israel. I have always remembered that day when reading of the endless wrangles between Jews and Arabs over the West Bank that are still unresolved thirty-seven years later. In 1955 the State of Israel was

*Military Operations 4 which dealt with the Middle East. Bredin was already one of the most decorated officers in the Army, holding 3 DSOs and 2 MCs.

only seven years old, Nasser was daily threatening to drive the hated Jews into the sea, and the Arab Legion held the high ground of the West Bank. It did not need much intelligence to see that if an unfriendly power held the West Bank, Israel could be cut in half within an hour by a surprise attack.

I was invited to dine with Glubb at his house in Amman. We were quite a small party which included his son, then sixteen and on Easter holidays from Wellington. I asked him what he was going to do when he grew up, and he replied: 'I should like to follow in my father's footsteps'. That of course was not possible, nor do I know what has happened to that quiet well-mannered boy, obviously still under the spell of his charismatic father. Though it was a black tie affair (almost mandatory in those days) the atmosphere was very informal and I sensed the paternal way in which Glubb talked about his beloved Arab soldiers. There was no imperial pomposity about him. He was a highly professional soldier and a very loyal servant of Jordan. At the dinner party Glubb made two particular points: first, he was not 'almost an Arab' and likely to support Jordan should the King and his government adopt policies that were damaging to British interests; and second, Israel was likely to attack Egypt in 1956 as by then she would be strong enough, and Egypt was receiving large quantities of arms from the Soviet bloc. A pre-emptive strike would be the best solution. (This is of course exactly what happened.) Historians and biographers have compared Glubb with Lawrence, and there is a certain similarity; however, he was a far more orthodox soldier who understood the Arab mind better than Lawrence, but who was not destined to play such a leading role on the Middle Eastern stage. As I shall shortly relate, he, like so many others, underrated the power of Nasser at this time and had to leave Jordan a broken man barely a year later.

We also visited the British armoured regiment at Aqaba (the Queen's Bays) and drove up to Maan, almost following in Lawrence's footsteps of 1917.

From Jordan we flew to Iraq and stayed with the RAF at Habbaniya on the Euphrates not far from Baghdad. It was then considered to be the most comfortable and well appointed RAF station overseas. A signpost outside the gates read: 'London 3,287m. Baghdad 55m'. Somehow I don't think that sign is still there. I bought two Bokhara rugs whilst we were there, one at Habbaniya from a carpet dealer who regularly visited the officers' mess, and the other from Kashi's in Baghdad, who of all the traders in the Bazaar was considered to be the least likely to sell you rubbish. I looked through his selection and saw nothing that I particularly liked, and was about to leave when an old man staggered in with a load of rugs which he had washed in the Tigris, and had been drying in the hot sun on a mud wall. I found a deep red one that I liked and we agreed £15. The one at Habbaniya had cost £12. Flying RAF we were of course able to carry relatively bulky items like rugs as personal baggage! They both still adorn our drawing-room nearly forty years later.

The Iraq army was extremely kind to us and we met General Ghazi Daghastani* the Chief of Staff in Baghdad, who asked after 'my old friend General Templer'. We toured the northern passes and lunched with a group of Iraqi and Iranian officers at the entrance to the Ruwanduz Pass. The atmosphere was very friendly. I think that at this stage the Iraqis genuinely thought that there was a real threat from Russia. We met our Ambassador, Sir Michael Wright, and were told that British support was welcomed, and indeed needed.

Our last port of call was the Gulf Shaikhdoms. We stopped briefly at Kuwait, spent a day at Bahrain and met Sir Bernard Burrows, the Political Resident (PR) and senior British diplomat in the Gulf. Finally we touched down at Sharjah to visit the Trucial Oman Scouts, a British-officered Arab force responsible for maintaining law and order in the seven Trucial States and answerable to the PR. We were accompanied for this leg of the tour by Brigadier Robert Baird who was then Senior Army Officer Persian Gulf (SAOPG). I had worked with him some fourteen years earlier in the Western Desert when he was our principal link with the local Bedouin tribesmen. Baird was an experienced Arabist in the Glubb mould but preferred working on his own, and was not entirely at ease commanding troops. Nevertheless he was very popular, and I was delighted to meet him again. We bathed in the Gulf which in April was already hotting up, and visited one of the Beau Geste-type forts inland. Nine years later I was to find myself commanding this very force.

As soon as I got back Simone and the children arrived, accompanied by a new Norland nanny, Dinah, whom we were lucky to recruit just before departure. She was twenty and had only had one job before coming to us. Her air passage was paid for at public expense, a perk allowed to Lieutenant Colonels and above. To begin with we lived in a barely-finished villa on the outskirts of Nicosia in which we camped until something more suitable turned up. Within a month or so we found a comfortable ground-floor apartment in Lascaris Street, a quiet lateral road between the two main roads leading out of Nicosia to the

*He was to be assassinated with the King in the 1958 coup.

west. Our landlady, a Greek Cypriot, lived upstairs; her English was limited and we never got much further than calling her 'Mrs Upstairs'. I had ordered a new Morris Oxford in January and we took delivery straightaway. Wolseley Barracks was about a mile away. David, aged four and a half, was accepted at the English School and Caroline was to join him there the following year. Dinah made friends with several other English nannies, not to mention young officers from the South Staffords who were based two to three miles out of town at Waynes Keep.

On the surface it was a very peace-time and ordinary way of life. Then on April 1st, 1955 EOKA formally declared war by placing sixteen bombs in various vulnerable points, including the broadcasting station. In addition, Grivas issued what he called his first revolutionary proclamation: 'We have taken up the struggle to throw off the English yoke . . . ' etc.

EOKA increased its terrorist activities throughout that summer. A bomb was placed under the seat of the Governor Sir Robert Armitage at an Empire Day Film Show — which fortunately did not explode until after he had left. There were attacks on police stations designed (exactly as in Malaya) to intimidate, followed by bombs exploding inside army bases and causing a significant number of casualties. Perhaps the most serious incident was that sixteen EOKA key suspects escaped from the supposedly impregnable Kyrenia Castle.

This type of emergency situation did not materially affect our lives. We had to close the shutters of our flat at dusk every evening as we were on the ground floor; it was almost a hark-back to the blackout days at home during the war. Servicemen were not allowed within the walled city of Nicosia, and in particular Ledra Street which became known as the 'murder mile'. It was also the main shopping street and Simone occasionally had to buy clothes for me. I remember shoes were a problem. We were required to carry arms at all times, which sometimes raised embarrassing situations at cocktail parties; on arrival, the host relieved you of your revolver and put it along with others in a hall drawer. Several drinks later, you had to remember firstly to collect your weapon and equally importantly to check that it was yours and not somebody else's. On returning to our apartment, I would have to get out of the car and check the garage before Simone drove the car in. I often wonder what on earth I would have done if there had been a 'baddy' lurking in the bushes. Who would have shot first?

We were able to go for picnics to the north coast, particularly Kyrenia which was mainly Turkish. There was also sailing in the harbour. Compared to our second tour in Malaya when families were hardly allowed to leave Kuala Lumpur, there was much more freedom of movement. However, EOKA was just as active and effective a terrorist organisation as the CTs in Malaya had been.

The Turkish Cypriot minority who lived along the northern coast, the 'panhandle' (as the north-eastern point of the island is called), and in the northern part of Nicosia and Famagusta, were of course opposed to *enosis*, and were generally pro-British, but they were hopelessly outnumbered by the Greeks. It would not be fair to say that the Greek Cypriot population as a whole was anti-British, but they became increasingly intimidated by EOKA and Makarios's outpourings from the pulpit.

In the summer of 1955 I accompanied the C-in-C on a quick visit to Aden as some RAF Regiment officers had been ambushed and the security situation was uncertain. A British battalion (the Seaforths) were diverted there from the Canal Zone. We refuelled at Khartoum and I met for the first time Bill Luce, under whom I was to serve in both Aden and the Gulf in the years to come. He was then number two to the Governor of the Sudan.

In September 1955, in a move very similar to that of Templer's appointment as High Commissioner in Malaya in 1952, Eden (who had succeeded Churchill as Prime Minister in April) appointed John Harding, now a Field Marshal, as Governor to succeed Armitage. Harding had just handed over as CIGS to Templer.

This surprise appointment was of course greatly welcomed by the Army in Cyprus but viewed with suspicion by Makarios. Harding was not given the *carte blanche* powers that Templer had had in Malaya, and was dealing face to face with a clever and completely unscrupulous Greek Cypriot leader masquerading as a man of God. From a personal point of view I, too, was delighted that Harding had been appointed Governor. He was now Colonel of the Somersets and our paths had crossed a good many times since the early days in the Western Desert in 1940. Simone and I were privileged guests at Government House on several occasions. However, I had no official contact as my job was concerned almost entirely with the Middle East theatre as a whole.

Cracks had very quickly appeared in the Baghdad Pact. Egypt, blossoming forth under Nasser as leader of the Arab world, claimed that she had not been consulted about the Pact, and Jordan was not even a member. Considering that young King Hussein aged twenty (first cousin of Faisal of Iraq) had also been educated in England, and that we paid for and ran their very efficient army under Glubb, this was surprising, and with hindsight significant.

On November 27th HMG sent Templer (now CIGS) to Amman to persuade Jordan to join the Pact. A small groups of staff officers from GHQ, including my boss Brigadier Bill Williams and myself, also went over to advise as necessary on the state of forward planning so far. We were there about a week and I can remember attending some of the meetings (sitting behind the principals of course) and rather hoping that no fast balls were bowled. They were not; mainly I think because we never got as far as detailed planning. Egyptian propaganda had won the day; the Baghdad Pact was an imperialist plot to help Israel, and before we knew what was happening there were anti-British riots in Amman and the Government bowed to pressure. There was much worse to come in 1956 but I do not remember reading the danger signals at this stage. We returned to Nicosia with our tails between our legs.

Our position still seemed secure in Iraq. During that winter of 1955-'56 I was a UK observer at their army manoeuvres. About four of us, led by Brigadier John Hopwood of the Black Watch, joined an international party which included Americans, French, Turks and Pakistanis amongst others. The manoeuvres were held in the general area of the centre pass (the Penjwin) leading through the Zagros mountains into Iran and not far from Sulaimaniya. We were well looked after and the atmosphere was extremely friendly. Young King Faisal attended and on the last evening invited us all to a reception in a huge marquee, in the course of which we were all presented. Just two years later in 1958 he was to be shot down in a violent revolution which overthrew the monarchy and dismissed the British mission.

I always think of 1956 as the year of Suez, which of course it was, but Nasser did not nationalise the Canal until July 26th and events in Cyprus and Jordan during the early months were momentous enough to prevent us from being bored. Harding and Makarios held talks which lasted for five months throughout the winter of 1955-'56, and came very close to solving the Cyprus conflict. Harding wanted Makarios to denounce violence; Makarios's price was self-determination. After Harding had been to London for further instructions HMG came back with the famous double-negative formula: 'It is not the British Government's position that the principle of self-determination can never be applicable to Cyprus. It is their position that it is not now a practicable proposition'. Makarios refused to accept this delaying tactic, even though it represented a significant shift in the British position, and temporarily broke off the talks. He then consulted Grivas in his secret hide-out in the Troodos mountains, and came back with more conditions concerning an amnesty for EOKA fighters and Cypriot control of the police. Makarios was constantly upping the price for denouncing violence, and eventually Harding asked Lennox-Boyd, the Colonial Secretary, to come and join the talks. Sadly, the negotiations broke down though the British side had been willing to compromise again and again. As the talks dragged on Harding is alleged to have asked 'Who will rid me of this turbulent priest?' alluding to Henry II's famous remark about Thomas à Becket; it was almost as though his prayer was answered when in March HMG decided to deport Makarios to the Seychelles. We were told in great secrecy that this was to happen, and families were warned not to go out. The road to the airport came very close to our flat, and there were demonstrations with much flourishing of Greek flags and shouting of 'Enosis, enosis' but the army presence in and around Nicosia, which had been considerably increased since Harding's arrival, was able to keep law and order. It was now a case of open warfare between the Security forces and EOKA, and a State of Emergency was declared.

Very shortly after Makarios's deportation, my parents arrived for a three-week stay over Easter. In view of the security situation it was not an ideal time to choose, but the visit had been planned for some time and they were much looking forward to it. Everybody thought that they were very courageous to come. They arrived on one of the first BEA Viscounts, a new and very comfortable turbo-prop airliner. We were able to do quite a bit of sight-seeing and picnicking, and the nearest to an incident happened on their first morning, when they woke to an appalling clatter outside their window which turned out to be the local dogs scavenging our dustbins.

One Sunday evening that summer we had just returned from a picnic on the north coast, and were putting the children to bed, when there was a very loud explosion in Quaglino's, a restaurant immediately opposite our flat across the road. The plate-glass windows were blown out and there were obviously casualties. I ran across the road to see if I could help, saw the havoc inside and went back for some blankets. I was later nearly arrested as someone seen running out of the restaurant very shortly after the explosion. The total casualties were four killed and fifteen injured, some seriously, and all of them Cypriots. Most had been sitting on high bar stools and the blast came up from floor level. It was an alarming reminder of how vulnerable we all were.

We used to dine regularly in Nicosia at a restaurant called The Gourmet outside the city walls in a suburban area similar to Lascaris Street. It remained in bounds but was regularly checked by troops and police. The incident that really hit the headlines was when a bomb was found under the mattress of Harding's bed in Government House. He had slept on it and it had failed to explode.

At almost the same time as Makarios' deportation, an event occurred in Jordan which was to have considerable reverberations throughout the Arab world. King Hussein suddenly decided to dismiss Glubb Pasha immediately and without giving any valid reason. The events of February 29th and March 1st are graphically described by Peter Snow in his book, *Hussein*. Glubb (who was forty years older than the King) was slow to promote Arab officers in the Legion, and there was disagreement between him and the King over how best to defend the West Bank — but these differences were relatively trivial, and Glubb claimed afterwards that he had often told the King that he would resign at any time; Hussein had only to say. Most commentators are now agreed that the young King was determined somehow to show to his country and to Nasser that he was in charge in Jordan, and felt that there was no better way to do this than to get rid of Glubb at a moment's notice, with no pomp and ceremony. Glubb was initially given only two hours to pack up and leave, but this was later rescinded to eight o'clock the following morning. He had lived in Jordan for twenty-six years.

The RAF flew him to Nicosia and I remember seeing him arrive at Wolseley Barracks that morning to call on General Keightley, the C-in--C. He was in civilian clothes and looked a forlorn figure. It was a sad end to a most distinguished career in the service of Jordan. With hindsight one might say that he should have read the danger signals, announced his formal retirement perhaps a year earlier, and left in a blaze of glory. But he clearly felt that he was still needed both to defend Jordan and in particular the West Bank, and to help the young King, realising that the Israelis were stronger militarily than the Jordanians believed. Hussein did not want his help and felt embarrassed to have an elderly British general running his army for him.

As soon as Glubb's dismissal was announced there was wide-spread rejoicing throughout Jordan and the Arab world, and Hussein's position was greatly strengthened.

The Queen made Glubb a KCB as soon as he arrived home. All that Hussein gave him was a signed photograph of himself in a silver frame.

Early in July, 1956 I flew to Naples, piloted by Willie Tait, who was Group Captain Ops at HQ MEAF (Middle East Air Force). Tait was one of the most distinguished bomber pilots of World War II and had commanded the raid which finally sank the *Tirpitz* in a Norwegian fjord. He had the DSO and three bars. We were representing GHQ at a planning conference run by the NATO HQ in Naples. I was struck by Tait's meticulous inspection of the aircraft (a Pembroke) before we left. He must have had thousands of flying hours to his credit but was leaving nothing to chance. We night-stopped in Malta and I was able to stay with Andrew Willan and his family, as Andrew had a staff appointment at the RAF HQ. After the conference (about which I remember very little) we landed back at Nicosia on July 26th and were greeted with the news that in a speech in Alexandria Nasser had announced to roars of applause from a huge audience that he had nationalised the Suez Canal Company.

Nasser's timing was clever; the United States and Britain had both announced early in July that they could not finance the building of the Aswan High Dam, and the Soviet Union obligingly stepped into the breach; Egypt had recently negotiated an important arms deal with Czechoslovakia and could boast 300 modern Russian tanks and several squadrons of jet fighters; the last British soldier had left the Canal Zone base; Britain appeared to be as unpopular in her new Middle East base (Cyprus) as she had been in Egypt, and last but by no means least, it was a Presidential year in the US, and Eisenhower who was seeking a second term was known to be a man of peace.

The endless talks, plans and counter-plans which went on throughout August, September and most of October have been described by many historians, and I shall not go over well-trodden ground.

I do remember very clearly that in GHQ we all felt that Nasser had breached international law, and must be stopped. The Canal was an international waterway, and its safe passage was crucial to Britain. Over two-thirds of the fuel supplies of Western Europe passed through it. One-third of the 15,000 ships that used it were British. Nasser had 'his thumb on our windpipe' as Eden put it. All the foreign canal pilots (mostly French) were dismissed and the Canal was successfully operated by the Egyptians, through whose territory it ran; however much Britain and France wanted to find a good reason to use force and teach Nasser a lesson, there was no way in which they could do so that would win international support.

At GHQ we wondered why military action could not be taken quickly — no later than August, for example. 16 Parachute Brigade, an élite force of highly trained men, was in Cyprus.* Nobody thought

---

*Tubby Butler, then its Brigade Commander and later to reach the rank of full General, was probably the best-loved officer in the army of his time. He could rivet the attention of officers and men and inspire them. Never appearing to need more than a few hours' sleep, he liked whisky, rugby football, women and good soldiers. On a guest night at Minley Manor (part of Camberley Staff

anything of the Egyptian army. Why wait? Could we not re-occupy the Canal Zone before the politicians and pacifists had got their act together? There were of course good reasons for waiting, many of them political. The main military one (and I remember attending a meeting of the BDCC (ME)** at which this point was forcibly made) was that we were not at war, the Egyptians had a large number of modern tanks and aircraft with Russian advisers, and heavy casualties in an opposed landing would be unacceptable. Cyprus had no proper port facilities, troops from the garrison (except the Parachute Brigade) could not be spared, 20,000 reservists would have to be called up in Britain and a landing at Port Said mounted from Malta was not possible until mid-September at the earliest.

We then heard that opinion polls at home supported the Government's tough line, and it seemed certain that force was going to be used unless Nasser climbed down. General Keightley was put in overall command, and Lieutenant General Stockwell, who had been GOC in Malaya under Templer, was to command the invasion force. A special staff came out from home to serve him. Most of us in GHQ carried on with our normal duties as interested spectators. It was a slightly unreal situation.

Until the middle of October if seemed likely but by no means certain that 'Musketeer'† would go ahead. With hindsight I believe that the operation should not have been launched, and that we should have done a deal with Nasser accepting Egyptian running of the canal, only taking a tough line if free passage of Western shipping was interfered with. However *at the time* we were all in favour of force being used.

My 'normal duties' in mid-October were to take me away once more on a most interesting 'swan'. The DMO-designate‡ at the War Office, Major General Jack Hamilton, was on his way home from the Far East to take up his new appointment and GHQ was ordered to arrange a ten-day whistle-stop tour of British spheres of interest in the Middle East to bring him up to date. I was to meet him in Aden and conduct

College) he usually managed the difficult feat of going round the walls of the large ante-room without touching the floor. Having gone to bed at 5 am he would appear at 8.30 slightly paler but able to give a brilliant lecture on nuclear policy. When his new brigade major after a fortnight said; 'Sir, do you want me as a BM or a drinking companion?' the answer was a rapid 'Both', and Tubby went on writing.   (Tribute by one of his COs.)
**British Defence Co-ordination Committee (Middle East)
†The official codename for the Suez operation.
‡Director of Military Operations.

him round, a very pleasant assignment.

We duly met in Aden, called on the acting Governor and local service commanders and flew over to British Somaliland for a day to visit the Somaliland Scouts, a local force commanded by British officers responsible to the Governor Sir Tom Pike, whom we were later to meet in Berbera. We then flew to Bahrain for a night or two, and saw Sir Bernard Burrows, the Political Resident, and service commanders before going on to Baghdad. It was here, in talks with HM Ambassador Sir Michael Wright, that I realised the disastrous effect that military action against Egypt would have on Britain's position in the Arab world. The landings at Port Said had not yet taken place but there was every indication that D Day was imminent. Hamilton was made well aware of local feelings. British missions throughout the Middle East had — I suspect deliberately — not been given any details of what was to happen.

We were to have spent several days in Jordan where we still had British officers in the Arab Legion, and a RAF presence. Not surprisingly however, Hamilton's tour was cut short and we were ordered back to Cyprus as quickly as possible. I see from a note I made then that there was just time during a stop-over in Beirut to have a swim in the sea.

We arrived back in Nicosia on October 27th, two days before Israel attacked Egypt. Hamilton was booked into a hotel but I invited him to stay with us, which he was glad to do. He was with us for four days and I well remember his reaction when I told him that the Canberra force had just taken off to bomb Egyptian airfields. He simply could not understand what the Government was playing at (nor could I).

British collusion with Israel has been endlessly debated. At the time, at my level in Cyprus, we knew nothing about joint planning and regarded accusations of collusion as nonsense. When the Israelis attacked in Sinai on October 29th it came as a complete surprise to us. We now know, of course, that Eden and Mollet (the French Prime Minister) did secretly agree with the Israelis that they would attack first and go straight through to the Canal, which they did in a few days. It was the sheer speed of the Israeli advance that wrecked the Musketeer plan. By the time the invasion fleet had arrived off Port Said, the Israelis were at the Canal and there was no clear pretext for a landing that would obviously be opposed. Any further action was condemned by the United States and the UN, and viewed with grave doubt by public opinion in Britain.

Though both the bombing of Egyptian airfields by Canberras from

Cyprus, and the parachute landing at Port Said, went ahead and were successful there was no real justification for either action, and the cease fire on November 6th halted the Parachute Brigade halfway down the Canal with Suez almost in sight and no opposition in front of them. It was all an appalling anti-climax. Bredin, who was now commanding the 2nd Parachute Battalion and led the advance down the Canal, felt that whilst there may have been good reasons for not using force at all, there were none for stopping halfway. We clearly overestimated the fighting qualities of the Egyptian Army, and with hindsight should have attacked in August using the Parachute Brigade, the Commandos and one regiment of tanks. When Bredin was ordered to stop at El Cap just short of Ismailia, he was shown a signal from Whitehall warning of Soviet nuclear missiles being launched on London and Paris if the operation continued. He commented forcibly to me that signals like that should never have been sent to a CO in action. I agree! Two verdicts on the ceasefire are worth recalling: Churchill's only known comment was: 'I don't know if I would have dared to start, I would never have dared to stop'. John Foster Dulles, Eisenhower's Secretary of State whose position throughout had been ambivalent, said to the British Foreign Secretary Selwyn Lloyd: 'I can't understand why you didn't go on'.*

The Soviet threat to intervene was not taken seriously in either London or Paris, but there was an anxious moment in Nicosia one evening at the height of the crisis. An unidentified aircraft appeared on radar flying very high, and the sirens went. We put the children under their beds and lay low. The all-clear quickly came but I heard next day that it might have been a Russian recce aircraft. We were a target as the entire Canberra force was based two to three miles up the road from our flat.

One last point needs to be made. Despite our carefully prepared plans with the French and the Israelis, Nasser was able to sink forty-seven ships filled with concrete in the Canal, effectively blocking the main passage for months; and when the dust finally settled it was he who came out on top. Despite military defeat by Israel in Sinai, by the British-French forces in Port Said and on the Canal, and heavy damage to his military airfields by the bombing, Nasser was elevated to a national and international hero whose portrait appeared on every poster throughout the Arab world for years to come. It was not for nothing that Julian Amery thirty years on called Suez 'Europe's Waterloo'.**

*Quoted by Julian Amery MP in a special article in the *Sunday Telegraph*, October 26, 1986.
**Sunday Telegraph*, October 26th, 1986.

It is interesting to compare the three major set-piece military operations in which British forces have been engaged in the last forty years (not counting internal security emergencies in Malaya, Cyprus, Aden and Kenya). I refer of course to Suez, the Falklands and the Gulf War.

At Suez we invaded Egypt without American support to protect a vital international waterway which had been nationalised. There were over three months of talk and planning before anything happened; the actual fighting lasted seven days, but achieved nothing and very gravely damaged our standing throughout the Middle East. In the Falklands we landed to recapture British territory which had been invaded by the Argentinians. It took six weeks to mount the operation and twenty-four days to force surrender. The Americans gave us strong undercover support. In the Gulf War we entered Kuwait with the Americans to drive out Iraqi forces who had invaded and taken over the country. It took five months to plan, seventeen days of air war and 100 hours of land battle to drive the Iraqis out.

Perhaps the lesson is that if you go to war when your opponent is clearly in breach of international law, and you persist until you win, world opinion will cheer you to the roof. If on the other hand, you give up halfway, as at Suez and one might say in the Gulf War, whatever the reason, you will create a lot of trouble in the years to come simply because the job was not finished.

One of the surprising by-products of Musketeer was the arrival of the Somersets in Cyprus. They had very hurriedly mobilised in England in early August, been given 200 reservists and flown to Malta later that month. After several changes of plan they eventually arrived in Cyprus on November 13th after it was all over, and were put on guard duties in the Nicosia area. One of the young officers, Keith Shapland, wanted to marry a girl to whom he had become engaged in Malta, and who was able to join him in Cyprus. We had a spare room and offered it to Jackie and eventually she and Keith were married in Nicosia, the reception being held at our flat. What made it a particularly dramatic occasion was John Harding's acceptance of an invitation to attend. Security was very tight with soldiers on rooftops and armoured cars on every corner, but to everybody's delight he stayed quite a while. I have a photograph of our son David, then six, looking up at Harding and pointing a finger at him as though saying 'Who is that man?'

There was a considerable feeling of anti-climax in Cyprus after Suez. EOKA had their best three weeks of the entire four-year emergency causing thirty three deaths in November, and we seemed to have temporarily lost the initiative.

Eden resigned, a sick and ruined man, in January 1957 and Macmillan took over. Makarios was released from the Seychelles in April and allowed to return to Greece but not Cyprus. By then Harding had regained his pre-Suez grip and Grivas's gangs were feeling the pinch.

The 2nd Parachute Battalion returned to Cyprus after Musketeer and carried out a particularly successful operation against EOKA at Lower Platres in the Troodos range. Acting on what proved to be very reliable information, they surrounded the village at night and were told that several top terrorists were hiding in one particular house. The scene when they entered was blissful; a woman with a baby in her arms sitting in front of a large log fire, and no sign of anyone else. Suddenly one soldier noticed that there was very little ash around the fire. There was nothing for it but to move the mother and her baby, and the fire. Sure enough, the fire had been laid on the stone lid of a trap-door leading to a cellar. Someone shouted in Greek: 'Come up one by one, or we shall throw a grenade down'. Up came six leading terrorists. As the leader emerged blinking from the darkness, he recognised an intelligence officer who had accompanied the paratroops, and said: 'Captain C — I presume, sir'. EOKA had been after this particular thorn in their flesh for some time.*

In Jordan our fortunes were at a low ebb. In January an Arab solidarity agreement was signed between Jordan on the one hand, and Egypt, Syria and Saudi Arabia on the other. The Anglo-Jordan treaty was terminated on March 19th, and with it the British subsidy came to an end. Those few remaining British troops were to be withdrawn within six months.

I have dealt with Suez at some length because its repercussions were to play such a central part in Britain's relations with the Arab world for at least another decade. I think with hindsight that if there had been no collusion with Israel, and we had been able to carry out a quick joint operation with the French to take over the Canal, we might well have been successful. The Arab world (excluding of course Egypt) would have accepted strong decisive action by the two Western Powers who had dominated the Middle East since the demise of the Ottoman Empire. Both Pakistan and Iraq were known to support force and were disgusted by our half-heartedness. We would not of course have toppled

*This action was described to the author by Major-General Bredin who was commanding the 2nd Parachute Battalion at the time.

Nasser; we merely needed to teach him a lesson. It was not to be.

Since 1955 it had always been the intention to build a large joint Middle East HQ at Episcopi in the south-west corner of the island, west of Limassol. There was also to be a large RAF air base on the peninsula of Akrotiri as part of the complex. We used to visit Episcopi regularly to inspect progress and the move finally took place in April-May 1957. A new village of married quarters was built at Paramali overlooking some lovely sandy beaches. It was in many ways an idyllic spot — except that there wasn't much shade and Cyprus is very hot in summer; a temperature of 95-100° is not uncommon in Nicosia but it is always cooler by the sea.

Simone and I were allotted a comfortable, brand new detached house which was quite a change after our ground-floor flat in the Nicosia suburbs. It had virtually no garden but surprisingly boasted a fir tree which provided some shade, and climbing for the children. The main HQ office blocks were about two miles away. Access to the beaches was a slight problem as our 'village' was several hundred feet up and there was only limited access until the sappers (Royal Engineers) built a jeep track down to one beach and dug a tunnel through a headland connecting it to another beach, which had good access to Paramali. Excellent sea bathing at our doorstep was a great luxury.

Skiing at Troodos was for me the highlight of my free time. It was about a two-hour drive from Nicosia; the Army had a stock of skis and boots which we could use and there usually seemed to be snow in January and February. The highest point, Mount Olympus, is a rounded top 6,403 feet high just above the tree-line. We skied from the top for perhaps half a mile of gentle gradient into the trees, and were then driven back to the top in an army truck. There were no lifts. It was quite hard work but great fun and well patronised by anybody who could get away. On one occasion we skied down the road for several miles to the chrome mines at Amiandos.

We also took local leave in the summer at the Troodos Holiday Camp run by the NAAFI. It was delightfully cool and peaceful though the buildings were patrolled and surrounded by wire, to be on the safe side. We played tennis and went for walks in the pine woods, Caroline being led on a pony. There were no ambushes on the road up, which was of course steep and winding, but unlike the Malayan jungle the verges were more open and did not offer such good cover.

Our nanny Dinah fitted in very well and was excellent with the children. When we moved from Nicosia to Episcopi she stayed behind with a South Stafford family and later married one of the subalterns, Nigel Magrane. Twenty-five years later we were delighted to receive an invitation to the Magranes' Silver Wedding anniversary.

As part of the winding-down after Suez the Somersets went home by troopship from Limassol in early January 1957, and we went out by launch to see them off (there being no berths alongside). It was almost exactly nine years earlier that we had seen the regiment off from Bombay, and then quietly sailed ourselves in the opposite direction.

Early in the same year General Sir Geoffrey Bourne took over as C-in-C from Keightley. He came to us from being Director of Operations in Malaya, and had earlier made his name as GOC in Berlin during the 1949 airlift. As a young officer before the war he had lost an arm on the Cresta run at St Moritz. Keightley had borne responsibility for the military operations at Suez and was widely respected. As a man I found him a little less approachable than Bourne, who was extremely friendly from the start. He occasionally used to drive me down the jeep track to the C-in-C's private beach, which was quite exciting considering that it was narrow and steep and he had only one arm.

One of my last jobs at GHQ was to escort Randolph Churchill (Winston's son) round some army and RAF units on the island. He was then forty-six, had been through two unhappy marriages, served in the war in Intelligence, as a commando on the Salerno beaches, and with Tito in Yugoslavia, and had been an MP for five years, apart from joining his father at several of the major wartime conferences such as Casablanca and Teheran in 1943 and Yalta in 1945. He had certainly inherited some of his father's ability but probably suffered, as have many others, from being the son of a famous man. He was also inclined to drink too much.

Shortly before we left Nicosia John Harding had sent for me and said that he wanted me to return to the Somersets in the autumn as 2nd in Command to Bill Lawson, who would be the next CO.* He anticipated that when my turn came I would be given a command away from the regiment, probably in the Middle East.

We were sad in a way to be leaving so soon after the move to Episcopi, but that is service life. We would anyhow have been due home at the end of 1957 after three years, so it was not too much of a surprise.

We finally flew home via Malta in July 1957, leaving an island still deeply torn by strife; Greek Cypriot against both British rule and the

---

*As Colonel of the Regiment Harding naturally took a considerable interest in senior officer appointments in the only regular battalion. COs changed every two and a half to three years and there would often be a reshuffle on returning from overseas.

Turkish Cypriot minority. Sir Hugh Foot, brother of the prominent Labour politician, succeeded Harding as Governor in December 1957, and talks aimed at creating an independent republic acceptable to both Greek and Turk were concluded by August 1960. However, it was an uneasy peace. In 1974 the Turkish army landed to protect the Turkish Cypriot minority and the island became split as never before. The Greek Cypriots still regard Cyprus as a Greek island though they have abandoned *enosis*. A Green Line which is patrolled by UN troops cuts across Cyprus like a scar. There are two Sovereign Base Areas (SBAs) which remain British territory, the Episcopi-Akrotiri complex in the south-west and another administrative area at Dhekelia between Larnaca and Famagusta. Both are on the Greek side of the Green Line. Akrotiri is now the largest RAF base in the world and played an important part in the Gulf War and the recent release of hostages.

Despite the inability of Greeks and Turks to live peaceably together, the island is prosperous. 700,000 British tourists (more than all the Greek Cypriots living there) visited Cyprus in 1990, unemployment is under two per cent and Britain is her biggest trading partner, taking more than twenty-five per cent of the island's exports and providing more than ten per cent of its imports.

I remember being horrified to see photographs of Makarios as the first President of the Republic in the early 1960s sitting with the Queen at Commonwealth conferences, but that is part of the legacy of empire.

CHAPTER 19

A Lull at Warminster

WHEN we arrived home in July 1957 the Somersets were stationed at Seaton Barracks, Plymouth, and had been warned that they would be taking over as Demonstration Battalion at the School of Infantry, Warminster, in the new year. The move was to be phased over several months and, being due some home leave, I was not required to report at Plymouth. We were allotted a very comfortable married quarter at Warminster, one of a group of houses built pre-war to a high standard.* They were sited just below the edge of Salisbury Plain and gave onto wide open spaces for miles. Before moving in we did the rounds of our respective families at Gaddesden and Coolnakilly. There was a small private school called Draytons just down the road which took David and Caroline, then six and five. I took delivery of a Wolseley 1500, a completely new style of small car, which was a great pride and joy.

Demonstration Battalion at the School was theoretically an honour as we would be required to demonstrate all the latest infantry tactics to gatherings of officers ranging from subalterns just out of Sandhurst to command conferences for top brass, and foreign attachés. The disadvantage of the job was that we were totally at the beck and call of the school, and Bill Baily our CO had virtually no say in decision-making except if things went wrong, when he would be required to explain why.

There was, however, the interest of being at the centre of infantry policy at a time when the Cold War was at its height and nuclear thinking still in its infancy; but for me just back from the Middle East and expecting to be offered a command out there pretty soon it was all rather academic.

Though married officers and men were accommodated at War-minster itself, the battalion was located at Knook about four miles down the Salisbury road. It was a typical hutted camp built during the

*We used to call army barracks and houses built in the 1930s 'Hore Belisha type' after the then Secretary of State for War, who in some mysterious way found the necessary building funds. They still represent some of the best accommodation in the UK.

war; cold and draughty in winter, and just passable in summer. I spent much of my time there though I was able to watch most of the important demonstrations spread over quite a large area of Salisbury Plain.

The 'ghost' village of Imber, tucked away in a remote valley on the Plain, had some years earlier been entirely evacuated and taken over by the army to enable troops to practise street fighting and other skills. We used to drive out there sometimes at weekends to dig up snowdrops and replant them in our garden. It was a rather eerie sensation walking through a completely deserted village of derelict houses and overgrown gardens in the middle of England's green and pleasant land.

Over the winter of 1957-'58 I used to shoot occasionally with an army syndicate on the Plain. Bags were not large but it was great fun. I also tried my hand at fly-fishing on the Wylye, with singular lack of success.

After some months of marking time I was told in November that I was to be promoted Brevet Lieutenant Colonel, backdated to July 1st, 1957. This was a form of accelerated promotion, re-introduced after the war and now discontinued, which meant that one was guaranteed subsequent promotion to at least full Colonel. I was naturally sad not to get command of the Somersets or possibly one of the other Light Infantry regiments, but in those days selection for command was strictly in order of seniority.

In May 1958 the summons came. My next job would be to command the recently formed 3rd Battalion of the Aden Protectorate Levies, and I was required to fly out there in September. Married accommodation was available in Aden itself but as my battalion would be based in the Protectorate all the time there seemed little point in the family coming out. I could only expect to see them for occasional weekends.

My wife's eldest sister, Kitty Pryor, was then living alone at Gaddesden Place and had planned a world cruise; it was decided that Simone and the children would be based there whilst I was abroad. David and Caroline both started school in Hemel Hempstead that winter.

Air trooping had recently been introduced and because there was a ban on overflying Egypt for fairly obvious reasons, we were routed via Kano in northern Nigeria where we spent a very hot night, then east across central Africa to Stanleyville (now Kisangani) in the then Belgian Congo (now Republic of Zaire) where we refuelled before the final leg to Aden. The journey took about thirty-six hours in a rather noisy piston-engined aircraft.

CHAPTER 20

History repeats itself?

'IN classical times the south-western corner of the Arabian Peninsula was known as Arabia Felix — a perfumed oasis desert green enough to support agriculture and a large population. The legendary home of the Queen of Sheba . . .' *The Times*, June 7th, 1994.

Reflecting on my posting to the Aden Protectorate Levies (APL), it almost seems as though the Almighty decreed that I should follow as nearly as possible in the footsteps of my father and grandfather.

The Western Aden Protectorate (WAP), where I was to be for the next two and a half years, was very similar both in terrain and way of life to the Indian frontier. Social conditions have been likened to the Highlands of Scotland in the mid-eighteenth century.

Another coincidence is that in 1941 my father was posted to command an Indian brigade that was being sent to Aden. He was only switched to the Kohat Brigade (on the North-West Frontier) because it was decided in the end not to send a brigade to Aden. So I was to take his place as a CO commanding local troops seventeen years later! However, I am quite sure that the Military Secretary's department of the War Office which decides who should go where knew nothing of this titbit of family history. I had looked in at Aden several times before; first in 1920 aged four on my way out to India with my parents; in 1938 on my way to join the Somersets for the first time in India, and more recently in 1952 when we did a route march through the town early in the morning on our way to Malaya. In each case the reason for the call was to take on coal in the early days, and later oil.

To most travellers who penetrate east of Suez, memories of Aden are confined to a first view of barren spiky mountains looming up on the horizon long before the harbour comes into view, a subsequent frantic dash round shops during which you buy a rather more expensive camera than intended, and finally the taste of the water which lingers until your arrival at either Suez or Colombo. According to Sir Tom Hickinbotham, who was Governor from 1951-6 and had held several other appointments in Government before that, the first recorded mention of Aden is in the Bible (Ezekiel ch.27, v.23.) The Eden referred to is Aden — not in any way to be confused with the Garden of Eden. Because of its key position at the southern entrance of the Red Sea, it has been a trading centre for centuries and regarded with envy by rulers from the interior, particularly the Yemenis. Portuguese, Turks and Egyptians have all been would-be conquerors, but the only foreign power that came to stay was Britain in 1839 two years after Queen Victoria ascended the throne, probably because we wanted to control the only good harbour between India and Egypt. Commander Haines of the Indian Navy who led the 'assault', then ran Aden as a private fiefdom for fifteen years, and was prosecuted by the British Government for fraud when he retired.

The opening of the Suez Canal in 1869 brought considerable prosperity to this British settlement (it became a Crown Colony in 1937) though conditions were primitive. As late as the 1930s fresh water from inland wells had to be brought into the town. Aden was and still is a free port, owing its prosperity to its geographical position, its natural harbour and its freedom from import and export duties.

In 1953 BP completed a large oil refinery on the other side of the bay and by 1956, the year of Suez, over 5,000 ships a year were refuelling there. It was the busiest bunkering harbour in the world.

Inland from the port was the Protectorate, and I cannot do better than quote Lord Belhaven (a British Political Officer in the 1930s) from his book, *The Uneven Road*:

A coastal strip of desert, nowhere more than forty miles wide, leads to the foothills, its dunes rising like the waves of a sea and then dropping down, as it were in a fallen crest, to a deep hollow where hill and sand meet. Beyond the foothills the country rises steeply in jagged tumbled mountains, contorted and precipitous, some with great spurs of rock projecting from their flanks . . . Across these mountains the high block of the Yemen throws out a long spur, seven thousand feet high . . . North of this range, the country breaks away, in cleft and abyss, to the central desert plain of Arabia. Thus, in brief, the territory can be said to have three main features, a coastal plain and a desert plain, divided by a giant spur of mountains.

The country is big in every sense, going up to 9,000 feet in the Protectorate and 12,000 feet in the Yemen. However, despite this considerable height, *wadi* beds, with very few exceptions, are dried up for most of the year; only during the autumn rains do they rise suddenly and flood the whole valley in a matter of hours. Water for cultivation and drinking is all drawn from wells. Roads are almost non-existent, there being only four through trade routes to the Yemen on a frontage of 500 miles. Tarmac, with one very minor exception, does not exist outside the Colony. Cover is scarce, there being very few trees, but despite this the predominantly dark colour of the rock provides surprisingly good camouflage. Villages are almost all perched on the tops of hills, the houses being built of mud and stone with tiny windows and thick walls; each house is in reality a miniature fort.

Such are the bare facts. The country has its own harsh, barren form of grandeur, which cannot help but impress the newcomer.

By way of contrast with the Crown Colony of Aden the Protectorate was a real protectorate, that is to say, a group of protected states with recognised rulers exercising full authority outside the fields of foreign affairs and defence — not just a colony under a different name, as was often the case with British Protectorates in Africa. Most of the eighteen states had their own rulers who in some cases ruled direct, or, as progress continued, through a state council. There were six British Political Officers, known as Assistant Advisers, who advised the rulers on government policy. They in turn were responsible to a British Agent in Aden who was responsible to the Governor. The APL and, on occasions, the Royal Air Force were used by this administration to help preserve law and order.

Relations between Aden and the Yemen had been strained for years, one of the main reasons being that the exact delineation of the frontier had never been mutually agreed. A Boundary Commission, which was established in 1902, started work at Bab-el-Mandeb on the Red Sea and was supposed to cover the whole 700 miles. In fact it got as far as Dhala, some 150 miles up the frontier, after two years' work, and then gave up, due partly to the inaccessibility of the country, and partly to the innumerable tribal disputes which had to be resolved. The result was that the frontier from Dhala onwards was just a line on the map; there were no boundary stones, no wire, nothing in fact to indicate where the frontier actually ran.

Up to 1934, the Yemenis occupied quite a large portion of WAP territory and it was only as a result of the Treaty of Sana'a signed in that year that they agreed to withdraw.

For the last twenty-five years there had been a series of border skirmishes, which seemed to have achieved little beyond causing bitterness between the tribesmen living on either side. The Yemeni authorities had also been actively engaged in subverting WAP tribesmen by giving them arms and money and encouraging them to cause trouble in the Protectorate. One of the oddities of the situation was that there were some 40,000 Yemenis in the Colony, many of them servants in European homes. There was constant movement to and fro across the border, particularly on the main trade routes. *Suq* (market) days on the WAP side were well attended by Yemenis and to a lesser extent the same applied to the other side. Aden Airways which operated a regular Dakota service to two of the border towns, Mukheiras and Beihan, carried almost as many Yemeni passengers as those from the WAP.

The APL then consisted of three regular battalions of infantry with a fourth about to be raised. It had been formed shortly after World War I, was paid for entirely by HMG and until the early 1950s was officered by the Royal Air Force Regiment, because the RAF provided virtually all the service personnel in the Colony.

By 1958 responsibility had passed to the Army though each battalion had a RAF officer commanding one of its companies. Force HQ was in the Colony just outside Aden and was commanded by a brigadier (Derrick Worwald for most of my time). Major General Cecil Firbank (late Somerset Light Infantry and shortly to be Colonel of the Regiment) was Colonel Commandant of the APL, and I was delighted to welcome him to Mukheiras on an official visit during my first year.

Such was the background to my new job, a far cry from Demonstration Battalion at Warminster.

It was extremely hot in Aden when I arrived in early September, and after briefing I motored out by landrover to Zinzibar in the Fadhli Sultanate, where 3 APL was deployed in a reserve role. I was glad to hear that we were very shortly to move to Mukheiras in the Audhali Sultanate on the border with Yemen, the most popular station of all as it was 6,800 feet up and delightfully cool. The ruler was known to be very friendly and only too pleased to have the army as a back-up in case of incursions from Beidha, the Yemen town about ten miles away.

Mukheiras was perched on the high rolling plateau which formed the frontier with the Yemen at this point. There was an airstrip there (it could hardly be called a runway) and a tent served as terminal buildings. This was just as well as there was as yet no road up from the main Audhali plateau at Loder, only a very rough footpath which climbed 3,500 feet in six miles up the Thira Pass. We were flown in by RAF Beverley, a cumbersome but reliable work horse specifically designed for short take-off and landing (STOL), and were subsequently supplied entirely by air with all the necessities of life: rations, mail, spare parts, equipment and so on.

My battalion group included a company from the Northamptons (the rest of the battalion having to sweat it out in Aden), a section of twenty-five-pounders and a troop of Ferret scout cars. One of my companies was based at Loder and controlled the bottom of the Thira

Pass, which I walked up and down on a number of occasions; there was a good deal of competition as to who held the record for the climb. Par was about two hours. Battalion HQ was in a white-washed mud building which had in the past served as rest-house and customs post. Covered in red and mauve bougainvillaea it had a certain romantic charm, and was quite comfortable.

The Ruler of the Audhali Sultanate, Sultan Saleh bin* Hussein, lived in his capital Loder, and delegated the running of the Mukheiras plateau to his brother Naib Ja'bil, with whom I was to deal. Sir Charles Johnston** in his book *The View from Steamer Point* describes the brothers well: 'Squat, thickset with a round face, high cheekbones and a flat turban like a soufflé placed square on the top of his head, Sultan Saleh had a slightly withdrawn, Far Eastern look about him . . . Naib Ja'bil is a prince of a very different type. Known to his British friends as "the choirboy", he has an angelic air of youth and innocence combined with a strong taste for devilry which he has been known to gratify to some effect when provoked by aggression from over the border'. After I left Aden Naib Ja'bil called on us at Gaddesden when visiting Britain. I remember meeting him off a bus! He was suitably impressed by the Halsey ancestral home looking down on the Gade Valley, being used to living in a 'tower-house' himself.

We had hardly settled in before I was told that the Duke of Gloucester (the young Queen's uncle) was visiting Aden shortly and that the Governor proposed to bring him up to Mukheiras for a tea party with the Ruler and his family. I was also told that HRH did not drink tea; he preferred whisky and it had to be Black Label. We went into top gear, erected a smart marquee, repainted anything that could do with a lick or two, including stones, and had the dhobi working flat out on perfectly starched khaki drill. The only problem was the Black Label; we had Red but not Black and only in the nick of time did Aden Airways oblige with a bottle. The great day arrived; the sun shone (as it did practically every day), HRH arrived, pleasantries were exchanged and we went into the marquee for tea. The precious Black Label was discreetly produced; HRH appeared not to notice it, and drank tea! As the royal aircraft taxied away we made a concerted dash for the mess, and had soon made amends for the Duke's abstinence.

Another visitor that winter might have upset relations with the ruler had he not been so naturally polite. A signal arrived† saying that Lord

---

*'bin' means 'son of' in Arabic.
**Governor of Aden, 1960-63.
†Our only communication with Aden was by HF wireless. It was sometimes possible to talk loud and clear but all routine traffic was in morse, taken down by Arab signallers whose English was limited or non-existent.

Belhaven would be visiting Mukheiras by Aden Airways and it would be nice if he could meet the Ruler. Fortunately I had done my homework and knew that Lord Belhaven (then the Master of Belhaven) had been a Political Officer in the WAP some years earlier and had written an excellent book* about the area. So again we alerted every everybody and the Ruler and I met the aircraft. Out stepped a tall, languid-looking Englishman accompanied by his wife. I advanced and said something like: 'Welcome to Mukheiras, Lord Belhaven,' to which he replied 'My name is Claud Hamilton; I am on a visit to an old friend Maurice Heath [the Air Officer Commanding] from Kenya, and he kindly suggested that I might like to have a quick look at Mukheiras'. Knowing that Hamilton was the family name of Belhaven I had by this time introduced him as Lord Belhaven to the Ruler, who had not a clue who he was, and it was all rather embarrassing. What had happened was that somebody on the AOC's staff in Aden had wrongly assumed that Lord Claud Hamilton (to give him his full title) must be Belhaven, whereas in fact he was a son of the Duke of Abercorn, and not connected with Belhaven at all.

We all had tea together (no Black Label this time) and Hamilton invited me to visit him on his estate in Kenya — which I was unfortunately never able to do.

One of my first jobs was to learn some basic Arabic so that I could communicate, however amateurishly, with my soldiers. I bought an excellent text book entitled *Aden Arabic for Beginners* and engaged a *munshi*** who spoke good English, to go through the various exercises. After three months I passed the Lower Standard Colloquial Exam and was rewarded with a small language grant. I was surprised to find out afterwards that neither of the other COs had taken the exam and spoke to their men almost entirely through an interpreter.

I had about ten British officers, all seconded from British service, and about twenty Arab officers. Amongst the Majors were Stuart Smith and Pat Creagh from the Royal Leicesters, Frank White from the North Staffords, Dick Holman from the Suffolks and two excellent Squadron Leaders from the Royal Air Force Regiment: George Foskitt and Kingsley Oliver. Bill Heber-Percy, Welsh Guards and then about twenty-four, was Adjutant for my last year. Their tour of duty was eighteen months but could be extended. There were also a few British specialist NCOs such as signallers, fitters, armourers, clerks and medical orderlies. Our doctor, Robin Lush, had recently qualified in England

*The Uneven Road, John Murray, 1955.
**Language teacher.

and was doing National Service as were several other young officers. It was a happy and very informal mess. We all lived 'over the shop' and theoretically were on duty all the time; there were no 'office hours' as such. The climate was delightful, and though we wore khaki drill it was seldom too hot. However, occasional dust storms could be trying.

My soldiers were all tribesmen from the WAP. They enlisted initially for four years and were then permitted to re-engage year by year, which the majority did. Recruiting was no problem, as the pay and standard of living (in particular the food) were considerably better than in any other form of employment outside Aden. Several hundred tribesmen, all of them supermen according to their shaikh, would appear before a recruiting officer who might only want about fifty. Men who were well over age and probably tubercular would try to pretend that they were only eighteen and completely fit. Needless to say, Robin Lush played an important part in any recruiting drive.

The laws of Islam were strictly observed in South-West Arabia, and this could present problems in the Levies where the men were all Muslims. It was, for example, unusual to plan operations during the thirty-day fast of Ramadhan.

As soldiers the men excelled at moving quickly over the perpendicular hills of the WAP carrying a rifle or LMG or even a 62 Set manpack. Their fieldcraft was good, but they knew little about minor tactics and were not quick to learn. A platoon commander would find his way from A to B because he knew the country anyway, or by asking locals, rather than by using such modern aids to navigation as maps and compasses.

The men were extremely cheerful and willing and once they got to know their British commander would do almost anything for him. In the conflict of loyalties between tribe and the *geish* (army) the personality and leadership qualities of the British officer played a decisive part. Arab officers, particularly platoon commanders, tended to be 'old sweats' because commissioning in the past had been largely based on long service and good contact. We tried to select officer material early and commission likely candidates in their early twenties.

From time to time during those early months suspect Yemenis were picked up and questioned by one of Naib Ja'bil's men. He had at his disposal a force known as Tribal Guards, local tribesmen who were recruited specifically to maintain the ruler's authority.

One day a Czech-manufactured armoured personnel carrier (APC) drove over from the Yemen to seek asylum. A Beverley was quickly sent up to collect it but disappointingly it had no special intelligence interest.

Since the frontier in the Mukheiras area was relatively peaceful, and the high plateau was cool and had a certain charm, we tended to get all the VIP visitors. I was particularly pleased to receive Bernard Fergusson who was then writing for the *Sunday Times*, having retired from the army as a brigadier. Commissioned in the Black Watch and Wavell's ADC before the war, he made his name as a Chindit* leader in Burma. He later vividly described his exploits in two best-selling books: *Beyond the Chindwin* and *The Wild Green Earth*. He was subsequently to become Governor-General of New Zealand and awarded a life peerage as Lord Ballantrae. I took him round the OPs (observation posts) on the frontier, and we had a very jolly evening in the Mess.

Sir William Luce, the Governor of Aden whom I had very briefly met two years earlier in Khartoum, also came up for several days and stayed in the official Government rest-house. He toured the frontier with Sultan Saleh and Naib Jab'il and I provided him with a suitable escort. A fluent Arabic speaker and a man of commanding presence, I have always regarded him as one of the last great British pro-consuls. He was much respected by the Protectorate rulers and by all walks of life in Aden. His brother Admiral Sir David Luce was to be First Sea Lord, and his son Richard Luce became an MP and Minister under Mrs Thatcher, and is now Vice-Chancellor of Buckingham University — altogether a most distinguished family. I served under Sir William not only in the Aden Protectorate but also later in the Persian Gulf when he was Political Resident.

One of my regular commitments was to escort a convoy northwards along the Yemen border to supply a fort at Merta'a manned by Government Guards who formed the first line of defence against Yemeni raids.

It was an extremely isolated spot and supply vehicles had been shot up on several occasions. We normally had a Shackleton on call which was a powerful deterrent.

The use of the Air Arm (i.e. the RAF) both for border reconnaissance, but more particularly in Internal Security work which usually meant bombing or using rockets, was inevitably controversial and condemned by armchair critics. Sir Tom Hickinbotham in his book *Aden* very clearly argues the case for using the air weapon in mountainous country like the WAP. He writes: 'imagine that a breach of the peace has occurred and the Ruler has asked Government to help him

*The name given to the brigade which Wingate led far behind the Japanese lines in 1943. Wingate wanted to call the brigade by the name of an animal. *Chinthe* is Burmese for lion. A *Daily Express* reporter later used the name Chindit and it stuck. They became the lions of the Burmese jungle.

bring the guilty party to account. Offenders are called upon to surrender but ignore the summons. The Ruler orders a fine to be paid and this also is ignored. Air photographs are probably then taken and actual towers or houses identified. Twenty-four hours' notice of air action is given and the transgressors warned to remove their belongings. A further warning of one hour is given immediately prior to action. The operation takes place; it is very accurate and no unnecessary damage is caused. Quite often', says Hickinbotham, 'the offenders and their friends gather on a nearby hill feature to watch the aircraft in action. The incident is over. There have been no casualties, there were not intended to be; only material damage has been done. I do not recall . . . at any time, any casualties as a result of such operations. To have inflicted the same punishment in the more remote parts of the Protectorate, with land forces, would certainly have resulted in casualties on both sides . . .'*

In the late summer of 1959 3 APL (to use my battalion's official abbreviation) was relieved at Mukheiras and we moved down into the much hotter and dustier plains. We were then ordered to Ahwar on the border with the Eastern Protectorate in the Wahidi Sultanate nearly 300 miles east of Aden. It was wild country and had hardly ever been visited by Government forces. In this case disaffected tribesmen had been causing a lot of trouble stealing livestock such as camels and goats, and there had been some pillaging and burning of crops and houses.

The area was accordingly 'proscribed' and we moved in. I was allotted an Arab Political Officer who spoke good English and might be described as the local equivalent of a good English 'bobby'. We established two strong patrol bases in the centre of the area and were soon able to confiscate a considerable number of camels and goats. This quickly resulted in tribesmen coming in and offering themselves as hostages for the good behaviour of their fellows. We had an RAF officer with us acting as a Forward Air Controller (FAC) to direct fighter and bomber aircraft onto specific targets.

After three weeks of patrolling and some air action we had collected nine hostages representing (according to my Arab bobby) almost all the sections of the dissident tribe, and had returned all livestock to their rightful owners.

It was on this operation that I first encountered 'blue men', which is the simplest way to describe really wild tribesmen who cover their bodies all over with an indigo dye; it is said to keep them cool in the summer and warm in the winter. An equally plausible explanation is

*pp. 106-8. Published in 1958

that the dye provides an ideal camouflage against the predominantly dark rock of the Protectorate. Blue cotton 'kilts' reaching to the knee are held in place by a leather cartridge belt which in turn supports a *jambiya* (dagger.) Stripped to the waist, they present a fearsome appearance which is topped by a mane of curly black hair. Their rifles are certainly loaded, probably with a round up the 'spout'. Rough leather sandals complete the picture.

Whilst we were at Ahwar an RAF Whirlwind helicopter landed in the dried-up *wadi* bed where my HQ was and sank into the sand and all three rotor blades snapped off. The pilot was cut about the face when the perspex hood of the cockpit shattered but otherwise nobody was hurt. In this remote valley where Western civilisation had hardly ever penetrated it caused quite a sensation. Recovering what was left of the helicopter presented quite a problem but the RAF won in the end.

We also managed to drive our section of twenty-five-pounder guns forty miles up the same *wadi* bed, a remarkable achievement by the British gunners and their gun towers, the standard Bedford three-tonner.

Our regimental Christmas card that year depicted a camel carrying a heavy No. 62 wireless set and batteries on each side of its hump.

We were able to conclude this particular operation in time to have a few days off at Christmas back in the Abyan plain, forty miles east of Aden on the coast. This was a fertile delta rich in silt where flood water from late summer and autumn rain in the mountains had been harnessed, and an irrigation system developed to spread precious water over several thousand acres. A Development Board had been set up by Government and long staple Egyptian cotton successfully introduced.

We were loaned a villa outside Zinzibar, the main Arab town, and were entertained by the British manager of the Cotton Board and his wife. It was a very welcome break; I can remember playing tennis and shooting some duck.

During that Christmas I met Hilary Hook, then a Major commanding the APL armoured car squadron. He had originally been commissioned in an Indian cavalry regiment, had transferred to British service and was now on secondment to the APL. He was an extremely keen shot, and ran a most enjoyable duck shoot at Abyan, one of the few areas for hundreds of miles along that desolate coast where there were fresh-water feeding grounds for duck. Hilary would motor out from Aden along the beach with some of his friends, arriving before dawn and positioning us in the half-light at various prepared butts. He reserved what he called 'the Kaiser's butt' for his most important guest. The morning would end with a splendid breakfast including kippers from the fridge and Cooper's Oxford marmalade. Over twenty years

later, Hilary was to make his name as a television personality and
author when he returned home from Kenya and described what it was
like to have to fend for oneself in England, after living in some style as
a safari-leader game-warden in Africa. The tabloid press reported that he
received many proposals of marriage from women who felt sorry for
him. He was certainly a very colourful character.

In January 1960 my battalion was ordered to take over the Dhala area
of the Yemen border. This was the most westerly of the three battalion
sectors (the other two being Mukheiras in the centre and Beihan in the
north-east). Some eighty miles almost due north of Aden, it boasted a
so-called road, and we were not therefore on air supply. The 'town' of
Dhala is 4,500 feet up on a flat table-land dominated by Jebel Jihaf, an
imposing massif rising 3,000 feet above the plateau. Sir Charles
Johnston* describes the scene well: 'There is a special magic about the
early morning mists smoking up the perpendicular face of the Jebel
Jihaf. I have never seen the North-West Frontier of India, but imagine
that it must have given very much the same impression; castled hill-tops,
towering peaks with tented camps at their foot, strategic tracks through
narrow gorges along which we would proceed, in military pomp, led by
a troop of the 11th Hussars with coloured pennants flying from the
antennae of the armoured cars, immediately escorted by jeep loads of
Federal Guards, and watched by Marine Commandos operating walki-
talkies from salient points beside the track.'

The 'road' from Aden gradually wound through foothills following
dried-up *wadi* beds until just below the Dhala plateau, when it climbed
up the tortuous Khoreiba pass and suddenly emerged onto a flattish
cultivated plain. The APL base was entirely tented on a low flat hill just
above the cultivation. Dhala itself, also on a low hill and consisting
mostly of tower houses, was about three-quarters of a mile away. Most
houses in the Protectorate were fortified in some way with thick walls
of mud or stone, flat roofs, parapets and very small windows through
which one could shoot without presenting much of a target oneself.

This sector of the border was important for two reasons: there was
a direct road from Qataba (the Yemen town opposite Dhala) to Aden,
and as recently as 1956 and 1957 the Yemenis had staged an overt attack
across the border and a campaign of internal subversion with the object
of seizing Jebel Jihaf. The then Political Officer had been besieged with
a small group of Government Guards at a remote fort on the border
and relieved by British infantry in a dramatic operation which hit the

*The View from Steamer Point, p.71.

London headlines.

Consequently, in addition to my battalion I had a company of the Royal Warwicks, a section of twenty-five-pounders and a troop of Ferret scout cars from the 11th Hussars who were then stationed in Aden. I remember John Charles Harding (the Field Marshal's son), then serving with the 11th, spent a night with us at Dhala. We were supplied once a fortnight by convoy; there was also an airstrip which was regularly used by RAF Twin Pioneers, invaluable work horses which could take off and land virtually on a postage stamp.

Dhala was distinctly more exciting than Mukheiras. There was always the chance of being sniped at from Jebel Jihaf, or coming up the Khoreiba pass; our guns had defensive fire (DF) tasks registered on possible approaches, our tents were sand-bagged and we were always out patrolling. I sometimes thought of my grandfather leading the 5th Bombay Mountain Battery armed with 2.5 inch seven-pounder 'screwguns' in the 1890s, and my father leading his Pathans, Punjabis and Sikhs of the 1st/13th Frontier Force Rifles in the 1930s. Both were then serving on the North-West Frontier of India but the terrain must have been very similar for all three of us.

Sir Tom Hickinbotham describes how on his first visit to Dhala as Governor he was received by a seventeen-gun salute from cannon which were less dangerous to be in front of than behind. They had a tendency to explode if too much black powder was used in the charge, and there had been several accidents. On this occasion the gunners were unable to fire seventeen rounds on his first day, and chose the following day in the middle of a feast given by the Ruler for Hickinbotham to fire the last round. He describes the scene in his book, *Aden:*[*]

It was at this moment, while the silence was profound and everybody's attention was occupied with the food, that it happened. There was a shattering explosion, and the pungent smell of gunpowder filled the room. The whole building shook as the ground trembled and plaster fell from the ceiling on to the food. The whole assembly, with the exception of three, came rapidly to their feet and looked wildly round while daggers were drawn, and I saw one of my personal servants with commendable presence of mind seize and draw the dagger from his neighbour's belt, thereby providing himself with a weapon and disarming a potential enemy in one swift movement. The three exceptions were the Naib, the Political Officer and myself, and to this day why we remained unmoved I really do not know, because normally speaking the noise and surprise of the explosion would have made me jump out of my skin. Possibly I had some subconscious realisation of the cause of the disturbance.

[*]p.114.

The Naib looked at the startled company and spoke: 'The cannon,' he said, and smiled.

The people of Dhala have one serious vice; they grow and eat qât, a small green leaf which absorbs a great deal of their vitality and practically all their money. As a result they are physically well below the ordinary standard of the Protectorate's population. Wherever one went one would meet local tribesmen with one side of their mouths distended by a ball of qât which they were chewing. It was not a pretty sight.

It is appropriate here to mention health in the Protectorate. Very few qualified doctors were available and Robin Lush had a considerable civilian practice in addition to his normal work of looking after the troops. Tribesmen from far and wide, including Yemenis who may well have made a special trip across the border, came to see him, and the part that he played in cementing Anglo-Arab relations was out of all proportion to his appointment. On one occasion a tribesman with a very serious dagger wound in his stomach (incurred, as was usually the case, in a domestic quarrel) was brought in on a donkey from a nearby village. Robin did what he could but doubted whether the unfortunate man would last the night. Miraculously he did and was 'casevaced' by the Royal Air Force when it was considered safe to move him. He recovered in the large modern Queen Elizabeth Hospital in Aden.

After we had settled in and registered our guns in the unlikely event of a surprise attack, I was told that the War Office at home wanted to make a recruiting film featuring a young officer leading an adventurous life in defence of British interests in distant lands. The Aden Protectorate had been chosen as the location, and in particular, Dhala. A production team from Associated British-Pathe including several actors would be arriving shortly from the UK, and I was to give them every assistance. They must have been with us about three weeks and proved good value but somewhat distracting. Various incidents had to be staged, including the ambush of a convoy on the Khoreiba Pass. The special effects man was in his element and an old BLR* Bedford truck went up in a ball of fire. We also had RAF Hunters strafing a target which had been identified by the 'hero' (the young officer). As part of the plot an innocent local family party, riding on donkeys with their belongings on a camel, were to be filmed. There was a problem: Arab men were delighted to be involved, particularly as they were well paid,

*Beyond Local Repair

but their women could not possibly be allowed to take part. It was accordingly arranged that two British soldier volunteers would be suitably disguised and ride the donkeys. It was not difficult to arrange as the 'women' would be heavily veiled. We also had to paint their legs dark brown from the knee downwards as they nearly touched the ground on each side of the donkeys.

About a year later, after leaving Aden, I was invited to attend a preview of the film in a studio off Wardour Street. The family all went and the children were thrilled. I never heard how successful the film was; the British Army was already running out of 'outposts of empire' where a life of adventure could be realistically portrayed. It was all too soon to be only Germany or Northern Ireland.

In the early summer of 1960 I had hoped to fly home for a family wedding at Gaddesden. Caroline was to be a bridesmaid to Addie Pryor, a niece of Simone's who was marrying Digby Raeburn of the Scots Guards. At the last minute I had to cancel my trip, since I was ordered to leave a much-reduced garrison at Dhala and move my battalion to the Upper Aulaqi Sultanate about 200 miles to the east, where a major operation against dissident tribesmen was to be launched. It was in fact about the only area of importance in the Western Protectorate where British influence had not infiltrated. The Aulaqis are a virile and warlike clan, and according to Hickinbotham* were the most powerful race in this remote corner of Arabia before the Christian era.

We were flown in Beverleys to a remote airstrip near Ataq. From there, a penetration group, consisting of the fighting element of the battalion accompanied by a gunner OP party and FAC**, walked into some of the most mountainous and inaccessible country in the WAP, an area which had never before been patrolled by Government forces. Support weapons, wireless sets, reserve ammunition and bedding rolls were carried on camels and we took an airdrop of rations every other day. We never saw our transport for nearly a month. Contact was made with dissidents on six separate occasions, but it was always at long range and the main gang that we were after eventually fled across into the Yemen. Just after one air drop of supplies the heavens opened and it simply poured. The brightly-coloured pink nylon parachutes used to drop supplies were useful in providing some sort of cover. The shallow valley which we were in at the time was quickly flooded but as quickly dried up.

*Aden, p.117.
**Forward Air Controller.

On another occasion we carried out a rather tricky move by night along a remote, winding *wadi* bed. There was little moon and visibility very limited. The men were not used to a manoeuvre of this sort and were rather jumpy. Somebody let off a round by mistake and there was a minor panic. It took us British officers a little time to restore calm. This incident taught me not to expect local tribesmen to be as highly trained as some of their counterparts in the British Army.

At one stage of this Aulaqi adventure — and it was really more of an adventure than a strictly text-book military operation — we were ordered to construct an airstrip which would take Beverley transports. I had two or three hundred men levelling ground and marking the edges of the runway with stones for several days. It later became known as 'Freddie's Field' and is (or was) actually marked as such on official War Office Survey Directorate maps of the area.*

Dhala seemed quite tame after a month or so of constant movement in a totally undeveloped part of Arabia. We had no casualties and I certainly don't remember being shot at, but that doesn't mean that there was not a certain amount of indiscriminate shooting at nothing in particular, a bad habit which British officers with similar experience to mine will, I am sure, agree was extremely difficult to eradicate amongst Arab soldiers.

My most vivid memory of Dhala will always be David Shepherd's visit because his painting looks down on me as I write. In his book, *The Man who Loves Giants*,** Shepherd tells how, at the age of nineteen, the Slade turned him away with the comment: 'Failed, talent lacking'. He was then under the wing of an established artist, Robin Goodwin, and spent several years painting London scenes under his guidance. In 1954 Shepherd had his first painting accepted at the Royal Academy's Summer Exhibition. Now on his own, he specialised in painting aircraft at London Airport and then switched to railways and in particular steam locomotives; some of his most well-known early paintings were set at Crewe, Swindon and King's Cross.

Readers must be wondering what this biographical note has to do with Aden. In 1960 Air Marshal Sam Patch, the AOC, invited Shepherd to come out and record for posterity the end of empire in Aden with special reference to the role of the RAF. That, as Shepherd puts it, 'changed my life'.

Up at Dhala I was informed that an artist called Shepherd would be

*Sheet 687B Series 1404 World 1:500,000 1962, for anybody who is interested.
**Hodder & Stoughton, 1975.

on the next convoy and would like to stay the night. I had vaguely heard of him and hoped that he might have time to do a little sketch for me. On arrival he said that he had a bad headache, and wished to go to bed at once; however, if I woke him early the next morning and showed him what I wanted, he might consider it. In his book* he describes the Dhala convoy and says that it took over twelve hours to cover the ninety miles from Aden, so I can understand the headache.

Next morning at about 6 a.m. I took him in my Land Rover to a small hill above Dhala town looking across at Jebel Jihaf which towered over us, our tented camp just visible down below, and said 'What about this?' Shepherd took a few feet of 8 mm cine film and some transparencies and spent perhaps a quarter of an hour pencil-sketching in a notebook. On our way back to camp for breakfast he said: 'When you're next home on leave, give me a ring and I will try and knock something up for you'. The resultant painting now has a place of honour in our dining-room, and is reproduced in part on the jacket of this book.

Later, Shepherd's *Dhala Convoy* became one of his most famous Aden works, second only to *Slave Island*. It was originally intended for the Royals whose Ferret scout cars featured prominently. However there was an argument about the price and eventually Shepherd sold it to the Federal Regular Army (as the APL was later called), painting out the white faces and substituting Arabs. I have a print of the Arab version. Another painting which I very much liked was of a Beverley landing on a desert strip. To quote Shepherd: 'By reversing the pitch of its propellers, it would almost stand on its nose and stop dead. It had to, otherwise it hit the mountain at the end of the runway. The whole aeroplane, except for the tip of the tail, would disappear in a sandstorm of its own creation. This would then take half an hour to subside, after which the aeroplane would re-emerge, apparently none the worse for wear. This astonishing scene was a subject I recorded on canvas for three different RAF units.'**

After his very successful visit to Aden the RAF flew him to Kenya and it was there that he started painting jumbos and many other wild animals; it is as a wild-life artist that he has been acclaimed world-wide.

Our last distinguished visitor at Dhala was the CIGS Field Marshal Sir Francis Festing, who flew up by Twin Pioneer. An imposing man, I suspect that he was the only British Field Marshal ever to visit such a remote outpost of empire.

*pp.62-5
**pp.58-9.

IN the autumn of 1960 I was told that my next job was to be Brigade Colonel of the Light Infantry, based at Shrewsbury. I was to hand over 3 APL in early January 1961 and start at Shrewsbury in April after leave. It meant promotion to full Colonel and a 'red hat', which was pleasing.

My battalion was relieved at Dhala before Christmas and I spent my last fortnight or so at Zinzibar on the coast. There were the inevitable farewell parties and presentations. I was given two *jambiyas* by the Arab officers and men. Reading again the English translation of the farewell speech made by my senior Arab officer (which is now carefully preserved on the back of the *jambiya* box) I see that I was 'never afraid from death . . . and good in all my actions'. Had my Brigadier seen this extravagant and eulogistic tribute and, much more important, agreed with it, I would have gone far! As it happened, I was very pleased to be awarded the OBE in the New Year's Honours List which came out just before my departure.

So ended my two-and-a-half year command appointment, a very different affair from being CO of a British unit in BAOR. In many ways it was great fun; career-wise it was probably a dead end. The WAP tribesmen were very likeable and I cannot recall an occasion when there was any genuine ill-feeling. My British officers and NCOs were a good lot, we had some exciting moments but there was seldom any real danger. The country was 'big' and romantic. One was fit and there was a real job to be done.

The final British departure from Aden came seven years later in 1967. In the 'fifties Tom Hickinbotham, the Governor, had seen the need for a joint organisation of states in the WAP though there were age-old traditions of jealously and hostility between some of them. By 1959 (my first full year) a Federation of Ten States made a treaty with HMG under which we were mainly responsible for defence and foreign affairs, but also committed to financial aid for economic development.

The next stage was to be union with the Crown Colony and this proved a far more difficult problem, even though Aden and its hinterland were intricately involved with each other and completely inter-dependent; for example, Aden's water, much of its labour, and most of its fruit and vegetables came in from the Federation, and the latter in turn was almost entirely dependent on Aden for its communications with the outside world.

In 1961 there came, surprisingly, a distinct improvement in relations between Aden and the Yemen, and a corresponding decline in the fortunes of the dissident leaders in the WAP. In November the APL was ceremonially handed over to the Federation and became the Federal Regular Army (FRA).

Throughout 1962 talks went on to try to create a merger of Aden and the Protectorate which would be acceptable to all parties and, of particular importance to HMG, secure the British base. But just as agreement, however flimsy, seemed to have been reached, there was a revolution in the Yemen; the Imam was deposed, tanks rumbled into the streets of Sana'a, and the Yemen Arab Republic was created.

As David Holden of the *Sunday Times* wrote in his book, *Farewell to Arabia*: 'The merger had to be — if it was going to be anything at all — an old fashioned shot-gun wedding'.* The battle-lines were now finely drawn between Aden nationalists, Yemeni revolutionaries aided and abetted by Nasser against the British, and the reactionary Federal Rulers.

The security of the Aden base was considered so important at this time that HMG had no alternative but to refuse recognition of the new regime in the Yemen and, to be blunt, back the reactionaries. In 1963 Aden Colony became Aden State, its Governor became High Commissioner and it was formally incorporated into the South Arabian Federation.

Throughout 1963 and the following year the security situation deteriorated; political strikes in Aden increased, the National Liberation Front (NLF) began an intensive terrorist campaign inside the base and in the Radfan, and an Egyptian army of 70,000 was supporting the republican regime in the Yemen. The new Labour Government in Britain announced that independence would be granted to a South Arabian state by 1968, or sooner if possible. By 1966 HMG went further and announced that the Aden base would also be handed over by 1968 at the latest. The Federation Rulers, in particular, felt let down.

1967, the last year of the Raj in Aden, was sad and barely escaped becoming a shambles. There was no responsible party who seemed capable of providing the structure for the successor state. Mutinies occurred in both the Federal Army and the police. British troops were heavily committed to maintaining order in Crater, the densely populated site of the original Aden in the heart of the main volcano of the peninsula. By September the Federal Government was no longer functioning, many of the sultans went into exile in Saudi Arabia and the evacuation of British troops had begun. The only possible authority to whom we could hand over was the NLF who, given the chance, were still prepared to shoot British troops in order to preserve their

*p.164. Faber & Faber, 1966, p.56.

nationalist image. By November 30th, 1967, after 129 years, Aden was
no longer 'red on the map'.

When one considers that during those last fifteen years we had a
series of extremely able and experienced Governors and later High
Commissioners — Tom Hickinbotham, Bill Luce, Charles Johnston,
Ken Trevaskis, Richard Turnbull and Humphrey Trevelyan* — it is
hard to believe with hindsight that any major wrong decisions were
made, except possibly that in the political field HMG under-estimated
the influence of Nasser, mostly through 'Saut al Arab'** in the Arab
world, and in the military field we over-estimated the importance of
Aden as a Middle East base.

The NLF took Aden and the Protectorate further to the left than
most citizens could have expected. The People's Democratic Republic
of Yemen (PDRY), as the new State was called, proved itself a whole-
heartedly Marxist Soviet satellite, a development unique to the Middle
East.

In 1986, nine years after the British withdrawal, there was a fierce
outbreak of fighting in Aden which led to the temporary evacuation of
the foreign community. Finally, in 1990 North and South Yemen
merged into one multi-party state, the Yemen Arab Republic, and an
Aden Free Zone was opened in 1991. Oil was struck at Marib in North
Yemen in 1987 and at Shabwah in South Yemen in 1991. It seemed
possible that some of Aden's old commercial importance might hence-
forward return.

But as I write in 1994, to quote *The Times*: 'Twenty seven years after
the British beat a bloody and undignified retreat from Crater, the crack
of gunfire and crash of exploding shells are once again shaking the city
of Aden. North and South are once again at each other's throats, the
marriage of 1990 was as 'dry as the desert sands'. We read that Scuds
acquired by the breakaway South have been fired at Sana'a, and that the
army of the North has occupied Aden. It seems that the old frontier
which we guarded [in my case at Mukheiras and Dhala] should once
again be recognised.'

*Trevelyan was appointed by George Brown, Foreign Secretary in Wilson's
Labour government, because he had been Ambassador in Cairo at the time of
Suez and was liked and trusted by Nasser.
The service chiefs during the last years in Aden were equally distinguished:
Air Chief Marshal Sir Sam Elworthy, 1960-63, later became Chief of Defence
Staff and a Life Peer: General Sir Charles Harington, 1963-65 became DCGS
and Admiral Sir Michael LeFanu, 1965-7 became First Sea Lord.
**Voice of the Arabs* (Cairo Radio)

CHAPTER 21

Peace and Quiet in a Gentleman's Residence

THE Light Infantry Brigade Depot at Copthorne Barracks, Shrewsbury, was then the home of the Light Infantry which consisted of four regiments:

The Somerset and Cornwall Light Infantry (SCLI)
The Kings Own Yorkshire Light Infantry (KOYLI)
The Kings Shropshire Light Infantry (KSLI)
The Durham Light Infantry (DLI)

Each regiment consisted of one regular and one territorial battalion. At Shrewsbury all recruits were trained for ten weeks before being posted to one of the four regular battalions. We also had a company of junior soldiers who came to us straight from school at sixteen.

The Depot was commanded by Lieutenant Colonel Michael Elcomb who was responsible for all training and the day-to-day running of the barracks. As Brigade Colonel I had a small office alongside the depot commander's. My job was to ensure as far as possible that the four regular battalions were receiving the drafts that they needed to keep up to strength, and that Light Infantry officers were posted either to regimental or staff appointments. At this time there were around 200 officers on our books, of whom only 120 would normally be serving with one of the battalions, or at 'regimental duty' as it was officially termed. The remainder would be on the staff or at 'extra-regimental employment' (ERE) which covered a wide range of duties at home and overseas such as attending a course, serving with the TA, language training or being an ADC.

Executive action to keep battalions up to strength and to post officers was taken by the appropriate War Office branch, usually after consultation with my office.

When I took over at Shrewsbury in April 1961 the four regular battalions were located as follows: 1 SCLI was in BAOR (moving to Gibraltar), 1 KSLI was also in BAOR, 1 KOYLI was in Malaya and 1 DLI was in Berlin. I had a small staff of one major and a retired brigadier.*

*Brigadier John Snow, late Somerset Light Infantry and father of Peter Snow of television fame.

163

Finally I was responsible to the Colonels of the four regiments (all retired generals) for the well being of the Light Infantry as a whole, and also to HQ West Midland District in Shrewsbury for local administration.

Thus described, it may well seem a very loose-knit and fragmented sort of job, and in some ways it was. I regarded myself as being at the centre of a large army family. I knew most of the middle-ranking and senior officers and had served at different times with my own regiment, the Somersets before amalgamation with the Duke of Cornwall's Light Infantry (DCLI), as well as the KOYLI and the DLI: and Copthorne Barracks had been the home of the KSLI for many years. So it was not difficult to brief oneself on the latest state of affairs.

Simone and I were allotted a very comfortable Victorian house called Hazelwood which the Army had just bought to go with the job. It was only a stone's throw from the barracks. I also had a batman and the Army paid for a cleaning lady, so we were well looked after.

Caroline attended Shrewsbury High School, an excellent GPDST* establishment, and David was already in his third year at Lockers Park Prep School, Hemel Hempstead, as a boarder.

I was summoned to an Investiture to receive my OBE from HM the Queen in June 1961. Simone and both children, then aged ten and eight, were also invited. I shall always remember the glitter of the Throne Room, the string orchestra, the uniforms and the perfection of the ceremonial.

It was an introduction to Snowdonia which I enjoyed most during that first summer at Shrewsbury. We were only two hours by car from North Wales, and I used to take groups of junior soldiers up there regularly to climb Snowdon, including the Horseshoe if the weather was right. Mountains were beginning to have a certain fascination for me. There had been lots of opportunity for climbing in the Aden Protectorate, very limited scope in Cyprus and virtually none in Malaya, unless one counts hill walking as plodding up a steep, leech-infested path through primary jungle and only knowing that one was at the top because the path started going down. I think it was probably Aden that whetted my appetite, and Shrewsbury's nearness to Snowdonia that developed in me a love of hill walking that has remained a favourite pastime. I deliberately do not say mountaineering because rock climbing and rope work, which I have experienced only under instruction, are for the experts. Abseiling is a skill that can be taught without undue exposure; we found a simple rockface a few miles

*Girls' Public Day School Trust

out of Shrewsbury at Pontesbury, and introduced a number of junior soldiers and the family to this enjoyable form of simple 'mountaineering'. David and Caroline first climbed Snowdon that summer.

I also visited the Army Outward Bound School at Towyn in the centre of Cardigan Bay. Charles Howard, late of the Somersets, from whom I had taken over temporary command in India in 1947, was now a retired brigadier and the Commandant at Towyn. I was introduced to rock-climbing on the Flying Buttress in the Llanberis Pass, very much under instruction. I remember clutching my rope, thankful for the expert above me who was leading, and looking down at the road which seemed an awfully long way almost straight below us.

Adventure Training in the early '60s was still being introduced into army training. Now, thirty years later, it is commonplace to read that an army team is climbing in the Himalayas or crossing Greenland by sledge. We are told that 250,000 people now walk, hike, bike and climb over Snowdon every year. Then it was still quite an adventure.

That first summer at Shrewsbury I was asked to lecture at the Staff College, Camberley, in connection with an exercise with an Arabian background which students had been set. It was appropriately called 'Hot Rocks'. One of the DS, Bill Scotter,* had visited me at Dhala the previous year, and had worked out a suitable location. I was required to speak in general terms about the terrain, the political scene and local forces. Fortunately I had taken several films of transparencies up at Dhala and was thus able to illustrate my talk, but nevertheless I found it quite an ordeal despite having been a wartime DS there myself. However, it seemed to go down all right, and the Commandant Reggie Hewetson** was complimentary.

I was allowed, indeed required, to visit regular battalions once during an overseas tour and was particularly glad that all four were in fact abroad. In February 1962 I was able to visit the DLI in Berlin, and attend the Light Infantry inter-regimental ski race at Lermoos in Austria, where my time for the downhill was at least twice that of the young officers who were racing. I also visited Munster, where Mike Carver was then commanding the 6th Infantry Brigade which included 1 KSLI. We had met occasionally in the Western Desert. He was later to become a Field Marshal, Chief of the Defence Staff and a Life Peer. A man of outstanding ability, he did not tolerate fools gladly and those under his command had to watch their step.

*Later Lieutenant General Sir William Scotter, KCB, MC, VCIGS.
**Later General Sir Reginald Hewetson, GCB, CBE, DSO, Adjutant General.

Robin Handley, who had been one of my platoon commanders in Malaya twelve years earlier, was then serving with the KSLI and took me to see the reconstructed Mohne Dam which Guy Gibson* and his dambusters had destroyed in 1943. I remember being astonished to see Germans happily selling postcards depicting the Dam 'before and after'.

In Berlin Jack Burgess, formerly of the Somersets, was commanding the DLI. He had also been in my company in the KOYLI in 1948, and later with us at Warminster. His switch to the DLI illustrates well how officers were transferred to other regiments, but, it must be emphasised, always within the family of the Light Infantry.

With the Cold War at its height, Berlin was an extraordinary mixture of luxury in the Western sectors and poverty in the Russian zone. The DLI barracks was on the western edge of the British zone and was watched by Russian frontier guards from their look-out towers. One had to remind oneself that there were 100 miles of Russian-occupied Germany between us and the edge of the Iron Curtain. It was a rather eerie situation. I was taken through Check Point Charlie into the Russian zone and visited the Meissen shop where one could buy cut-price samples of this lovely china.

In May I was off again, this time to Gibraltar to witness the presentation of new colours to the SCLI by Field Marshal Lord Harding (as he had become). I flew RAF by a rather circuitous route, firstly by train to Bodmin, the former DCLI depot, and then by Shackleton from RAF St Mawgan to the Azores where we spent a night before flying slightly south of east to Gib. Each leg was about 1,200 miles. This was essentially a training flight which could accept passengers like myself 'by arrangement'; — for several hours we flew low over the Atlantic which was quite hairy. The CO at the DCLI Depot, 'Toots' Williams, was a well-known figure in Cornwall, and undoubtedly knew the station commander at St Mawgan.

May is normally a reliable month in Gib. as far as the weather is concerned, but that year thirty-six hours of torrential rain and gales preceded the day of the parade and it was touch and go whether a postponement would be necessary. In the event, the rain stopped but the parade ground, normally sandy, was a sea of sticky mud which inevitably stuck to men's boots. The other problem was the wind, and whether chinstraps should be worn up or down. The final order was 'down' and all went well. However that was by no means the end of

---

*Churchill describes in Vol V of his *Second World War*, *Closing the Ring*, how in 1943 he took Gibson with him on the *Queen Mary* to the Quebec Conference because Roosevelt liked meeting young heroic figures. Gibson wore only three ribbons; the VC, DSO and bar and the DFC and bar.

13. Our wedding at Gaddesden, July 1944

14. HE The Governor (John Harding) talking to Jackie and Keith Shapland at their wedding reception in our flat, Nicosia, 1956

15. Derek Sutcliffe with an
iguana at Baling, 1949

16. Vice-President Nixon talking to Oliver Eley and jungle patrol, at Ulu
Langat. Author on left, 1953

17. Visit of Bernard Fergusson when reporting for the *Sunday Times*, Yemen
Frontier, 1959

18. Beverley unloading at Freddie's Field during operation in Aulaqi country,
1960

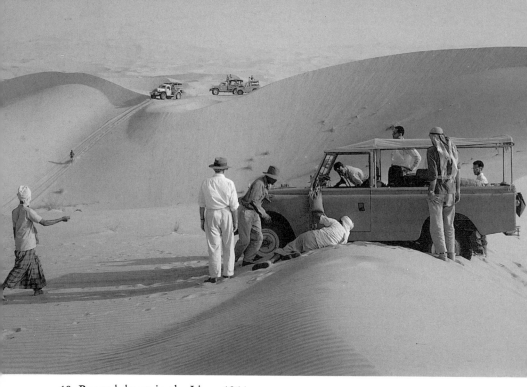

19. Bogged down in the Liwa, 1964

20. Jahili Fort, Buraimi, 1965

the story. David Shepherd, who had been commissioned to paint the ceremony, had been unable to attend the final dress rehearsal, and to quote his own words: ' . . . all I could see were the massive backviews of three large army chaplains, an impenetrable barrier to my line of sight. I panicked. Dashing hither and thither, I fired off photograph after photograph, not really knowing what I was pointing at'. Lord Harding could hardly be asked to go through this moving and solemn moment in the regiment's history again! 'Back in England, the yellow box of film returned from Kodak, and I knew that disaster had struck — when transparencies are successful they are sent back in a little flat box, but when they are not they are sent back in a little square box. Sure enough, a considerable footage of absolutely blank black film unrolled; not one picture had come out.'*

Not to be outfaced he came up to Shrewsbury and asked for help. In the cookhouse 'we found a tiny little lance-corporal about 5ft 5in high, peeling spuds, hauled him out and asked him to play the part of Lord Harding. He did not seem unduly perturbed, indeed he entered into the spirit of the thing most wonderfully. We tied an army blanket to a broomstick and got him to present the "colours" to another lance-corporal, in filthy overalls, who had been working on an army lorry. I did the whole painting with the invaluable help of these two gentlemen, and it was their finest hour!'**

The final act in this drama was over the chin-straps. Should they be painted down as they had been worn on the day, or should artistic licence prevail and show them up, which would certainly look much smarter? Shepherd was first told to paint them down (which he did) and then six months later was asked to paint them out. Describing the event, Shepherd says that dark paint underneath a lighter colour can show through after a time, and he was afraid that it would eventually look as though the men all needed a shave! I have a reproduction of this painting and Shepherd's prediction has proved correct, though it is only the principal officers in front who appear to have beards (and only the Royal Navy are allowed to sport beards). It is a fine painting nevertheless. Since the parade ground was at Europa Point and the painting is facing north, the Rock is shown end on and is not immediately obvious. I often quiz visitors and am surprised how many do not immediately recognise the setting.

Our time at Shrewsbury was to prove the most tranquil and settled three years in England that we had had, both since the War and until

* *The Man who Loves Giants*, p.135-6.
** *Ibid*, p.136.

I retired. My job was not demanding, we had a very comfortable house and were well looked after.

Shrewsbury was an attractive old market town and the surrounding countryside was delightful. On one occasion after we had returned from a weekend at Gaddesden, the police called and asked if they could interview my batman, P — *. It happened that the parents of a young girl who lived near the barracks had gone to the police because their daughter had been out all night and, on being asked the next morning where she had been, said that she had spent the night with a soldier in a comfortable bed in a large house very near the barracks which she was told belonged to the colonel. Her description of the room answered exactly to our bedroom. P — hotly denied the allegation and the police did not press charges, but it seemed likely that either P — or a friend of his had taken advantage of our absence to entertain a girlfriend, and enjoy our bed!

Peter Snow used to regularly visit his parents who lived in Shrewsbury. His face was already well known on television as an ITN newscaster. We had first met him at Warminster, where he was doing National Service with the Somersets. He sometimes used to look in on us for an evening drink, and Caroline, then ten, still remembers how he used to go up and kiss her goodnight. Peter told us he was often recognised by the girls working in Shrewsbury shops, and had to beat a hasty retreat.

In August 1962 we drove to the Atlantic coast west of Bordeaux and stayed for a fortnight at a small hotel in Le Grand Picquet on the Basin d'Arcachon, recommended by Alban Coventry who had been one of my Intelligence officers in the desert. He had married a French girl and settled in Bordeaux after the war. The weather was perfect, the bathing excellent, and the food good.

The following summer we found an equally good hotel in Guethary on the coast between Biarritz and St Jean-de-Luz. The children were keen to report that they had been to Spain, so we walked them up to the top of La Rhune, a prominent hill at 900m on the frontier. There was a shop on the summit and they both hankered after little Spanish guitars which needless to say we ended up by carrying down, along with other impedimenta.

On another occasion we drove over a lowish Pyrenean pass at Roncevalles and stayed a night in Pamplona, famous for its bull stampedes. The only thing I remember about that night was that I was

*Cliff Richard was making his name as a pop star at this time and I remember that our batman slightly resembled him!

nearly arrested for wearing shorts (to this day I am not sure why), and that all four of us had to squeeze into one bedroom.

The winter of 1962-'63 was one of the most severe since the war. Snow lay from shortly after Christmas until March. During the Christmas holidays the children made an igloo which housed four people on the lawn, and it remained almost intact until Easter. We skied on several occasions on the hills towards Welshpool and near Church Stretton. However, the most dramatic event was that the Severn froze over completely on the reach just below our house on The Mount and the children were actually able to walk across. But we nearly lost our Jack Russell, Pru, when she went through the ice. David rescued her by lying flat on the frozen river and just reaching the struggling dog with hands outstretched whilst Simone, herself on the ice, held onto his legs and pulled them both back.

In the spring of 1963 I was able to visit 1 KOYLI in Malaya where it formed part of the Commonwealth Brigade at Terendak, the new military base near Malacca. The Emergency had been officially declared over in 1960 and shortly after my visit the State of Malaysia, consisting of Malaya, Singapore, Sarawak and Sabah was created.* Charles Rome was commanding the KOYLI. I knew him well from my eighteen months with the battalion in 1948-9. Everything was very peaceful and one could understand why Malaya in peacetime had been a popular station in which to serve — except perhaps for the climate.

From Malaya I went on to Hong Kong to visit the DLI, which was accommodated in a comfortable barracks near Kowloon on the mainland. I had never been to Hong Kong and was delighted to be given the chance of a visit. A conducted tour of the New Territories, including looking through field-glasses at Kwantung Province of China from a forward OP, was included in the programme, as of course was Victoria Island. It was a fascinating place to be in for a few days but I know that troops based there feel cooped up after a time. There are a lot of guard duties, too, which can be exceedingly boring.

I was away for about a fortnight and considered myself very lucky to have visited two of our four Light Infantry battalions at such interesting 'outposts of empire'. I think I can still just call them that.

In July 1963 I led a small team of six from the depot on the Three Peaks Expedition. We were merely required to stand on the summit of Ben Nevis, Scafell and Snowdon within a period of twenty-four hours using only our feet and army transport. There was no M6 in those days

*In September, 1963.

and only a ferry over Loch Leven at Ballachulish. The goal-posts must have been moved closer together several times since those early days. The party consisted of two officers: myself and a subaltern, Tony Makepeace-Warne;* one corporal, one private and two junior soldiers. Two staff cars were provided plus experienced drivers.

We drove up to Ayrshire on the first day and camped at my brother-in-law's house that night. On day two we arrived in Fort William in time to spend two hours climbing on the south side of Glen Nevis as a final hardening-up exercise, spending the night at a TA drill hall in Fort William. We planned to start the timed expedition at 6 p.m. on the top of Ben Nevis, so we spent a leisurely morning and started the climb at 2 p.m. in good weather, arriving at 4.40 p.m. without hurrying.

At 6 p.m. we ran down to the two cars in one hour and ate a prepared evening meal whilst being driven to the Ballachulish Ferry. We were clear of the ferry by 8 p.m., reached Glasgow by 10.0 and Carlisle by 1 a.m. having had one short stop for a snack. We reached Wasdale Head at 3 a.m. but waited until 3.30 before starting the climb as it was too dark. We were on the summit of Scafell at 5.0 in time to see a very red sunrise over Helvellyn. The heavens then opened and it rained almost continuously all day. We ran down to the Old Dungeon Ghyll Hotel in Langdale, the cars having been driven round via the Hard Knott and Wrynose Passes. The descent took two hours in bad conditions and we arrived at the cars tired and soaked. Goretex had not yet been invented.

After a hurried breakfast prepared by our gallant drivers we arrived at Pen-y-Pass via the A6 and A5 at 12.45. We climbed Snowdon by the Pyg track in driving rain and, towards the top, gale force wind, arriving at 2.30 p.m., twenty and a half hours after leaving the summit of Ben Nevis. I hasten to add that there was nothing special about our time. Had we not descended Scafell into Langdale, and instead returned to Wasdale, we could probably have beaten twenty hours. In my official report to HQ West Midland District I said: 'This is an immensely worthwhile expedition involving careful planning and team work, good driving and a fairly high degree of physical fitness. It is probably more of a strain on the drivers than on the climbers'. Apart from myself (forty-seven), the others were all under twenty-five.

A sad but inevitable family upheaval occurred that year. My father decided to sell Coolnakilly and move over to England. He had asked me whether I would wish to live there myself in due course, and after some

*Later Major General and Colonel of the Light Infantry.

soul-searching I had said no. We were Protestants in a ninety-nine per cent Catholic land, and were regarded as Anglo-Irish. It was well-nigh impossible to become involved in local affairs; the most that my father managed was to be Treasurer of the tiny Church of Ireland church at Glenealy, and Honourary Secretary of the RSPCA. Nevertheless, it was very sad to be selling an attractive small country house with sixty-four acres in County Wicklow, and one which had been in the family since 1850. It is almost unbelievable to recall that the property went to an Italian Papal Count, Colonna by name, who it was said wanted a quiet little place in Ireland to escape the nuclear holocaust! He paid £15,000 and never lived there.

In the autumn of 1963 the War Office asked me whether I would be prepared to return to Arabia early the following year and command the Trucial Oman Scouts, an Arab force with British officers responsible for keeping the peace in the Trucial States.* It was an unusual job in an unusual place, which was why I was asked whether I would go. Normally one had no choice. As I was allowed to be accompanied (that is, have my wife with me) and there was a house which went with the job, I accepted. The next three years were to be far and away the most interesting and exciting of my soldiering career.

In February 1964 I seized the opportunity, before leaving England, to take ten junior soldiers up to Aviemore for some elementary skiing. We travelled up by train and stayed at Rothiemurchus Lodge which was then run as a sort of youth hostel. It was a remote spot in the middle of a deer forest at 1,400 feet, accessible only by a jeep track. We were there for a week and every day walked, carrying our skis, to the bottom of the main Cairngorm ski complex. It was over three miles by a rough track and an ascent of 700 feet. The skiing was very elementary but the boys loved it, as did I. We used to meet quite a number of roe deer in the forest, particularly on the way back in the evenings, and sometimes red deer on the open moor.

Packing up at Hazelwood after three years of putting down our roots was a nightmare. Both children were due to change schools, which was an added complication. David started at Eton in January and Caroline was due at St Mary's, Calne, in September. We decided in the end that Simone would stay behind at a guest house in Shrewsbury for the summer, and join me at Christmas.

*Now the United Arab Emirates (UAE).

CHAPTER 22

Keeping the Peace in the Lower Gulf

I FLEW out to Sharjah, HQ of the Trucial Oman Scouts (TOS), in March via Aden as the GOC, Major General John Cubbon (whom I did not know), wished to meet me and give me a run-down on the general situation. It was three years since I had left Aden and there were many more British troops about. The atmosphere was fairly tense; I was told that things were much more peaceful in the Gulf. Cubbon was absolutely right; there was an entirely different feel about things from the moment I stepped off the plane — even though in Sharjah we had at the time a very pro-Nasser ruler (Shaikh Saqr bin Sultan), and 'Saut al Arab' was listened to almost as widely as in Aden.

To understand the reason for this difference in atmosphere one has to go back a little in history, and I am indebted to Donald Hawley* and Glen Balfour-Paul** for much of the background information which follows. The Arabian coastline from the Qatar Peninsula to the Straits of Hormuz had been known as the Pirate Coast since the days of the Napoleonic Wars, when the English East India Company, out to dominate trade with Asia against all comers, set about establishing security at sea along both routes to India (through the Gulf and round the south coast of Arabia); and it was against the Company's ships that acts of what it regarded as piracy were committed by the 'fleets' of the Gulf Shaikhs who resented such forceful interference (and for whom tribal raiding at sea was as traditional as tribal raiding on land). They, and in particular the Qawasim of Ras al Khaimah, had to be brought to order. After a preliminary canter in 1809, a Company expedition bombarded and captured Ras al Khaimah in 1819-'20 and proceeded to destroy large numbers of fighting ships there and in other Shaikhdoms as far west as Abu Dhabi. Treaties were then signed with the six ruling coastal Shaikhs, first of the Cessation of Plunder and Piracy and in mid-century of a Maritime Truce between each other (largely in the interests of the local pearling industry). Undertakings to cease the traffic in slaves

*Political Agent Dubai, 1958-61.
**Political Agent Dubai, 1964-6.

172

were also extracted. Finally in 1892 Britain's monopoly of influence in the Gulf was achieved by 'Exclusive Agreements' with all Rulers, ingeniously designed to keep other powers out. No consular representation by others — even the Americans — was permitted.

Of equal historic importance is the fact that for nearly three centuries the East India Company had mostly used the Persian coast for its trading, as well as Kuwait and Bahrain. It was the back door to India (whereas the Arabian coast was a cul-de-sac which offered nothing but piracy). It was only in 1946, in the context of British withdrawal from India, that the British Political Resident in the Gulf moved his headquarters from Bushire to Bahrain, and only then that the Arabian shore became so overwhelmingly important with the discovery and exploitation of its massive oil reserves, both on and off-shore.

From the mid-nineteenth century onwards the Raj authorities certainly had no desire to embroil themselves with the internal affairs of the bickering shaikhdoms; but the separation of internal and external affairs became increasingly awkward, and as the decades passed the oddity of our treaty relationship with the Rulers put us in an absurdly ambivalent position. The seven Trucial shaikhdoms had always been self-governing, and could and did reject advice from British representatives if they so chose, even in the days of that great imperialist Lord Curzon, Viceroy of India.

This was the essential difference between our presence in the Gulf and Aden. Aden was a colony with a British Governor; the Protectorate, though it consisted of many small sultanates, was to all intents and purposes also 'red on the map'. We needed the base and there was no question of negotiation. In the Gulf on the other hand, any British defence requirements, for example the RAF airfields at Sharjah and Bahrain, and the small Royal Navy base at Jufair, had to be negotiated with the respective rulers.

Similarly, in 1932 HMG had negotiated an agreement with the Ruler of Sharjah to enable Imperial Airways to be granted facilities including a rest house for passengers. It was built in the form of a fort for local security, and guarded by the Ruler's men. In 1937 an agreement was also made with the Ruler of Dubai allowing Imperial Airways to land flying boats on the creek. Passengers were then driven ten miles over the desert (there was no road) to Sharjah and spent the night at the Fort before continuing their flight to India or Australia.

Up until World War II, and even later, there was constant inter-tribal rivalry between the shaikhdoms; a state of war existed between Abu Dhabi and Dubai between 1945 and 1948, and looking at the seven states as a whole, it used to be said that your friend would not be your neighbour but the sheikhdom beyond you (the latter being at a safe remove and unable to plunder your borders). It was British policy to try and bring the rulers closer together, and after the formation of a Trucial States Council in 1952 it was decided to raise a force called the Trucial Oman Levies* to act as a police force for the whole area, there being no police at the time except Rulers' guards. When its formation was first envisaged, the object was recorded in London as simply to prevent the traffic in slaves (not slavery itself, which was an internal affair). Later, the declared objectives were (a) the protection of British political officers(!); (b) to help in the maintenance of law and order; (c) assistance to the Rulers in fulfilling their treaty obligations in regard to the slave trade. The force would be paid for by HMG and ultimately responsible to the PRPG but would work closely with all the Rulers.

The Trucial States (now called the UAE) are about the size of England and consist mostly of desert which becomes increasingly difficult to cross the further south (that is, into the Empty Quarter, the interior of the Arabian peninsula) one goes. The Gulf coast is largely *sabkha* (salt flats) into which even four-wheel-drive vehicles can bog down very easily. There are a series of sea creeks stretching right along the coast from Ras al Khaimah south-westwards, of which the most important are at Dubai and Sharjah. They were ideal hide-outs for pirates in the early days. A spinal chord of mountains, the Hajar range, ascends to 1,000 metres** and runs from north to south just inland from the Indian Ocean, and the eastern frontier with the Sultanate of Oman includes a sixty-mile strip of coastline on the ocean. It is extremely hot and humid on the Gulf coast from March to October and pleasantly warm from November to February. Thirty to forty miles inland from the coast in the Liwa it is exceptionally hot in the summer, temperatures of 50°C being not unusual. Rainfall varies between five inches and nil per annum.

Of the seven Shaikhdoms the westernmost, Abu Dhabi, is also the largest (some eighty-six per cent of the entire country) and richest in oil both on and off-shore. Next comes Dubai, the main commercial centre with its navigable creek, then Sharjah, the former RAF base and HQ of the TOS; the smallest Shaikhdom is Ajman, a mere 100 square miles; then there is Umm al Qawain (in Arabic 'the mother of twins') which is not much larger; and finally, near the northern tip of the Gulf coast, Ras al Khaimah. The seventh Shaikhdom, Fujairah (450 square miles and

---

*Field Marshal Templer, when CIGS, changed 'Levies' to 'Scouts' in 1956.
**Up to very nearly 3,000 metres in the Sultanate of Oman.

independent of the Qawasim only since 1958), is the strip of coastal plain and mountainous interior on the Indian Ocean coast. The best way to describe the frontiers between Shaikhdoms is to say that they resemble a patchwork quilt of many colours. Several shaikhdoms have enclaves in the middle of a neighbour's territory; for example Sharjah owns a strip of coast on the Indian Ocean.

The total population in the 1960s was estimated at less than 200,000. Thirty years later it is estimated to be at least 1.6 million, an 800 per cent increase which includes a huge number of non-indigenous immigrants from India, Iran, Pakistan, Iraq, Kuwait and Jordan.

One final feature which must be mentioned is the oasis of Buraimi, which lies ninety miles inland of Abu Dhabi, has always been the focal caravan crossroads of this part of Arabia, and consists of a group of nine oasis villages. Britain had been supporting the Abu Dhabi claim to six of them and the Muscati claim to the other three. The Saudis insisted that the principal (nomadic) tribes in the area once owed allegiance to *them* and that the whole group lay within Ibn Saud's ancestral domain. They were also encouraged by their legal advisers, hired from ARAMCO (their oil company), into maximising the area of the latter's oil concession. As the focus of the resulting Arab-Saudi dispute that was submitted to Arbitration in 1954, and particularly when the British member of the tribunal, followed by the Belgian President, resigned in protest at Saudi bribery of the tribe involved,* Buraimi probably became better known in the West than the rest of the Shaikhdoms put together.** The immediate antecedents of the Arbitration were the occupation of part of the oasis by Saudi soldiery in 1952. After the collapse of Arbitration, they were ejected from Buraimi by a combination of the TOS and tribal soldiery from Oman and Abu Dhabi.

I found myself dealing directly with all seven rulers, an interesting and varied group of men; Shakhbut bin Sultan of Abu Dhabi was supposedly the most important since he ruled by far the largest Shaikhdom under which were massive oil reserves. At least five of his predecessors had not died in their beds; local history had it that three brothers succeeded each other, each one having murdered the brother before him, so Shakhbut was taking no chances. By 1964, at the age of sixty-one, he had been ruler for thirty-six years partly due to the sagacity of his mother, Shaikha Salama, who made her four sons swear not

*They even tried to bribe Shaikh Zaid, who had been born and brought up in the oasis and was currently the Ruler of Abu Dhabi's representative there. (He is now the Ruler of Abu Dhabi himself and President of the UAE.)
**Hammond Innes's book *The Doomed Oasis*, published in 1960 and a best seller at the time, is a highly fictional version of the affair.

to kill one another. He was already a very rich man though he refused
to keep his money in a bank. It had to be paid to him by the oil
companies in brand-new Indian rupee notes which he was alleged to
have counted himself note by note, and then stored in old petrol tins
and suitcases and locked away out of sight and use. Having finally
accepted the existence of a bank (though more than once he asked to be
shown his cash) he still did not understand cheques, and on a visit to
London wrote out a cheque and sent his secretary all the way back to
Abu Dhabi to cash it, and bring the money back!*

Rashid of Dubai, then fifty-two, was very different. A merchant
prince with an acute business acumen, a keen sense of humour and
considerable dignity, he was undoubtedly the key figure among the
rulers. Even though Dubai's development was in those days still in its
infancy — it used to be called a sort of decrepit Arabian Venice — and
oil had not been struck, it was already the commercial centre of the
Lower Gulf.

Rashid was clever enough to collect around him a small team of
reliable and highly professional British expatriates who ran Dubai's
banks, the water supply, the police, customs and shipping. He trusted
them and they did not let him down. I was to get to know, like and
respect all of them. Saqr of Sharjah was again completely different. A
poet and collector of stamps in his spare time, and outwardly friendly
to us, he listened to the endless propaganda from Cairo that was being
beamed at the Gulf, and made no attempt to improve the lot of his
suffering subjects. He was already collecting some oil revenue from
concessions, and HMG paid him rent for the RAF base. Sharjah creek
was not dredged and the town was dingy and run down. Water was
drawn from saline wells in the desert, collected in old petrol tins and
carried round the streets by donkey.

Rashid of Ajman looked like a handsome stage pirate. His
Shaikhdom was tiny; it was sometimes called a garden state (something
of a misnomer as there was no garden). Extremely friendly whenever I
called, he had no revenue except from granting permission to British
companies to issue stamps bearing his portrait, and from crumbs which
fell from the rich man's table further down the coast. On one occasion
when I called at the Eid, which marks the end of the fasting month of
Ramadhan, he was not ready to receive me as his radio had stopped
working, and consequently he had not heard the news from Mecca and
was a day out, having no other means of knowing the date.

Ahmed of Umm al Qawain was an old man who had been ruler for

*Farewell to Arabia, David Holden, pp.189-90.

thirty-five years. He was friendly, not conspicuously active, had a deserved reputation as a peacemaker and was often used as such by his neighbours. Saqr of Ras al Khaimah was a cousin of Saqr of Sharjah. They were both members of the Qasimi tribe, against whose piracy the East India Company had waged war over 100 years ago. He was clever, had ambitions for his state and was not always overscrupulous in pursuing them.

Finally, Muhammad of Fujairah, known as 'Fudge' after the name of his Shaikhdom (not because we doubted his honesty) was penniless and friendly.

When I took over the TOS in March 1964 this little 'private army' consisted of a large HQ set up in Sharjah alongside the RAF Station, a training squadron and five operational squadrons, of which four were permanently deployed. Apart from my HQ, there was the reserve squadron, a signals squadron, a transport squadron, a workshop, a stores section and a boys' school. In all, I had about 100 British officers, warrant officers and NCOs and 1,500 Arab officers, NCOs and men. British personnel were all volunteers on an eighteen-month unaccompanied (by families) tour except for COMTOS*, who was allowed to be accompanied and had a house provided.

It used to be said (rather unkindly) that officers volunteered for the TOS because they had wife trouble or were broke. This certainly applied in some cases, as it did to many other out-of-the-way postings abroad, but I hasten to add that I had some extremely good officers and, indeed, needed them because, particularly on detachment, a wrong decision about a local problem could have far-reaching consequences.

Apart from a deputy commander who was a lieutenant colonel (John Emerson Baker and later Bob Feltham) I had two principal staff officers. I also had two rather unusual officers, both of whom were to prove indispensable in different ways. One was Major Tim Budd, who had already served with the Scouts since they were raised twelve years earlier and before that had been in the Sudan. He spoke his own special sort of Arabic, of which a purist would disapprove, but which was readily understood by rulers and all the local tribesmen with whom we were constantly dealing. He was officially Intelligence officer but in practice I used him as my adviser whenever I was stuck over any problem, which was often, in those early days.

The other was Major Jack Briggs who had been a guardsman in the Scots Guards, then a Palestine policeman and finally a police officer in

*My title: Commander TOS.

Qatar before joining the Scouts to look after the Police Troop. Unlike
Tim Budd, he had learnt Arabic by sitting at the back of an Arab school
class and going through the whole process as though he were a
schoolboy. As a result he spoke the language like an Arab and was
invaluable in many different ways. A man of great integrity and charm
of manner, I was not surprised when, a year or two later, that wily old
statesman Shaikh Rashid of Dubai persuaded Jack to join him and run
the Dubai Police, which he did with great skill for many years.

Amongst the Arab officers were two young shaikhs: Abdul Aziz bin
Muhammed, a first cousin of Saqr Ruler of Sharjah; and Faisal bin
Sultan, whose father had been Ruler of Ras al Khaimah until 1948 when
he was deposed by his nephew Saqr. Both were members of the Qasimi
family and very influential in different ways.

Our uniform was colourful. We wore blue-grey cotton shirts with
the shirt-tails outside khaki drill slacks and a red and white check
shemagh and black *argl*.*On ceremonial occasions we wore Sam Brownes
instead of webbing belts. After initially being shocked, I found it a very
practical and smart kit in that harsh climate. A *shemagh* can protect one
from both sun and sand, and looks right in that environment.

HMG was represented in the Gulf by a senior diplomat of Grade 1
ambassadorial rank at Bahrain, known as the Political Resident (PR), Sir
William Luce, my old boss from Aden where he had been Governor,
five Political Agents (PAs) and a Consul General in the Sultanate of
Oman. I was to work closely with the two PAs in the Trucial States:
Hugh Boustead** based in Abu Dhabi, and James Craig† based in Dubai
but required to deal with the remaining six Shaikhdoms. Both were
outstanding men in their different ways: Hugh's career was unique. A
mid-shipman in the Royal Navy, he was serving in HMS *Hyacinth* off
East Africa in 1915 but, feeling that this was a backwater, deserted and
joined as a private soldier a South African Brigade, which was destined
for the Western Front. Wounded at the Battle of the Somme in 1916,
he was commissioned in the field and later won an MC and bar, having
been wounded at least twice. After the war he served for a year in
Russia with the White Army, spent a year at Worcester College, Oxford
reading Russian and boxing, before being given a regular commission in
the Gordon Highlanders in 1921. It was said that he was the only
officer ever to have been given a King's pardon for having deserted from
the Royal Navy! Extremely athletic, he was entered for the Modern
Pentathlon (running, riding, fencing, swimming and shooting) and cap-

---

*A headcovering and headrope which kept the *shemagh* in position.
**Later Colonel Sir Hugh Boustead KBE CMG DSO MC.
†Later Sir James Craig GCMG HM Ambassador, Jeddah.

tained the British team at the 1920 Olympics in Antwerp, where they were beaten by the Swedes. Badly injured in a motorcycle accident, he missed the Pentathlon at the 1924 Olympics in Paris.

Hugh found peacetime regimental soldiering boring (who doesn't!), volunteered for the Egyptian Army and served in the Sudanese Camel Corps, eventually resigning his commission in the Gordons in 1935 and joining the Sudan Political Service. Having climbed a lot in the Alps and also acquired some Himalayan experience, he was selected for Ruttledge's Everest expedition in 1933 and reached 25,500 feet, which was almost as high as anybody got in those days. He served throughout World War II with the Sudan Defence Force and played a leading role in defeating the Italians in Ethiopia.

After the war he served successively in the Sudan as a District Commissioner, in the Hadhramaut (Eastern Aden Protectorate) as Resident Adviser for nine years, and finally as Development Secretary, Oman before becoming Political Agent, Abu Dhabi in 1961.

A man of enormous charm, he was loved by us all. He never married, feeling it would be unfair to ask a girl to share the hardships of life in the desert. Duncan Slater, the young career diplomat who worked under him at Abu Dhabi, had many anxious moments accounting for Foreign Office telegrams which somehow got hidden under cushions in Hugh's sitting-room. His ghosted autobiography *The Wind of the Morning* is well worth reading (though now out of print). Paul Brickhill (author of *The Dambusters*) came out to the Gulf to write Hugh's life story but gave up in despair because it proved impossible to pin him down to facts.

James Craig was a totally different person. Probably the best Arabist of his day in the Diplomatic Service, he had won a first class Honours Degree at Oxford in Oriental Studies, and was a lecturer in Arabic at Durham University for seven years before becoming Principal Instructor at the Middle East Centre for Arabic Studies (MECAS) in the Lebanon. Unlike Hugh, who was to retire at seventy in 1965, James was just beginning a diplomatic career which later took him to Saudi Arabia as British Ambassador.

Taking over a new job in a foreign land can often be difficult. One's predecessor is doing a round of farewell parties, one feels in the way, and longs for him to go. I accordingly arranged for Tim Budd to take me round the out-stations — an invaluable introduction by somebody who knew the form. The flies were particularly bad and by the time we got back to Sharjah I had to retire to bed with violent tummy trouble, and wasn't even able to get up to bid a final goodbye to Hugh

Bartholomew, my predecessor.

The first major event in early April was the formal opening of the BP oil terminal at Jebel Dhanna, about 150 miles west of Abu Dhabi. It was the only place with deep water on an uncompromising coast. Oil was pumped from the main on-shore field seventy-five miles to the east through a sixteen-inch pipe to the terminal. Two thirty-six-inch sea lines then connected the terminal to tanker berths three miles off-shore. This was the first oil to flow from the mainland of the Trucial States, and Abu Dhabi Petroleum Company, (ADPC) a subsidiary of BP, was determined to advertise the fact. Invited guests arrived from all over the Middle East and even the UK at the remote airstrip, and were entertained to lunch in a huge marquee erected in the middle of the desert. The only snag was that a *shamal* had blown up, a high wind from the north causing rising sand, and very poor visibility. I arrived in a Gulf Airways Dakota from Sharjah and remember being vastly impressed by the skill of the pilot, who landed in what appeared to be a severe sandstorm on desert which was unrecognisable as an airstrip. However, all was well; the marquee did not collapse, the meal was good, the right speeches were made and Shaikh Shakhbut turned the wheel which caused the oil to flow. We were then all given black morocco leather wallets from Asprey's.

Very shortly after this Simone brought the children out for the Easter holidays. My official residence was a modern four-bedroomed bungalow next door to the officers' mess and overlooking the airfield. We had a splendid-looking Pathan bearer named Khan and a Goanese cook, Alex.

One of the main attractions was a stable of sixteen Arab ponies that belonged to the Scouts and had been imported from Iraq shortly after the Force was raised. They were looked after by Pakistani *syces* (Urdu for grooms), and we could and did ride them whenever we wished. Officially they were on our establishment for ceremonial purposes and, indeed, were on parade on a number of occasions, but in practice they provided an exhilarating break in that barren environment. A gallop across the sand either before breakfast or in the evening was a wonderful form of relaxation.

The Scouts also owned several catamarans and dinghies down on the Sharjah creek, and we could take them out whenever we wanted. One had to take care outside the creek as the wind could get up suddenly and there were sharks about. I never heard of anybody being taken but I saw them in large numbers quite close in when flying along the coast in a helicopter.

Simone had the use of a BLR (beyond local repair) Land Rover which the Scouts Workshop would lend her pending local sale. She went shopping in it and the children, then fourteen and twelve, learnt to drive out in the desert on the salt flats. There were virtually no civilian cars in those days. Movement outside the towns was almost entirely by Land Rover, Dodge, pick-up or three-tonner. Vehicles were fitted with sand tyres which were kept at low pressure.

There were some shops in Sharjah but we usually went to Dubai where the main European community lived. There was then no road and the trip involved about ten miles of picking one's way through patches of *sabkha*. It could be tricky at night, particularly after a party, and on occasion several Scouts officers were bogged down until daylight.

All too soon the Easter holidays were over and the family flew home. We planned that they would come out again at Christmas after Simone had settled Caroline in at boarding school.

Calling on all seven rulers and making myself known took quite a time. Tim Budd usually came with me, though when I first met Shakhbut of Abu Dhabi I was formally introduced by Hugh Boustead. Shakhbut held his *majlis**** in a large fort on the edge of the ramshackle collection of mud huts and lean-to shacks that was Abu Dhabi in those days. Hugh would knock on the huge heavy wooden door with his ebony cane, and possibly blow a whistle. The guard inside, who probably knew he was on the way, would turn out with much clatter and shouting, and we would then be admitted through a small aperture in the door, a relic of the days when an unwelcome visitor's head could easily be cut off as he bent forward to enter. After inspecting the guard we would be escorted to the *majlis* and exchange pleasantries with Shakhbut after the inevitable tiny cups of coffee had circulated. The pattern was the same whichever 'palace' one visited. The only difference was in the plushness of the furnishings, depending on whether the Ruler was receiving revenue from oil concessions. My Arabic was still very limited. After three years at home I had forgotten much of what I learnt in Aden, and Gulf Arabic was slightly different anyway. Serious discussions regarding such matters as border disputes or illegal immigration would usually take place in the presence of an expert Arabic speaker such as James Craig or Jack Briggs.

In reality I served three masters: first, the Political Resident in

*Literally, 'sitting' in Arabic. Rulers held a *majlis* daily, usually in the evening; it represented a form of tribal democracy, or at least of checks and balances. Any of the subjects of a Ruler could come and present grievances there in the open, and if the justice dispensed by a Ruler was inadequate, his tenure of office would be at risk from rivals.

Bahrain, Sir William Luce, to whom I was ultimately responsible,* and under him the two PAs in the Trucial States, Hugh Boustead and James Craig who I would see frequently. I would not, for instance, re-deploy any of my squadrons without consulting them. Second, the Brigadier in Bahrain (SAOPG, Senior Army Officer PG) to whom I was responsible for army administration; and third, the seven Rulers who provided my soldiers. I would not normally agree to any request from them which was out of the ordinary without checking with Hugh or James.

This may sound complicated but in practice it worked very well. I always knew to whom I could turn for advice, and was also my own master in many ways — for example, the Brigadier in Bahrain could hardly turn up unannounced, as there was no road and the RAF would always warn me of any unscheduled flight. It was nonetheless vital to get on well with all concerned.

That first summer I seem to have spent most of my time 'swanning', firstly in the Liwa, the famous land of high sand dunes on the edge of the Rub' al Khali (the Empty Quarter), and the southern border of Abu Dhabi with Saudi Arabia. Hugh Boustead said that he must go to 'chat up the locals' (of whom there were extremely few), would I like to join him? The answer of course was yes. I was warned that nobody normally visited the Liwa in the summer — it was quite simply too hot — but encouraged by Noel Coward's famous song, 'Mad dogs and Englishmen go out in the midday sun', and already totally hypnotised by Hugh's career and personality, I felt flattered to have been invited. I took with me a young Scouts officer, Michael Baugniet, who was seconded from the RASC and therefore knowledgeable about Land Rovers, which I was emphatically not. He was also physically tough and a good companion. Hugh brought with him Graham Burton** who had recently joined the Diplomatic Service, and fitted exactly the role of ADC to somebody rather special. The four of us had of course various essential support staff such as bearers, cooks, wireless operators, fitters and drivers. For me it was a fascinating experience — except that I have never been so hot in my life and would never wish to go there again in the summer. From Hugh's point of view (and the heat did not seem to bother him unduly) it was a good time to tour because the Bedouin moved south in the summer to harvest dates in the various oases, and it gave him a chance to meet them.

It is not easy to describe the Liwa and I cannot do better than quote

*The Scouts were sometimes called the PR's private army.
**Now HM Ambassador, UAE

Donald Hawley: 'The northern slopes of these dunes were gentle, though the sand was soft and the going difficult. On the south side, however, the dunes were sheer, and descending them in a Land Rover or truck was exciting. A great bow-wave of sand in front of the vehicles grew larger and larger as they approached the flat ground at the base of each dune, and sometimes it seemed impossible that a car could tackle such faces without mishap'.* We got stuck several times but there were enough men around to dig us out. One of the disadvantages of driving in the high dune country in the summer was that the heat almost melted the sand. It was much softer than in the winter, and sand tyres and low pressures were absolutely essential.

Hugh was one of those rare (and audacious) Brits who could when irritated use the rudest terms in addressing 'the natives' without causing resentment — largely because in the next breath he would be laughing with them and saying 'Well done'. He had a servant called Bakri, a Hadhrami. Bakri would just smile and get on with it. So would my huge Pathan bearer, Khan. By now Hugh had served in the Sudan and the Arabian Peninsula for nearly forty years and had earned the respect and almost love of those with whom he was dealing.

Glen Balfour-Paul, who was to succeed James Craig, recalls how he once met Bakri, after Hugh's retirement, in a queue at Bahrain airport taking the same plane to Heathrow. He said he was going to join 'the Pasha' (as he called Hugh). He admitted he had no idea where the Pasha was living but said 'When I get to London airport, they will surely know'. Glen next heard of him in Morocco, safely restored to Hugh's service. He was an appalling cook but devoted to Hugh — and Hugh to him.

After two or three days the heat really hit me. In the afternoons I would lie on a damp towel on my camp bed in a tent, stark naked and still sweating. It was impossible to sleep and all one wanted was a cold drink. We had water but it was not cold. Michael Baugniet was, rather to my surprise, more overcome than I, but neither of us was exactly fit for battle. It was an experience that I shall not forget.

My next swan was out to the Far West as far as the Qatar border, which was nearly 400 miles from Sharjah. I started off in July by visiting the Scouts squadron at Mirfa where I collected Ivan Loosemore, a young Somersets officer who had recently joined us on an eighteen-month tour. We then drove on past the ADPC oil terminal at Jebel Dhanna, and faced the notorious Sabkhat Mutti, a twenty-five-mile stretch of salt flats reaching inland fifty miles which Wilfred Thesiger

*The Trucial States, p.214

crossed by camel in the winter of 1947-'48, and describes so well in
Arabian Sands, still today the most authoritative book on the Rub' al
Khali. He writes thus:

Next day we crossed the Sabkhat Mutti. We decided we must make a
detour and cross these salt flats near their head, otherwise the camels might
become inextricably bogged, especially after the recent heavy rain. They
would only have to sink in as far as their knees to be lost. Camels are
always bad on greasy surfaces, so we fastened knotted cords under their feet
to stop them from slipping. Here the salt flats were divided into three arms
by crescent-patterned drifts of sterile white sand. The flats themselves were
covered with a crust of dirty salt which threw up a glare into our faces and,
even through half-closed eyes, stabbed deep into my skull. The camels
broke through this crust and floundered forward through liquid mud. It
took us five unpleasant anxious hours to get across.*

We did not experience liquid black mud, partly I suspect because it was
summer and there had been no rain for at least six months. However,
I do have a splendid photograph of one of our two Land Rovers bogged
up to its axles, and Ivan stripped to the waist, the mud well over his
ankles, wondering where we went from there. We drove for at least 100
miles along that barren coast without meeting a single other vehicle. I
remember that there was only one landmark near the Qatar border. It
was not surprisingly called 'Seven Trees' because there were seven
withered dried-up tamarisks still alive at this stop. We would have given
our position by WT to Sharjah as Seven Trees.

In August I was off again, this time to call on my opposite number
in the Sultanate of Oman, Tony Lewis, who commanded the Sultan's
Armed Forces (SAF) and had by coincidence taken over at almost
exactly the same time as me early that year.

The drive by Land Rover to Muscat by the inland route was both
exciting and spectacular. I took Tim with me and we went via our
squadron at Buraimi and, after crossing the border, took the inland
route via Ibri, Nizwa and the Sumail Gap to the coast at Muscat. The
track (it could hardly be called a road) through the Sumail Gap was
particularly impressive: the Jebel Akhdar (Green Mountains) towered
above us to the north-west, rising to 10,000 feet. It was about 300 miles
from Buraimi and took us two days of fairly hard driving.

SAF was a rather larger 'private army' than the Scouts but very
different in organisation. Most of the men were Urdu-speaking Baluchis
from what is now Pakistan, and the force owed its allegiance to the

*p.241.

Sultan, Said bin Taimur (as opposed to HMG), a remote ruler in the Shakhbut mould, who lived at Salala on the Indian Ocean coast about 500 miles 'round the corner' of the Arabian Peninsula from Muscat. British officers were seconded or on contract (vulgarly known as 'hired assassins') and there were also a few Muscati officers being trained to take over the senior posts in due course.

Tony took me up by Beaver aircraft to Saiq at 6,500 feet on the Jebel Akhdar. The terrain up there was of course totally different from the arid plains. Local tribesmen offered us bunches of grapes but they did not make wine: that would have been strictly forbidden in this essentially Muslim country. It was in these mountains that in 1959 the SAS had fought and winkled out the rebel tribesmen, claimed by 'Saut al Arab' to be 'our progressive and freedom-loving Omani brothers', who had defied the 'reactionary Sultan of Muscat'.

I envied Tony his environment, which was large and richly varied. However, his boss the Sultan was obviously a difficult man to deal with, and hardly ever appeared in public. It was a pity, too, that his men were not locals, as were the majority of mine.

Both Tony and I were commanding private armies operating mainly in a police role in this remote corner of the Arabian Peninsula, and it was extremely important that we worked together, particularly at certain key points such as the Buraimi oases.

In the autumn Michael Holme, the Brigadier in Bahrain, went home on a month's leave and I was required to deputise for him. This meant staying in Bahrain, and proved a useful visit as I was able to meet the Royal Navy and RAF commanders (known as SNOPG and SRAFPG) and also Sir William Luce, our overall master. The 3rd Battalion Parachute Regiment was stationed there, commanded then by Tony Farrar-Hockley* who had made a name for himself when, as adjutant of the Glosters, the Chinese had tried to brainwash him after taking him prisoner in Korea. Tony was later to bring his battalion down to the Trucial States for training exercises with the Scouts. Bahrain is a relatively small island some thirty miles by ten, and not at all suitable for army training.

Almost immediately after I returned to Sharjah James Craig was relieved after three years as PA, Dubai, and posted to be 1st Secretary Beirut, where I was to stay with him the following year. We laid on a special guard as he flew out of Sharjah. His successor, Glen Balfour-Paul**, came from Beirut where on January 23rd, 1963 he had invited

*Later Sir Anthony Farrar-Hockley, GBE, KCB, DSO, MC
**Later HM Ambassador to Iraq, Jordan and Tunisia.

Kim Philby to dine the night that he defected. Philby's wife Eleanor turned up alone; her husband had just disappeared.

Glen and his wife Marnie were a charming pair and we were to see a lot of them (and share some fairly traumatic experiences) in the two years to come.

Our visitors' book has fifty-three names in it for those first nine months up to the end of 1964. They include several major-generals, brigadiers, oil men, MOD civil servants (checking to see that we were not spending too much public money), journalists and a number of Scouts officers from outlying squadrons who came in to Sharjah for a break. Entertaining was relatively easy as Khan was excellent as bearer-cum-butler, and Alex was a very adequate cook, well able to cater even when the memsahib was not around.

Simone brought the children out for Christmas. David Mack of the National Bank of Dubai and his wife Betty were particularly hospitable and gave a children's party almost the day that the family arrived. David was an interesting example of the type of British expat. whom Rashid recruited. The story goes that having decided that he wanted a bank of his own, Rashid asked the Bank of England for help. David Mack had just retired to his native Dundee, having worked with Grindlays in India and East Africa. The call came when he was playing golf: 'A small country in the Lower Gulf wants to start a bank; would you be interested in setting it up?' David had never served in the Arab world, which was perhaps a good thing as he had no preconceived ideas about it. Although speaking not a word of Arabic, he was an instant success and became one of Rashid's most valued financial advisers. In those early days Dubai's prosperity did not depend on oil. It came from commerce in many forms, the only dredged creek for hundreds of miles and an extremely go-ahead ruling family, the al Maktoum.*

Gold smuggling was then at its height, and there was a recognised drill. Every woman in India wants to adorn herself with gold: necklaces, bracelets, rings, anklets; the demand was insatiable but the official price was too high. Rashid and a select band of merchants would order gold bars to be flown in from London, Paris or Zurich and David Mack would deposit them in his bank's vaults. Dhow captains would then be alerted that a cargo was ready and, when the weather was right, away they would go.

The system was that before entering Indian territorial waters (since the Indian Navy could not properly arrest or sink them outside) the

*Now internationally famous as the largest and richest owners of race horses in the world.

Dubai launches transferred their cargo under cover of night to small Indian boats, which smuggled the gold to land. The Indian operator then sold it privately to eager villagers in exchange for rupee notes, which they took to banks in Bombay, or wherever, and changed into rupee coins. For some inexplicable reason rupee coins were worth, in the Gulf states, twice their value in India. Accordingly when the coins were taken to Dubai, the entrepreneurs to whom they were delivered could effectively buy the same amount of gold in Europe again for nothing, by converting the rupee coins into sterling in Dubai. Allowing for expenses, interceptions by the Indian Navy and other accidents, the average profit on a turn-round was said to be about eighty per cent. Everyone in Dubai with a rupee to his name was in on the business, and plane loads of gold ingots could be left overnight, piled up unguarded on Dubai airstrip, because no one would steal them.

The Indian Trade Agent in Dubai was primarily there to report the departure of suspect launches to the Indian Navy. Glen Balfour-Paul recalls that he was once invited on a day's pearling trip by an ostensibly innocent Dubai dhow owner, who deposited him afterwards at Umm al Quwain by arrangement, and on saying goodbye disclosed that he was not returning to Dubai but was off to India, having used the Political Agent as cover for the load of gold he had in the hold, so the Indian Trade Agent would not be suspicious! The Indians eventually interrupted the business by withdrawing rupee coinage from the Gulf — though even then Dubai merchants found ways of carrying on the business by more sophisticated methods, until the discovery of oil provided an easier source of revenue.

Illegal immigration into the Trucial States was a running sore throughout my time. There were two incentives for immigrants: oil had been struck, therefore there must be jobs and good money; and second: pilgrims en route to the *haj* at Mecca were led to believe by unscrupulous Indian or Pakistani ship-owners that they would be put ashore in Arabia and Mecca was just round the corner. In fact, it was 1,000 miles away across some of the worst desert in the world. RN frigates used to intercept dhows that were crowded with pilgrims, who would have had little hope of ever reaching Mecca, even if they had eluded naval patrols. It was a tragic situation and many died of starvation or disease.

Early in the New Year of 1965 it was announced that HRH Prince Philip would be visiting us — for about an hour — on February 15th whilst his aircraft was being refuelled en route from Saudi Arabia to

Karachi. As there was not time for him to call on the Ruler in his 'palace', it was decided that courtesies would be exchanged in my house, which was on a slight rise just above the airfield. Meeting him would be the Ruler Shaikh Saqr, Glen Balfour-Paul the Political Agent, the RAF Station Commander Squadron Leader Jerry Jonas, my deputy John Emerson Baker, Jack Briggs who would be in charge of security, and myself.

Glen's most vivid recollection of the visit was when HRH stepped out of the plane, looked out from the top of the gangway for the normal crowd of British ladies in hats to wave at, and said 'Kind of quiet here, isn't it?' His staff had evidently not told him of the orders received by Glen to forbid the community from assembling to cheer the Prince, in order to make the stop-off as confidential as possible. The ladies were distinctly resentful. We drank coffee in our sitting-room and gifts were exchanged. The Ruler gave HRH a heavily jewelled *khanjar**, which after thanking him he passed to his private secretary with the words, 'I hope I shan't have to use it!', and in turn the Ruler was given a photograph of the Queen. HRH had been playing polo in Saudi Arabia and told Saqr all about it. I sensed that he was not interested in this Western frivolity, and in any case relations between the Trucial States and 'big brother' Saudi Arabia were not particularly good, but conversation flowed as much as it ever can through an interpreter in these sort of situations.

Shortly afterwards, I was invited to join the Luces and Hugh Boustead on a trek in the Liwa. In winter the dunes are relatively cool and hard; sand tyres seldom bog down and one is able to enjoy the empty vastness of this incredible country in comparative comfort. This was a rather special occasion as Hugh was about to retire, and Bill and Margaret Luce had brought along two old Sudan friends, Charles de Bunsen and John Rintoul. Many reminiscences were exchanged as we all sat on the crest of a sand dune watching the great ball of the sun sink below the horizon, and gazing at the never-ending sand sea to the south. We would then repair to our camp where ice-cold drinks would be handed round by servants brought from the Residency in Bahrain, helped by Bakri and Khan.

There is one rather special spot in the Liwa: a tiny oasis called Usub much favoured for camping. To the north of the well and its attendant date palms is a very high dune, much too sheer for a vehicle to descend but just right for tobogganing down on a tea-tray and creating the

*Gulf equivalent of the Adeni *jambiya*.

'singing of the sands' which was in effect a mini sand avalanche, while marvelling at this freak of nature. Scorpions were one of the few hazards. My driver was somehow immune to their sting and I have a remarkable photograph of a large scorpion crawling up his bare forearm.

I suppose that the real charms of a Liwa trek were the silence, the view of infinitely extending dunes and the feeling of being away from the bustle of life in rather distinguished company. For Bill Luce and his friends it was a real rest; my only concern was that the Dodges and Land Rovers did not break down, and that the wireless worked (we had of course to keep in radio contact with the outside world), as I was required to produce both. I need not have worried.

Early in March Simone flew out to join me and we immediately set out on a long drive to the remotest corner of the Trucial States, Umm al Zamul, a well in the middle of nowhere at the junction of three disputed international frontiers: the Trucial States, Sultanate of Oman and Saudi Arabia. It was 225 miles almost due south of Buraimi, and very seldom visited by Europeans. Not even Tim Budd, our faithful companion on swans of this nature, had been there though he had then served with the Scouts for thirteen years.

We had with us a Bedouin guide whom Tim had produced. As there was no road or even track, and international frontiers were involved, it was important to know roughly where one was. We planned to cover about 100 miles a day, which meant three nights' camping. I remember crossing ridge after ridge of dunes and, as we crested one, wondering exactly where we would cross the next. Our guide was good but unpredictable. On one occasion after we had safely crossed a ridge of dunes and there was a good view south, he asked whether he could borrow my glasses. I feared the worst: he was lost. But no; he could see through the glasses some black specks in the distance and his face lit up. 'My wives', he said; 'we must call'. Call we did, and wasted a good deal of time drinking interminable cups of coffee. Tim said that our guide had borrowed my glasses to check before our arrival that his wives — I can't remember whether he had the regulation four — were behaving themselves, but I think that this interpretation is a little far-fetched.

On we went and duly arrived on the second day at the Well, which was identifiable only by a forty-gallon oil drum covering its opening and nothing else at all. Nevertheless, we felt elated at having arrived at this furthest of frontier posts, which I don't think even the Scouts had visited more than once or twice in their history. We should of course have ridden on camels as Thesiger did, but I can only plead that this would have taken too long.

Our camp sites were rather fun. There was no need for tents; we simply stretched a lean-to shelter out from the Land Rover to provide shade from the inevitable sun, and at night slept under the stars. What was particularly fascinating was that in the morning, sipping our tea brought of course by Khan, we were able to trace the tracks of several desert animals including the desert fox (no relation of Rommel), hares and jereboas (desert rats), all of whom must have come to look at us whilst we slept.

David and Caroline came out for the Easter holidays. This was their third visit and they almost came to regard Sharjah as home. The Balfour-Paul children were much the same age and they had a lot of fun together. The Scouts owned a dhow which was officially used for patrolling at sea, particularly against illegal immigration, and occasionally for putting men ashore to show the flag at remote spots. We were allowed to use it for picnics and fishing when it was available and this proved very popular.

Hugh finally left on retirement on May 1st, but not before we heard that he had been knighted on his seventieth birthday. We were all delighted. I laid on a special parade for him at Sharjah and he rode onto the square wearing diplomatic service winter uniform (that is, navy blue as opposed to white, with a cocked hat), and was escorted by our ceremonial ponies. I can't imagine what a Guards RSM would have said but I could within reason move the goal posts when I chose.

Hugh's final departure was also quite unusual. He had decided to trek in the Himalayas before going home and was booked on a BI boat to Bombay which called at Dubai, but could not of course enter the creek. So a special dhow was laid on to take him out. I had a guard of honour on the jetty and he sailed away to the lament of 'Speed bonny boat, like a bird on the wing, over the sea to Skye,' played by our pipe band. Most of the ladies who came to say goodbye were in tears, and I suspect that some of the men were too. It was a very moving occasion.

Hugh's successor as Political Agent, Abu Dhabi, was Archie Lamb*, a career diplomat of forthright manner who had served as a pilot in the RAF during the war and won the DFC. After training at MECAS he had served both in the Bahrain Residency and Kuwait. Twenty-eight years younger than Hugh, I anticipated a new broom and was not wrong.

Early in 1965 it became apparent that Nasser, acting through the Arab League, was trying to detach the Trucial Shaikhs from their

*Later Sir Archie Lamb, KCMG, DFC, MBE.

allegiance to Britain by an offer of £5 million development aid which the League (i.e. Egypt) would administer on the ground. The Deputy Secretary-General of the League toured the Lower Gulf to spread the gospel and despite a visit by George Thompson, Minister of State at the Foreign Office, the five smaller states, led by Saqr of Sharjah, fell for the 'bribe'. At this point Sir William Luce flew to Ras al Khaimah, met the five Rulers and persuaded them to think again. A cable was sent to the Arab League saying that contributions were welcome but only if paid to the Trucial States Council (which we in a sense controlled). The £5 million never came. Glen told me afterwards that the Arab League take-over bid was the most difficult situation that HMG had to face during his time in Dubai.

At the end of April a ceremony took place which, in the light of what was to happen two months later, might be described as badly timed. A twenty-five-pounder gun suddenly arrived by air and I was instructed to hand it over to Shaikh. Saqr, Ruler of Sharjah, as a gesture of goodwill. It was to replace an ancient canon* at the entrance to his palace and was to be used entirely for firing salutes. Live ammunition was not of course included in the gesture. With hindsight it would appear that this relatively small gift was an attempt to win Saqr over to cooperating with us. A good deal of publicity was made of the occasion: we all turned out in our best bibs and tuckers and there were lots of smiles for the cameras.

Any weapon, and particularly one that makes a really loud bang, is an important status symbol in the Arab world. None of the other Trucial States Rulers could boast a highly-polished twenty-five-pounder gun in front of their palace, so Saqr was one up in this respect. What he really thought I do not know; the gesture made little difference to his attitude towards us. Sharjah was run down. Despite a modest revenue from oil concessions (both on and off-shore), and from HMG for the RAF base, there was little development in terms of such essentials as hospitals, drainage, roads or piped water. Saqr did announce a £1 million jetty project to provide deep water anchorage and thus divert some of Dubai's profitable trade; we felt it a waste of money and Glen was allowed by Saqr to put his views to the assembled citizenry in the *majlis* but they were all one hundred per cent in favour.

Saqr was interested in education and supported the Kuwait Education

---

*On one occasion when I was taking a walk down town I noticed a crowd round the canon, and on closer inspection was horrified to discover that an unfortunate man was strapped to the barrel and being flogged. The crime was theft. In Saudi Arabia he would have lost his right hand, so I suppose he could be considered lucky.

Office which set up many schools, especially in the Shaikhdom of Sharjah. Most of the teachers were of course Egyptian. There was also a small Trade School run by a British headmaster.

The real trouble was that Saqr was extremely unpopular within his own family, who one and all wanted him to be deposed. I was only too aware of this through Abdul Aziz, his first cousin, who was one of my most able and influential Arab officers. The Qawasim, as I have already mentioned, were and still are a very large and powerful family in the Lower Gulf. Saqr got on all right with his cousin Saqr bin Muhammad, Ruler of Ras al Khaimah, three Shaikhdoms up the coast, but with no one else.

He made no secret of his strong pro-Nasser sentiments and his apparent dislike of any form of British base on his soil — despite the fact that we paid handsomely for the facility. We also provided a peace-keeping force in the shape of the TOS, at no cost to him, and indeed another valuable source of revenue to the Shaikhdom as we employed a lot of local labour. It was a very delicate situation. The issues were of course entirely political and not directly my concern. It was my duty to ensure that if the military became involved in any way, they would obey orders and behave with total impartiality.

If things went wrong the Sharjah base could become untenable. With the withdrawal from Aden having been set for 1968 at the latest, the availability of facilities for stationing British troops in the Gulf would be increasingly important. Bahrain, where the MOD was to base its new (reduced) HQ on the approaching withdrawal from Aden, was only a small island. There was plenty of open space in the Lower Gulf for training.

Eventually a letter signed by all the leading members of the Qawasim requesting his resignation as Ruler was given to Saqr. He agreed to go quietly and was flown to Bahrain and subsequently sought asylum in Cairo. His cousin, Khalid bin Muhammad (Abdul Aziz's eldest brother), took over. Shaikh Rashid of Dubai, who was no friend of Saqr, had been kept informed of events and supported the family's action.

That evening the new Ruler was 'at home' in the *majlis* at Sharjah and rubbed shoulders with all and sundry. He was a quiet, unassuming man whom we came to like and respect. Little did I suspect at the time that seven years later Saqr would attempt a remarkable come-back; but that is another story.

I have said little so far about oil: drilling and prospecting was going on constantly in Abu Dhabi, Dubai and Sharjah and to a lesser extent in the small Shaikhdoms up the coast. Politically, off-shore drilling was a good deal more complicated than on-shore. Each state theoretically owned the 'continental shelf' reaching out from their coastline to a median line in the middle of the Gulf, the boundary with Iran. Surveying and agreement of such marine boundaries is intrinsically difficult and it is not surprising that Rulers sometimes disagreed about ownership when wells were drilled near the boundary. Das Island and the operations of ADMA (Abu Dhabi Marine Areas) was a case in point. Das, 100 miles off-shore from Abu Dhabi, had been uninhabited until the early 1950s. In ten years this barren island, measuring about one mile by three-quarters, was transformed into a thriving oil community with an artificial harbour, air-strip, prefabricated houses and offices, hospital, vast storage and tanker-loading jetty. By 1966, when I was suddenly ordered to visit ADMA, there were some 150 Europeans and 1,200 Arabs and Indians working there. Oil had been struck at two separate locations, one twenty and the other sixty miles from Das, at an average depth of 9,000 feet. Oil from the first location, the Umm Shaif field, was being produced at about 120,000 barrels per day and then pumped to Das for degassing and loading.

Shaikh Shakhbut, Ruler of Abu Dhabi, suddenly decided that DPC (Dubai Petroleum Company) was drilling into the continental shelf across his border, and that ADMA through its common shareholding with DPC was supporting this. He promptly withdrew his representative, and it looked as though there might be trouble within the labour force, who owed their loyalty to Abu Dhabi. I flew there and was briefed by the ADMA General Manager, Peter Mann. At the same time my squadron at Mirfa was stood by to be flown in if necessary. In the event the affair blew over, and production was not affected. That year Shakhbut was receiving about £8-9 million from the Umm Shaif field alone, a not inconsiderable sum in those days.

In true Arab style, Shakhbut was prepared to spend his oil revenue not where it was needed but where it would give him heightened prestige amongst his peers — on a private army of his own. In vain did Bill Luce and Archie Lamb reason with him — he was adamant: 'I must have my own army,' he said. Thus the Abu Dhabi Defence Force (ADDF) was born in 1965 and almost immediately I was asked to give up one of my most experienced squadron commanders, Major 'Tug' Wilson, to command it. Though the ADDF was not an operational force of any consequence for several years, its formation started a chain reaction, inevitably undermining the role of the Scouts. We were essentially a military force whose role was to keep the peace throughout the seven Shaikhdoms, and be available to support any ruler who might have an internal security problem. We were also available as a defence against improper occupation from outside (conceivably, for example, from Saudi Arabia as had happened in Buraimi in 1955). However, HMG paid £2 million a year to man the TOS and rulers undoubtedly knew that control rested ultimately with the PR. Yet I suppose they could argue that if the PR had a private army why should not they?

Within a few years Rashid of Dubai followed suit with the Dubai Defence Force; Sharjah and Ras al Khaimah were not far behind. It was a sad turn of events at a time when the Trucial States were crying out for peaceful investments of revenue in roads, piped water, drainage, hospitals and schools. Law and order in the Trucial States was very important to the many different oil companies operating both on and off shore. As COMTOS I was responsible for ensuring that as far as possible tribal disputes, sabotage or any local disturbance did not interfere with the flow of oil. This was just as much a vital interest to the Rulers as it was to HMG.

In July the Royal Navy kindly invited me to spend twenty-four hours at sea in HMS *Ashanti*, one of their Tribal class frigates. I was collected by helicopter from our parade ground at Sharjah and taken out to the ship, which was lying just offshore. We steamed up the coast past Ras al Khaimah and turned into the Elphinstone Inlet*, an almost Norwegian-type fjord cut deep into the Musandam Peninsula which forms the northernmost tip of this corner of Arabia. We crept slowly up to the head of the inlet and anchored, whilst a few of us went ashore and climbed to a low rocky col from which we could look out into the Indian Ocean. Quite a few of the ship's company enjoyed some fishing whilst we were otherwise engaged.

I was taken by helicopter to call on the local emir at Khasab in the Sultanate of Oman, the northernmost village on the mainland. The dates were ripening and we were given armfuls to take back to the ship. It was the helicopter pilot's birthday and when we landed on the pad he was presented with a highly decorated cake.

On our way back *Ashanti* intercepted a dhow crammed full of illegal immigrants trying to enter the oil-rich Shaikhdoms. We carried a small interrogation team on board for just this task and the dhow had to be turned back. I felt sorry for the unfortunate passengers — though they probably waited until we were out of sight and then made another run for the coast.

*Named after the Hon. Mounstuart Elphinstone, Govenor of Bombay in 1820.

I may have given the impression that I was out 'swanning' all the time and and hardly ever in my office at Sharjah, or dealing with the routine matters that are the lot of any commanding officer. This was not so: much time was inevitably taken up with office work. After an early morning ride I would spend perhaps four hours or so in the office and visit one or two of the administrative units at base, such as the signal squadron or the REME workshop or the boys' school. I might call on the RAF station commander and hear his latest news. Though the RAF shared the runway with a few civil airlines almost all the air movements were RAF: a Hunter squadron on a training exercise, regular Twin Pioneer or Beverley flights to our outlying squadrons or to Muscat or Masira Island, and VIP flights using Sharjah to refuel. There were only four or five civil movements each week.

In the afternoons I tried to avoid the office, sleep for a bit, and then go for a sail in the creek or outside the bar if the weather was right. I had two staff-college trained officers, one on the G side (General Staff) and the other AQ (Administrative), both of whom knew their jobs well; and if anything came in during the afternoon or evening I would either go to the office where we had the operational maps, or deal with the problem from my house. There was no telephone except to Dubai. All other communications, for example to Bahrain or to my four outlying squadrons, were by WT. We were a close-knit community 'living above the shop', and situations were dealt with as and when they occurred, at any hour of the day or night, seven days a week.

The four outlying squadrons were all self-contained and self-supporting. One was in what we called 'the Far West', 200 miles from base in the oil country, one at Buraimi ninety miles south, in what David Holden described as 'an absurdly romantic whitewashed fort that looks as if it had strayed from Beau Geste'*; and two were only ten miles apart in the central plain and the foothills of the Hajar, forty miles east of Sharjah. They were all sited to cover strategic trade routes that had been used by camel trains for hundreds of years. In the same way that I could scarcely be surprised by the Brigadier in Bahrain descending unannounced on me, the squadron commanders reckoned that they were kings of their own little castles. It was an extremely responsible job for an infantry major on secondment and I was lucky to take over three who had already served with the Scouts for considerably longer than the official eighteen-month tour. There were many others who did extremely well in this difficult environment, and quite a few volunteered to extend their tours. As a result I seldom had to worry about what went on in the outlying squadrons.

*Farewell to Arabia, p.201.

Visitors from the UK, either from the Services or on business, usually came in what was called 'Directors' weather' — that is, October to February. One VIP who came in the hot weather was Admiral Peter Hill-Norton* who was on his way home from the Far East and stayed the night. It happened to be a particularly humid evening and I debated whether to offer him a drink in our air-conditioned sitting-room, or outside on the verandah. I chose outside and apologised about the heat. Hill-Norton rounded on me, saying: 'Don't apologise. This is what you are paid for!' His abruptness and direct manner were well known, I was subsequently told.

Two other very charming VIPs who visited us were General Sir John Hackett, then Deputy Chief of the General Staff at the MOD, who had commanded the Trans-Jordan Frontier Force shortly after the war. I had known him slightly in the Western Desert when he was a very dashing young 8th Hussar. The other was Admiral Sir Michael Le Fanu, the last Service Chief in Aden who later became First Sea Lord, only to die in office.

In November an American aircraft from ARAMCO at Dhahran called at Sharjah to deliver a generator for the American hospital at Buraimi. As there was a good deal of spare room on the plane a number of families came too for the ride. We entertained a very friendly USAF colonel and his wife, the Leahys, and took them to the suq. A few hours later their Dakota staggered off the ground laden with brass coffee pots, silverware and khunjars, which apparently were difficult to buy in Saudi Arabia.

There was one remarkable silver merchant based in the suq, known as 'Robin Bastard'. He was an Iraqi who had drifted down the Gulf and found a niche in Sharjah. He used to buy ingots of silver in London and have them sent out. He then melted them down and could copy almost any ring, brooch or badge very accurately. One of our most treasured pieces of silver is an Omani coffee-pot which he copied from a Nizwa original, and which was given to us as a leaving present by the British Sergeants' Mess. Robin earned his unusual nickname because British visitors used to call him 'that robbing bastard' — which was hardly fair as his goods were of high quality. However, he had a nice sense of humour, knew perfectly well what he was called, and with a broad smile on his face would introduce himself to new customers as 'Robin Bastard'.

Three months later we were to return the colonel and his wife's call

*Later Admiral of the Fleet Lord Hill Norton, GCB, Chief of the Defence Staff.

under rather different circumstances. Simone and I, accompanied by Tim, decided to drive by Land Rover from Sharjah to Dhahran, a distance of 550 miles. It was not the distance that presented a problem but the fact that for an important section of the route on the Saudi border there was no recognised track at all and one just had to drive across the desert by compass.

That winter, the rain such as one got in the Trucial States (two to three inches average per year), came late and by February 4th, the day we left, there had not been a drop on the coast. However, no sooner had we cleared Dubai than the rain started and the track across the sabkha became a lake as the rain invariably lies on the surface and takes a long time to drain away. We had rashly forgotten to take side-curtains for the Land Rover and arrived at Mirfa 190 miles from Sharjah that afternoon fairly damp but determined to press on if possible. We accordingly borrowed a pair of side-curtains and drove on the sixty-five miles to Jebel Dhanna, our planned first night stop where ADPC had their ocean terminal. The first major obstacle was the notorious Sabkhat Matti. Despite the previous day's rain the coastal track which crosses the marsh at almost its widest point was quite firm. Twice it crossed a shallow tidal creek but by dint of wading ahead on what I believed to be the track we drove the Land Rovers through without difficulty and by midday were clear of the sabkha and making steady progress across a low sand plateau. It was about now that we crossed the frontier from Abu Dhabi into Saudi Arabia and really had to start serious navigation. Our plan was to reach the Saudi frontier post at Salwa that evening and then drive the 150 miles to Dhahran on the third day.

Shortly after crossing the frontier we came across a much-used spring which gushed forth highly sulphurous water and gave off an unpleasant odour. It was no doubt drinkable by camels and possibly Bedouin but not by Europeans except in dire emergency. Tim said that he had heard previously of this water but was not sure of its exact location. We decided to turn north and drove by compass for fifty miles over a mixture of low rolling sand dunes and *sabkha* salt flats. Shortly before dusk, just when we were hoping to glimpse the palm trees of Salwa and the sea, we unexpectedly hit a tarmac road running roughly east and west. Which way to go? Was the road in Saudi Arabia or Qatar? I elected to turn right. It was soon obvious that we were in Qatar territory and that Salwa was the other way, so we rapidly retraced our steps and arrived at the Qatar Police Post on the Gulf of Salwa about a mile from the Saudi village, just as it was getting dark. Needless to say the Qatar police were very surprised to see us. Who were we? Why had we not got visas and how had we entered Qatar territory in TOS vehicles? They were sorry but it was quite impossible to cross the frontier that night. They would speak to Headquarters in Doha on the radio telephone and ask for instructions. Meantime *tafadhl* (welcome), would we please make ourselves comfortable in their smart new police station. Disappointed but realising the inevitability of the situation, we drank coffee and unrolled our valises. After an excellent meal with our 'captors' a very smart police car drove up and out stepped Bill, an old friend who had visited us in Dubai the previous year. He had been sent from Doha to check on these strange visitors.

We were suitably apologetic; a slight compass error had taken us about five miles east of our intended destination, we had no intention of trespassing inside Qatar territory, we thought that his police were very efficient and hospitable but could we please cross into Saudi territory as early as possible the next morning? Bill thought that this could be arranged but he reminded us that the Saudis never started work before nine o'clock at the earliest. With that he returned to Doha and we settled for the night. The next morning, full of hope and after quite an appetising breakfast of dates, rice and coffee we shook our Qatar friends warmly by the hand and drove across the mile of sand to Salwa itself.

Salwa, which we were to get to know rather better than we had expected, was a collection of decrepit buildings housing customs, immigration, police, dispensary and telegraph offices with an outer fringe of *barusti* (palm-frond dwellings) and tin shacks. Even the mosque was basically a tin shack. I doubt whether the population exceeded a hundred or two. It was very much a back-door into Saudi Arabia so obviously nobody bothered much. We were received on arrival by the Emir, a grandiloquent title for the representative of central government in so remote a spot. He was polite but quite inscrutable. We were ushered into his *majlis*, which surprisingly enough was in a square pointed tent with a brightly-coloured lining that one might have expected to see at a jousting pageant. Coffee was served and our passports were taken away by his equally inscrutable passport officer. We explained the reason for our visit and why we had inadvertently strayed into Qatar territory. The Emir listened attentively. No, we had no visas, but the British Embassy had been assured that we would be allowed through. Surely, we said, the Emir had been warned by the Governor of the Eastern Province at Dammam that we were coming? No, he regretted that he had not been warned. Jeddah, we must understand, was a long way away, and he took his instructions from Dammam. But we must not worry; permission would come *inshallah*; he had radioed Dammam and meantime he hoped that we would sit with him and drink coffee and talk.

The morning dragged by — we had arrived on the dot of nine — tea in tiny glass tankards followed by coffee, warm milk followed tea and then we went back to coffee. The *majlis* emptied and filled again; the Emir sat inscrutable as ever. What was it like in the Trucial States he asked: were there any trees, was there enough water, was there good grazing for goats, what was the fishing like, was it true that Dubai was becoming quite a large city? The conversation was interspersed with long periods of silence whilst the Emir digested each new bit of information. The time for midday prayer came and the Emir devoutly led his flock on a patch of sand outside the tent. He then invited us to lunch in an adjoining tent and we sat down to our second rice meal of the day. I realised by now that our chances of going on that afternoon were becoming increasingly slim. It was at least five hours' drive to Dhahran, we had no guide and our map was to say the least sketchy. Assuredly, said the Emir, clearance would come during the afternoon. We were not so sure. We took our siesta in the majlis and by five o'clock had resigned ourselves to staying the night. The Emir was apologetic; we were of course most welcome to spend the night, beds would be prepared immediately and he would be delighted if we would dine with him.

The radio link with Dammam was situated in a building about a hundred yards from the *majlis* and we always knew when it was working because a small generator started up. Our hopes were raised every time we heard the 'phut, phut' of the engine but eventually even that spark of hope faded.

Simone and I went for an evening stroll round the village and returned sadly at dusk to unroll our valises yet again. Dinner with the Emir followed closely the pattern of lunch and shortly afterwards we bade him goodnight. As we turned in I saw the lights of the Qatar Police Post where we had spent the previous night winking at us across the bay only a mile away. If you mad English want to travel in out-of-the-way parts of Arabia you must be prepared for delays, they seemed to say.

The next morning (our fourth day) it seemed impolite to ask the Emir at breakfast, as we considered how to eat cold fried eggs with our fingers, whether there was any news. It was whilst we were taking our morning stroll round the village that the news came. I saw the Land Rover come to fetch us. But alas, the news was bad: the Emir was extremely sorry, he had instructions from Dammam that we were to return at once to Abu Dhabi territory with an escort. It was no good arguing — what could we do — our passports were returned and, feeling

thoroughly frustrated, we had a hurried lunch, said goodbye to the
Emir and set forth into the desert. Our Saudi escort in their Chevrolet
pick-up obviously knew the way well and we found ourselves back on
the sandstone plateau inside the Trucial States territory well before dark.
After saying goodbye to our escort we decided to motor on about fifty
miles and camp at a derelict oil company site that we knew of. We
arrived there without incident and cooked our first meal from our own
supplies; it would have been most impolite to refuse the Arab food
offered us at both the Qatar post and in Salwa. As I climbed into my
sleeping-bag on our fourth night out I wondered whether the Saudis had
told our American friends that we were not being allowed in.
Otherwise I feared that search parties might be being organised as we
were now twenty-four hours overdue. My fears were to prove justified.
We turned in early and it was about 2 a.m. when I woke with a start to
hear the noise of vehicles approaching. After much gesticulation, Tim
came over and said that our Saudi friends had returned with two
vehicles to escort us back to Salwa as permission to proceed had now
been granted and would we please come at once as it looked like rain
and they did not want to get caught in the *sabkha*. I turned to Simone
who was by this time half dressed. Of course we must go, she said. I did
not need much persuading; so 3 a.m. saw us on the track once more,
following two Saudi pick-ups full of armed men. We had barely been
going half an hour before the leading vehicle veered sharply off the
track and we heard a shot followed closely by another. There was no
cause for alarm however — our Saudi friends were merely shooting a
desert hare for the pot. They got another later on. Just before dawn
there was a halt for prayers, but I was extremely concerned to see the
men wrap themselves in their blankets round the vehicles and go to
sleep. Would we ever get to Dhahran, I wondered, as I sipped a
welcome cup of tea and contemplated the shapeless forms of our Saudi
escort? To my surprise, after only half an hour or so, one sleeper woke
up and soon they were all throwing their bedding rolls into the trucks
and we were off again. I was full of hope, until somewhere just inside
Saudi territory at a spot where there was some dried scrub we halted yet
again and off came all the kit. This time it was boiled hare for breakfast.
By now we were past worrying about time. The hares were skinned,
firewood was collected and in a surprisingly short time we were being
served with coffee and dates whilst the hares boiled away merrily in the
pot. At one point a vehicle suddenly appeared on the skyline and a
truck of Saudis were off in a flash to investigate. They returned after ten
minutes or so to report that it was only a Qattari hunting party. I was
impressed by the alertness of these tough wild-looking men in their long

dark-coloured *kondoras* who obviously knew their way about the desert and were crack shots. I learnt afterwards that they were a detachment from the Geish Abyad (White Army), a force of irregulars which the King maintained rather as a private army to counterbalance the regular forces.

The hare was eventually ready and proved most tasty. We formed a small tight circle and silence reigned whilst we plunged our fingers into the pot. Arab meals may take a long time to prepare but they take a very short time to eat. In a matter of minutes we were being served with another round of coffee and shortly afterwards were mobile once more.

The rain, having held off since our first day, now decided to intervene and made the going tricky, but we were in Salwa before midday to be greeted by our friend the Emir as inscrutable as ever, but was there perhaps a twinkle in his eye as we shook hands?

Could he do anything for us, a guide as the weather was bad, petrol, a meal? We thanked him profusely, took the guide, refused the meal and sallied forth into the forbidden land which we had stared at for so long on our previous visit. The rain then really came down and I prefer to forget the next six hours. We only stuck once and that was in the *sabkha* a few miles out of Salwa, but it was hard going all the way. The windscreen wiper, unused for a year on our Land Rover, unfortunately refused to work and had to be operated by hand; we were tired, wet and dirty, and it was 150 miles to Dhahran. Apart from a few giant Mercedes lorries, we passed no other traffic and it was simply a case of choosing the best from amongst the several tracks leading north along the coast. Just after dark we hit the tarmac road linking Riyadh with Dhahran. It was still raining but nothing mattered now, and half an hour later we were driving past the impressive brightly-lit offices of ARAMCO in Dhahran — an amazing contrast to our experience of the last five days.

Our American friends the Leahys had indeed given us up for lost. The previous day when we were first overdue they had diverted aircraft to search for us and the British authorities in Bahrain had even sent up an RAF Shackleton to try and find us. Clearly, the Saudis had not told our hosts that we were held up at Salwa.

During two days of rest, refitting and sight-seeing in Dhahran we called on the Governor of the Eastern Province, Amir Sa'ud bin 'Abd Allah bin Jiluwi*, in Dammam. He and his father before him had

---

*The Ibn Jiluwi were notoriously ruthless. Their selection by Ibn Saud to govern the Province in his name was a tactical error, owing to their extreme unpopularity.

administered the Eastern Province of Saudi Arabia since the Turks were driven out in 1913. We found him an impressive and dignified old man, surrounded by a large number of personal bodyguards squatting outside the *majlis*, mostly armed with long curved swords. He was interested to hear about our travels and expressed surprise that we had taken so long. Was there perhaps a twinkle in his eye, too, when he said that he would ensure that we were not held up at Salwa on our return? He proved as good as his word and we were given every facility by our friend the Emir when we passed through Salwa on our way back. The whole 550 miles of the return trip only took us two days, thanks to Saudi co-operation, knowing the way and the sturdiness of our Land Rovers. My most vivid memory is of driving through nine miles of flooded *sabkha* not far east of Mirfa in the Abu Dhabi oilfield. The track was completely submerged and we might have been ploughing through a lake.

Early in 1966 Glen Balfour-Paul was promoted to Bahrain on appointment as Deputy Political Resident. We were sad to see him go as he and Marnie had been good friends not only to Simone and me but also to the Scouts as a whole. He was replaced by David Roberts* who came to Dubai from the British Embassy in Damascus. Like virtually all diplomats posted to the Gulf, he was an Arabist, which 99 per cent of us soldiers were not. I did, however, attend a special short course for service personnel and businessmen at Shemlan in the Lebanon that year. It was an intro-duction to the Arab world and Islam. The full MECAS course which most diplomats attended lasted a year.

Very shortly after David took over, we had a minor flap just up the coast at Hamriya. This was a tiny enclave belonging to Sharjah, squeezed in between Ajman and Umm al Quwain. The 'village' consisted of a fort and a few *barusti* huts on the end of a coastal promontory, and could only be approached along a narrow neck of land between the sea and a large creek. Hamriya had been involved in tribal disputes — and I suspect piracy — for over a hundred years, possibly because of its well-sited fort surrounded by water and a single approach which was easy to defend.

Apparently the local Shaikh was defying Shaikh Khaled of Sharjah and claiming to be an independent ruler. Would we (the British) please

*Later Sir David Roberts KBE, CMG, CVO, Ambassador to Syria, the UAE and Lebanon.

intervene and explain the position, asked Khaled. David Roberts scarcely knew where Hamriya was, and I had only been there once on a bathing picnic. I immediately alerted a squadron to move to the neck of the isthmus to effectively cut off Hamriya; I then drove there with David and a radio vehicle.

We 'parked' outside the fort and reviewed the situation. There were obviously a good many armed men inside and though the gateway was invitingly open there was also a large open window immediately above it which commanded the entrance. David was flying his Union Jack and it was perfectly clear who he was. There seemed no alternative but to walk straight in under the hidden eyes of tribesmen who must have been watching from that window. It was a slightly unnerving experience, particularly for David, new to the Gulf.

All was well. We were received with respect; coffee was served, local news was discussed, the Shaikh was honoured to meet the new Political Agent whose Arabic was impeccable, etc. etc. Eventually David politely and quietly told our host that he had come at the request of the Ruler of Sharjah to remind him that Hamriya was part of Sharjah Shaikhdom. Of course, said the Shaikh; it was all a misunderstanding. And that was the end of the affair as far as we were concerned. I withdrew the Scouts squadron, we drove back to Sharjah and told Shaikh Khaled what had happened. He was grateful; it was now over to him to sort out his recalcitrant subjects.

Back at my house David drank rather more gin and tonic than was probably good for him, before returning to Dubai. It had been a hot and rather tricky morning, but very illustrative of the role of the TOS: a request by a Ruler to the British Political Agent to help him sort out an internal matter which, without some muscle of his own, he could not do. It was of course the appearance of the PA plus a squadron of Scouts that cut him off from the interior which decided the recalcitrant Shaikh to call it a day.

In May we were visited by the new Emir of Kuwait, who had succeeded the great Abdulla Salem al Sabah on his death in 1965. He was touring the Lower Gulf to see how some of his 'have-not' brothers were faring. Oil had been flowing in Kuwait since shortly after the war and the Ruler was already immensely rich. He chose to lunch with Shaikh Rashid of Ajman, the old pirate whose Shaikhdom was about the size of a postage stamp. Though I attended the feast I do not know what passed between Rulers. Rashid must have received a handsome *pourboire*, not to mention prestige at having been selected as host. He was inevitably the poorest and therefore the most pro-British of all the

Rulers. On a visit to England he demanded to see the Queen — as an absolute monarch in his own territory he was entitled to ask this favour. The Foreign Office somehow fobbed him off with a conducted tour of Scotland instead.

Another distinguished visitor was King Hussain of Jordan, then aged only thirty. Shaikh Rashid of Dubai hosted the reception for him in the evening and we Brits wore civilian suits. Jordan is not of course oil-rich and I imagine that Hussain was on tour to meet the many Jordanians working in the Gulf as school masters or civil servants.

Among the many VIP visitors from the UK was the Minister of Defence for Administration, the Rt Hon. G.W. Reynolds MP, a young and extremely friendly Labour politician. It happened that his accompanying staff of three were all serving or had served in the Brigade of Guards, and my RSM, Mr M. Nicholas of the Coldstream Guards, in whose Mess the Minister lunched, arranged a gathering of former Guardsmen serving in the Lower Gulf.

Another trip that I was able to fit in involved sailing across the Straits of Hormuz to Bandar Abbas in Iran in the Scouts' dhow. An Australian couple who worked for BP in Sharjah, Les and Liz Rowe, were returning from UK leave and driving out overland in a new Mercedes. I had got to know them well through playing tennis on their court in the relative cool of the evenings.

A new dhow was being built for the Scouts and would be ready in July when Les and his wife were due at Bandar Abbas, so I offered to sail over and fetch them. However, as the summer wore on and the dhow neared completion I wondered whether I hadn't been a bit rash to have made that offer. It was obviously going to be extremely hot and not exactly a pleasure cruise. There were also tiresome complications over passports and visas owing to the Iranian claim to sovereignty over Bahrain. I had to have a passport clear of Bahrain visas, and also theoretically a permit to land. In addition the British Embassy in Teheran required all sorts of details about why I was going, the size and shape of my dhow and the composition of its crew.

Eventually however, armed with a shiny new passport, a *laissez passer* to the Governor of Bandar Abbas from his friend Shaikh Rashid of Dubai, and accompanied by Khan and Alex, I boarded the dhow in Sharjah creek, one hot Sunday evening. We were to sail on the high tide. The crew were all Arab and consisted basically of one family: two elderly brothers, their sons, one of whom, Ahmed, was the *nakhoda* (skipper) and various nephews and cousins — eight in all including a boy of about ten. Navigation was officially by an old ship's compass fitted into a small wooden box near the tiller; in practice, the *nakhoda* steered by instinct, the stars and sightings of land. No charts were carried and the only navigation light was an electric light bulb attached to the top of the flagstaff at the stern.

I had taken the precaution of consulting a Scouts officer who was an experienced ocean sailor. He had borrowed a chart for me and marked on it what appeared to him to be the best course with bearings and distances.

Immediately after crossing the bar at the mouth of Sharjah creek we ran into quite a stiff northerly breeze and began to pitch, which continued most of the night. After consultation with the *nakhoda* I decided to hug the Arabian coast until dawn and then turn north to cross the main shipping lane in daylight and arrive in Bandar Abbas about midday. The night passed uneventfully except for one anxious moment when we had a near collision with what turned out to be a Pakistani gold-smuggling dhow making for Dubai. We were virtually without navigation lights so I felt that the fault was more ours than theirs.

As dawn broke I rolled up my bedding where I had been sleeping on deck and checked our position against the jagged mountains which form the tip of this corner of Arabia. We passed within sight of the old naval coaling station dating from the Kaiser's war at Jazirat al Ghanam (the island of sheep) and then turned north to cross the shipping lane. I had been told by my old naval friend, Admiral Kyrle Pope, who had the unusual job of running the Persian Gulf Lighthouse Company, that about twenty-six ships passed through the Straits of Hormuz every twenty-four hours. I wondered whether this was an understatement since I counted at least six ships in as many minutes, some full of oil steaming east and others in ballast entering the Gulf.

By this time the wind had dropped and we were able to enjoy a smooth passage up to Qeshm, the long narrow island which guards the entrance to Bandar Abbas Bay. Ahmed and his family had taken it in turns to steer during the night. I had occasionally checked the bearing on the compass, but it was an unnecessary precaution. Once the helmsman had decided on a particular course he would make fast the tiller in the correct position by securing it with rope to one of the uprights on the poop. It might be described as a primitive counterpart to the automatic pilot installed in aircraft and known as 'George', the main difference being of course that the tiller could not itself make corrections.

There was an air of expectancy on board that morning as we chugged steadily north and the Iranian coast became clearer. Most of the crew had been on the trip before but it was obviously a bit of a jaunt, nevertheless. Almost exactly at midday and seventeen and a half hours out of Sharjah, we tied up at the rather rickety jetty at Bandar Abbas. I went ashore to be told that my friends had arrived the previous day and were staying with a Dutch engineering consultant about five miles out of town. After a visit to the imposing Police HQ where my smart new passport was immediately taken away, I took a taxi out to the Dutchman's house and found my friends, who were very relieved to know that we had arrived. We decided to sail back the following day as soon as their car was safely loaded — nothing happens in Arabia after midday as it is too hot.

We were down at the jetty by seven the next morning ready for loading the car. Les had been told that the lifting facilities were perfectly adequate but he had taken the precaution of asking me to bring some extra steel bars and chains to fit under the wheels. The crane itself proved pretty gimcrack and local lifting gear was almost non-existent. Despite the bits and pieces that I had brought, it was a most tricky and anxious business loading that Mercedes; perhaps we would not have worried quite so much if it had not been brand new and worth all of £3,000 at home (£30,000 today).

Most of the hangers-on of Bandar Abbas seemed to be on the jetty that morning and our job was not made any easier by tipper lorries full of magnesite loading a barge which was tied up next to our dhow. It was also of course extremely hot. After about two hours of gesticulation and manipulation the dramatic moment came when the crane took the strain and the car was swung out onto the dhow. It seemed to slip slightly just above the deck and landed with a bit of a bump, but no damage was done and it fitted like a glove across the beam amidships. Les decided that lashing down was unnecessary and in the event he was proved right, though I had qualms at the time.

We had an extra passenger for the return trip — an Arab who said that he was a *muttawa* (religious man) from Sharjah and had been convalescing from some dire internal complaint at Kerman in the mountains 300 miles north of Bandar Abbas. He had asked for a lift and when I agreed became embarrassingly attentive to my every want, insisting on accompanying me to Police HQ to recover my passport and later trying to assist Les over the final clearance of his car. On my return he appeared at my office in Sharjah asking for a job. I discovered eventually that he was quite well known locally and was thought to be slightly wrong in the head.

We finally sailed at about 11 a.m. with the sea glassy and not a breath of wind. It was all the more surprising, therefore, when we ran into a stiff southwesterly breeze after clearing the sheltered waters round Qeshm. We began to pitch and spray was coming over the precious Mercedes. Les, his wife and I were sitting in wicker chairs just aft of the car and so were well protected from the wind and spray. After a chat with the *nakhoda* I decided that we should steer straight into the wind, anyhow until dusk, in the hope that it would drop by then. The wind did drop but not until after dark. I was possibly more worried about the car than Les. He remained quite unmoved and assured me that it was firmly wedged between the gunwhales. He was right. Like all good Mercedes she rocked slightly on her springs but otherwise remained as unmoved as her owner.

I was determined to cross the shipping lane in daylight though the crew did not appear to regard 100,000-ton tankers as a hazard at all. About half an hour before dark we accordingly turned east and soon spotted the tankers; several monsters ploughed past and then it was dark and we were clear. The night was a short one as we saw the lights of Sharjah at 2 a.m. and entered Dubai creek at 4 a.m. We had to go to Dubai as there were positively no facilities for off-loading cars at Sharjah. It was an unusual experience arriving at that time of the night; the customs and immigration offices were not unnaturally closed so we chugged quietly up the creek and anchored until the respectable hour of seven.

Clearing the car proved a simple business in the end and I was impressed by the speed and efficiency with which off-loading took place. My last memory of this expedition is of Les driving me the ten miles to Sharjah in the Mercedes. I must have driven this route hundreds of times, but never in such comfort and so fast.

My last winter 'season' as COMTOS included a major training exercise with 16 Parachute Brigade who were flown out, less the 3rd Battalion already at Bahrain. They made a night drop in the central plain east of Sharjah after only the briefest of stopovers in Bahrain. Roly Gibbs* was then commanding the brigade and dropped with them. Being one of the exercise-directing staff, I collected Roly off the DZ. He told me that if you are over forty, over twelve stone and over six feet you should not parachute. He was all three, but jumped with the best of them.

On one occasion, I was taken up in a trainer Hunter by RAF Sharjah. When we were at about 20,000 feet the pilot said to me casually on the intercom: 'Would you like to fly upside down?' I could hardly say no so over we went. The first thing that happened was a cascade of

*Later Field Marshal Sir Roland Gibbs, Chief of the General Staff.

sand all over me which had accumulated in the cockpit area. I then felt the urge to hold on to something and grabbed a red handle sticking up between my legs. Had I pulled it hard I would have ejected upside down, which might have been uncomfortable. Fortunately my pilot saw what was happening and told me in no uncertain language to let go, assuring me at the same time that I was not likely to fall out. It was fun while it lasted (I think).

1966 was overshadowed by two events: the retirement of Sir William Luce from the Diplomatic Service in June, and the deposition of Shaikh Shakhbut of Abu Dhabi in August. The two are connected to the extent that Bill Luce tried throughout his remaining months in office to persuade Shakhbut either to spend his already vast wealth on development, or to hand over rulership to his charismatic brother Zaid, who was Governor and Ruler's representative in Al Ain, the most important of the six Abu Dhabi villages in the Buraimi oasis.

Sadly, Luce was unable to achieve this last diplomatic coup. He was widely respected by rulers throughout the Gulf and if anyone could move Shakhbut, he could; but Shakhbut remained convinced that every contract, whether it was for roads, hospitals, harbours, schools, housing, desalination plants or drainage, was suspect, and that he would be fleeced. I remember that he ordered a Rolls Royce (I cannot imagine why), which naturally got stuck in the sand. Shakhbut immediately assumed that he had bought a dud. I suspect that a Rolls is not designed to take sand tyres, and wonder whether in this particular case Shakhbut may have been badly advised.

I laid on a very special parade for Sir William when he came down to Sharjah to say goodbye on June 25th. We were of course by then well into the hot weather, and I knew that he was very tired and not in the best of health. However, he was determined to go through with the ceremonial, wearing his full dress white uniform and topee. As the Queen's representative he was entitled to a Royal Salute, which we were very pleased to give him. Our band played such tunes as 'The Barren Rocks of Aden' and 'The Green Hills of Tyrol' (the last sounds singularly inappropriate). The Parade was over by 9 a.m. and we retired to the Mess for breakfast. All the Rulers attended the Parade — except Shakhbut.

I was extremely sorry to say goodbye to Bill Luce, a man whom I, like many others, respected enormously, and sensed as I had in Aden that we were perhaps seeing the last of the great British pro-consuls. However, five years later both he and I were to be recalled from retirement to help with the withdrawal of the British military presence from the Gulf.

To describe what happened in Abu Dhabi that August I cannot do better than quote from John Bulloch's book, *The Gulf:** 'With the memory of what had happened in Sharjah still green, Shaikh Zaid decided in June 1966 to take an extended holiday in Britain . . . Meanwhile things were happening back in Abu Dhabi; there was a family meeting, and decisions were taken. As a result, Shaikh Zaid, the man unanimously chosen to succeed his brother, had quiet discussions with Glen Balfour-Paul, the immensely experienced Acting Resident in the Gulf, who duly went to Abu Dhabi on the morning of August 6th, and as protocol and courtesy demanded, immediately went to call on the Ruler, who was in his Palace. Shaikh Shakhbut appeared to have no inkling of what was coming, and settled down happily for coffee and a chat with his unexpected guest. Instead, he was abruptly faced with the news that the senior members of his family had decided that the time had come for a change, and that they wanted him to step down, a move which the Resident felt bound to say, would also be welcomed by Her Majesty's Government.

'Shaikh Shakbut was angry at first, and ridiculed the idea of any change; but as Balfour-Paul firmly explained to him the family thinking — and mentioned that all the senior figures in the al Nahayan clan were waiting at a nearby police station to hear his decision — reason prevailed. It would be far better to retire with dignity than to be hustled away like a criminal, the Resident suggested, and Shaikh Shakhbut reluctantly agreed. The Ruler left quietly for Bahrain with the Resident, then soon afterwards moved on to live for a while in Khorramshahr in a demonstration of his close links with Iran, before returning to Abu Dhabi and taking up permanent residence in Buraimi.'

Shaikh Zaid, like the Foreign Office, honestly believed that his brother was the main obstacle to the provision of a better life not only for the people of Abu Dhabi, but of the whole Gulf. As early as 1965 some of the far-sighted people in London had realised that at some time in the future there would have to be a form of federation among all the tiny statelets of the Gulf if they were to survive in the world: the removal of Shakhbut was a vital prerequisite for such a move, for Abu Dhabi then was the only one of the Emirates of the Lower Gulf producing oil in any quantity, and it would obviously be needed as the source of revenue for other States as well, if more oil were not discovered. Shaikh Shakhbut would never have allowed his money to go to other States, as he bitterly opposed most expenditure in his own, so he had to go. It was all done quite peaceably, with the announcement

*Century Publishing, London, 1984, pp.24-25

by the al Nahayan family that Shaikh Shakhbut had been deposed 'for failing to create an efficient administration, failing to govern, and not using the country's wealth for the benefit of the people'.

I had taken elaborate military precautions in case anything went wrong. Happily they were not needed and that evening Zaid hosted a huge banquet. It was appropriately not held at the palace. Everybody who counted in Abu Dhabi was there (except the First XI Brits who were on summer leave).

So ended the second bloodless coup during my term of office as COMTOS. It is pleasing to recall that after a short exile in Bahrain and later Iran Shakhbut returned to the Abu Dhabi Shaikhdom; Zaid welcomed him with open arms and invited him to live in honourable retirement in Al Ain, which he did until his death in 1989 at the age of eighty-three. One year he attended the Queen's Birthday Party in Abu Dhabi so it would seem that he bore us no grudge.

The children came out for their last Christmas holidays in this very unrestricted 'playground' (for them) and we went for a family trip in a dhow round the top of the Musandam Peninsula, with some special regimental friends then stationed in Bahrain: David Goddard had been one of our most successful platoon commanders in Malaya and he joined us with his charming wife Sue, their two children and Sue's sister Ann. The cruise involved sailing into the Elphinstone inlet once more, going ashore at Jazirat al Ghanam and then sailing right round the rocky peninsula which forms the tip of this corner of Arabia, and into the Indian Ocean. We then cruised down the east coast for seventy-five miles and went ashore at Khor Fakkan (in Sharjah territory), where there was a lovely sandy beach. We had a tent with us (more to provide shade than anything else) and Khan and Alex administered to our needs. We slept in rows on deck for two nights, and one night on the beach at Khor Fakkan. It was a very happy last jaunt which I still remember well.

In April BOAC had opened a weekly VC10 service from London to Dubai. We were all invited to watch the inaugural landing from the roof of the tiny airport building. Would the runway stand up to the weight of a large jet? There was polite applause as the VC10 came smoothly to a halt. However, the children's return by plane to school was not without drama. Driving to the airport across the *sabkha* from Sharjah, I said casually, "You've both got your passports, I suppose?" No, Caroline had not got hers. We turned round and roared back. About half an hour later we arrived at Dubai. The VC10 was there, the passenger steps had been removed and the engines had been started. Fortunately the steps up to the cockpit were still in position. I clambered over the barrier in front of the airport building and ran up the steps to the cockpit. The captain was understanding and the children were allowed on board, Caroline by this time in tears. It was an emotional moment and one which can only happen in a place such as Arabia.

In the same year came the opening of a tarmac road from Sharjah to Dubai, at which all the Rulers were present; Shaikh Rashid of Dubai ceremonially cut the tape.

In January 1967 John Cousens, a young gunner officer aged twenty-six serving with the Scouts, flew a Percival Prentice solo to Sharjah from the UK. He had applied for a further tour and was therefore entitled to home leave. Unknown to me he actually bought the aircraft in the UK and flew it out. Unfortunately he was badly delayed in Baghdad when the engine went u/s, and the offending part had to be flown out from home, which took time. John left the UK on September 27th, 1966 and touched down at Sharjah on January 7th, 1967, a rather longer flight than he (or I) had anticipated, having considerably overstayed his leave. He was typical of the enterprising young officers who volunteered for service with the Scouts.

Others were Anthony ffrench-Blake of the 13/18 Hussars who had already represented the Army on the Cresta run at St Moritz, and Allan Ramsay* of the Somersets who learnt Arabic properly, transferred to the Diplomatic Service and has already served as HM Ambassador in Beirut and Khartoum.

Sir Stewart Crawford, the new PR, had taken over in September 1966 and toured the Lower Gulf shortly afterwards. Unlike the majority of British diplomats serving in senior posts in the Middle East, he was not an Arabist in the strict sense of the word but was quick to learn. David Roberts and I took him around the Shaikhdoms. One call that I particularly remember, and it typified the scene, was on Shaikh Muhammed of Fujairah (Fudge). His palace near the Indian Ocean coast flew a Union Jack from the roof for the occasion and he and the PR were photographed together underneath it.

Shortly before my three years in command were up I was told by the British Consul-General Muscat, Bill Carden, that the Ruler Sultan Said bin Taimur was looking for an Organisation and Methods Adviser, and might I be interested? I was certainly interested, despite the family

*Now Sir Allan Ramsay, KBE, CMG, HM, Ambassador Rabat.

upheaval that such a job would entail. The RAF flew me down to
Salala, some 500 miles south of Muscat where the Sultan lived in almost
total seclusion. He received me very politely and we talked for perhaps
an hour with only an interpreter present.

I heard nothing until June by which time we were back in England.
The job was off, which was probably just as well from the family point
of view and the fact that Said bin Taimur was to be deposed three years
later.

Early in February, a week or so before we left, Sir Stewart asked me
to fly up to Bahrain to say goodbye. He and his wife put me up for the
night and Sir Stewart made some generous remarks about my period in
command.

I was due to hand over to my successor Pat Ive, a 17/21 Lancer, in
mid-February. Simone and I had decided some time earlier that we
would buy a Land Rover and drive home via Iran and Turkey, entering
Europe at Istanbul. We had to be back in time for the Easter holidays;
otherwise we might be unpopular with the children. Through the agents
in Dubai I ordered a short-wheel base Land Rover with canvas top at an
agreed price of £750. It had to be shipped out in a crate. On arrival in
Bahrain in January it was transferred to a dhow to be shipped to Dubai.
As I already knew, even the placid waters of the Gulf can turn nasty
and I heard afterwards that the dhow's *nakhoda* nearly pushed the crate
overboard on the passage south as his vessel was rolling so much. I duly
took delivery at Dubai early in February and told my REME workshop
to check it over, which they did most efficiently. New Land Rovers
were rare birds.

We finally sailed once more for Bandar Abbas on February 15th in
the new Scouts dhow, with our precious Land Rover lashed down
amidships. Our ceremonial departure was traditional and moving. My
official Land Rover was towed from our house by officers escorted by
the ponies, there was a large crowd of well-wishers down at Sharjah
creek plus our band, and catamarans from the sailing club escorted us
out to sea.

It had been an exciting three years: I had had more responsibility
than anybody of comparable rank in Europe, but being rather out on
a limb it was not the sort of job from which one might expect
promotion, as I knew from the beginning. It was fun, I was there at a
time when the British presence still meant a great deal, and we felt that
we were needed. It was peacetime soldiering at its best.

CHAPTER 23

Interlude at Greenwich and Shorncliffe

OUR drive home overland took six weeks and put some six thousand miles on the clock of our new Land Rover. It was an experience that neither of us will forget. We drove from temperatures of 80°F in the Lower Gulf to well below freezing in northern Iran and eastern Turkey, a fortnight later. Driving an unheated Land Rover with only a canvas hood was not the most comfortable method of travel on unmetalled roads which were often covered in several inches of snow.

In Persia, we marvelled at the sixth-century BC city of Persepolis, the blue and pink mosaics of the mosques and the abundance of rugs everywhere. We looked at them being made in Tabriz, bought a prayer mat in Isfahan and a pair of blue Kashans in Teheran. We seemed to eat nothing but *cheloh kebab* and frequently slept in dirty sheets.

We gazed at snow-covered Mount Ararat (17,044 feet) far away on the Russian frontier, where Noah's Ark is said to have rested after the Great Flood and which somewhat more recently was the route that Philby took when defecting to Russia in 1963. In eastern Turkey we crossed passes at eight thousand feet and discovered why the Black Sea got its name.

We tunnelled under the Alps in Austria, skied for a week at Bad Gastein and stayed with friends for a day or two at HQ BAOR. Finally at Dover we had a mild altercation with HM Customs who thought that our Land Rover, an export model on which we had not paid purchase tax, could hardly be classified as 'agricultural' as the canvas hood had talc windows. When we offered to remove the hood and give it to them, the matter was dropped.

As planned, we were just in time to extract our children from their respective schools for the Easter holidays.

My next posting was to attend the Senior Officers' War Course at Greenwich from April to July 1967. It was a refresher course for all three Services and proved a pleasant low-key interlude. We visited service establishments including Northern Ireland and Barrow-in-Furness where the first Polaris boat was then being built, and were lectured by

213

distinguished public figures including Denis Healey and Enoch Powell, who conveyed somewhat differing views on defence. Probably the most forward-looking of the talks, though I hardly understood a word at the time, was one on cybernetics which heralded the advent of the microchip.

The setting of the Royal Naval College at Greenwich is superb, and in particular the Painted Hall, one of Christopher Wren's most famous masterpieces, where we had our meals, waited upon by WRNS.

During the course I heard that I was to be made a CMG* in the Birthday Honours. This order is normally only given to members of the Diplomatic Service, and was in recognition of the political side of my job in the Gulf. I was naturally very pleased — and indeed surprised.

It was while I was at Greenwich that the Six Day war waged by Egypt, Jordan and Syria against Israel resulted in the total defeat of the Arabs, and Israel's annexation of the West Bank, Sinai and the Gaza Strip as well as the Golan Heights. At the time it all seemed rather remote but I heard afterwards that there were serious demonstrations in the Gulf against the British presence. Inevitably, after 1956 it was assumed that we were somehow involved on the Israeli side.

After Greenwich I was posted to Shorncliffe, just outside Folkestone, as Colonel in charge of Administration, South East District. It was not a very exciting appointment but I was told that it would not be for long as another job in the Arab world was likely to come up shortly. I was fifty-one and a further overseas posting would probably be my last before retirement, which was compulsory at fifty-five for most officers.

From the family's point of view Shorncliffe was fun as we were allotted a large Regency house which the Army had acquired. It was situated away from Shorncliffe Camp tucked under a hill and was appropriately called Underhill House. A gardener and cleaning lady were also provided. We only had five months there but they were happy ones; David, just turning seventeen, learnt to drive in the Land Rover. He had already had a go in the desert around Sharjah; now it was on almost empty military roads round Shorncliffe Camp.

In November we all attended another investiture at which HM The Queen gave me the neck order of the CMG.

---

*Companion of St Michael and St George.

CHAPTER 24

Quasi Diplomat in Cairo

SHORTLY after Christmas I was asked whether I would go out to Cairo as Defence and Military Attaché. I accepted, knowing that this would be a challenging appointment as HMG had only just resumed diplomatic relations with Egypt. Sir Harold Beeley, who had been British Ambassador from 1961-64, was reappointed and I would be required to re-establish the Attaché office in the Embassy from scratch.

Service Attachés have often been described as 'gentlemen spies' and there is a slight element of truth in this pseudonym. As serving officers they are part of the British mission of which the Ambassador is head, and are granted diplomatic status. Within this broad parameter they have three important roles: firstly representational, which simply means attending endless diplomatic functions in the foreign capital to which they are accredited, and of course hosting a good many dinner and drinks parties in return; secondly, overt intelligence-gathering regarding the armed forces of the country and reporting back to the Ministry of Defence in London; and thirdly defence sales, which means encouraging the country to buy British arms and defence equipment and generally helping with the sale where one is to take place. All three roles do not always apply — the country may well be buying from another foreign power, as indeed was the case in Egypt in 1968: she had been equipped with Russian arms since before Suez in 1956.

I attended a short briefing course in London in January, and we then packed up at Shorncliffe and repacked for what were to be three very social years. As hard liquor and wine (other than the local brew) were virtually unobtainable in Cairo we had to order several cases to be shipped with our 'heavy' luggage. Fortunately it was all tax free, as was a small Vauxhall Viva which we bought new and drove out as far as Genoa, where we boarded an Italian cruise liner which took both us and the car to Alexandria. It was the first long sea voyage that we had undertaken since the *Windrush* fourteen years earlier, and was a very relaxing few days in considerable luxury.

At the end of March we landed in Egypt and drove across the desert to Cairo in a minor sandstorm — quite like old times. On our arrival

215

the Embassy staff were extremely kind and helpful, particularly Patrick Wright,* Head of Chancery, whose father had been one of my tutors at Wellington. We were put up in the Semiramis Hotel (one of the famous old Cairo hotels) for a few days whilst a flat could be found, and David and Caroline were flown out 'on the Army' to join us for the Easter holidays. Quite soon we found a very nice old-fashioned, rather ornate 'apartment' (as opposed to a mere flat) on the Corniche-el-Nil overlooking the river, and quite close to the British Embassy. One floor below us was the Peruvian Ambassador. I'm not sure why Peru boasted an Embassy in Cairo but their man was certainly not overworked, judging from his leisurely lifestyle.

The first months saw me fully occupied starting up a completely new office on the top floor of our Embassy, calling on all the other embassies' service attachés, of whom there were over thirty, and trying to break the ice with the Egyptian military. The latter task was far and away the most difficult and the most important, as Sir Harold Beeley pointed out. The problem in a nutshell was that Egypt** was still trying to recover from the disastrous Six Day war with Israel, which had taken place only nine months before I arrived in Cairo. Although Britain was in no way involved, the memories of Suez twelve years earlier were still very strong. Russian influence was evident everywhere and particularly in the armed forces. They had a large Embassy in Cairo and a very considerable number of military 'technicians' spread throughout the army, navy and airforce. SAM† sites were located all round Cairo, covering key installations in the Nile Delta. The Suez Canal was a military zone barred to foreign diplomats, and particularly service attachés (except Russian). The whole of the Sinai Peninsula (Egyptian territory) was occupied by Israel.

Egypt was still officially at war with Israel and there were regular air battles over the Canal. Egyptian communiqués invariably told us that several Israeli fighters had been shot down without loss, claims which we took with a hefty pinch of salt. Russian warships used the dockyard facilities at Alexandria; these too were forbidden territory to foreign diplomats.

On a more personal level my staff car, which like all diplomatic vehicles had distinctive green number plates, was discreetly followed

*Later Lord Wright of Richmond, GCMG, Head of the Diplomatic Service.
**The country was officially known as the United Arab Republic. I prefer to use the universally-known Egypt, particularly since the Union with Syria had come to an end in 1961.
†Surface-to-air missile.

whenever we ventured outside Cairo, which we could do to certain approved places, but only after clearance. And of course our telephone was tapped.

Readers might wonder how we ever discovered what was going on; at Ambassador level however, the Egyptian authorities had to say something, and some attachés were luckier than others. Sovbloc and Arab diplomats were obviously told a lot more than we were. Although the United States had no formal diplomatic relations with Egypt throughout our three years there, they provided development aid in various fields and had a number of friendly and diplomatic contacts with officialdom.

That first summer I was allowed to call on Lieutenant General Abdul Moneim Riad, Chief of the General Staff, who had commanded the Jordanian Army during the Six Day war. He was friendly and I came away from our first meeting feeling that I just might be able to establish a personal relationship. Sadly, he was killed by a stray shell when visiting the Canal Zone in March 1969.

To turn the clock back briefly, there had undoubtedly been a love-hate relationship between Britain and Egypt which began in the 1880s when Cromer was Consul-General, wielding no executive authority but in effect acting as British trustee of the Egyptian people for some twenty-four years. When he retired in 1907 he left a country rich, contented and self-confident. Kitchener, though he spent only three years as 'trustee', was widely respected. With the outbreak of World War I Egypt was declared a protectorate and the last vestiges of Turkish suzerainty abolished.

By 1918 the first serious demands for independence were emerging; Egypt resented not being invited to the Versailles Peace Conference whereas certain Arab countries whom they considered greatly inferior to themselves were. Allenby's six years as High Commissioner (1919-1925) were far from easy even though it was he who persuaded the British Government to abolish the protectorate and recognise Egypt as an independent state. In 1922 Sultan Fuad was proclaimed the first king of an independent Egypt; yet only two and a half years later Sir Ian Stack, the British Commander-in-Chief of the Egyptian army, was assassinated. Somewhat unexpectedly Lord Lloyd, Allenby's successor, experienced four years of peace and stability and by 1936 a National Government in Britain was at last able to conclude a treaty of alliance under which the British 'occupation' was ended and was reduced to a military presence in the Suez Canal Zone; and at the same time the Egyptian government recognised the vital importance of the Canal as an international waterway.

Such had been the situation when I arrived in Egypt at the start of World War II. Farouk, Fuad's son, was King but wielded little power. Sir Miles Lampson* was British Ambassador and a very dominant figure; and the geographical position of Egypt, through whose territory ran the vital sea link to India and Australasia, made it the obvious British Middle East base throughout the' War.

From 1939-'43 I was to come and go through Cairo on numerous occasions, never sensing any real hostility to our greatly enlarged military presence; I am particularly reminded of the loyalty of the Egyptians to the Allied cause at the time of the Italian charioteer attack on the QE and *Valiant* in Alexandria harbour, and when Rommel was almost at the gates of Alexandria in July 1942.

Between the end of World War II and the Suez crisis in 1956 eleven years later, the British aim was simply to keep a relatively small garrison in the Canal Zone to protect the international highway; the Egyptian aim, on the other hand, was to be rid of British troops as quickly as possible. There was serious rioting in 1952 when Shepheard's Hotel and other symbols of British rule in Cairo were sacked and burnt down. Six months later, King Farouk was forced to abdicate and a military government took over. In 1954 Nasser began his remarkable reign as a military dictator which was to last until his death sixteen years later in 1970. Almost his first act (on July 27th, 1954) was to negotiate a rather flimsy agreement with HMG, under which all British troops would be withdrawn within twenty months and equipment in the Canal Zone base would be maintained by contractors. Almost exactly two years later Nasser was to nationalise the Suez Canal Company and create by far the most serious crisis in British-Arab relations this century.

To return to Cairo in 1968: HMG once more had diplomatic relations with Egypt and there was no doubt that our Ambassador got on well with Nasser. Beeley was not an Arabist; he did not speak Arabic, his background was academic and the Egyptian Government thus felt that they could trust him. However, his staff in the Embassy were mostly Arabists and I, with my background in Aden and the Gulf, was inevitably regarded with suspicion, though we all bent over backwards to be friendly. I knew that it was going to be difficult to break the ice, and so it proved.

There were several occasions when I thought that we were winning, only to be rebuffed. During our first winter (1968-'69) we used to motor

*Later Lord Killearn.

up to Fayoum (an oasis area sixty miles from Cairo) to shoot duck and snipe. We needed clearance, of course, and were undoubtedly under surveillance. We made friends with an Egyptian family who had a weekend villa down there, and stayed with them on several occasions. Quite suddenly, for no apparent reason, we were told that they could not see us again. I met an Egyptian of the old school at the Gezira Club and played tennis with him. That link also suddenly went dead.

In the summer of 1968 Simone and I took a trip to the Western Desert as far as Sollum on the Libyan frontier, which I had managed to clear with the authorities. By this time I was the proud possessor of an official hard top Land Rover. Off we went along that endless switchback coast road, the life line of the Eighth Army throughout the war in the desert, followed at a discreet distance by Egyptian security men in a car. We stopped at Maaten Bagush and I succeeded, with some local Bedouin help, in finding what was left of our dug-out complex in the sand dunes. At one point when we turned off the tarmac road and took to the sand our faithful 'escort' got stuck and we obliged by towing them out. Embarrassing for them; amusing for us.

The children flew out to join us for the summer holidays and we were able to rent a villa on the excellent beach at Agami, west of Alexandria. We were of course allowed into Alex (but not the dockyard) although we were invariably followed.

In October I found myself responsible for organising an interesting ceremony: wreath-laying at the three memorials at Alamein to commemorate the dead. The memorials are all characteristic of their countries: the British and Commonwealth is a large enclosed graveyard with headstones and bougainvillaea, designed to resemble a cloistered garden, with a memorial cross in the centre; the German is a huge dark granite structure resembling a fortress, all the names of the dead being carved on the interior of the granite walls; and the Italian is almost cathedral-like, marble everywhere, full of light, and with the names delicately carved on white walls.

Protocol required that the Ambassadors of the three countries, accompanied by their Service Attachés, should each lay wreaths at all three memorials. We were then expected to visit the Egyptian Alamein museum — which made those with a sketchy knowledge of the desert war think that it was really the Egyptians who won the battle. We then all lunched together. This ceremony still continues; Monty visited Alamein before he died, and I suspect lectured the Egyptian military on what had really happened, and his son and Rommel's son both attended the fiftieth anniversary in 1992.

By a strange coincidence, also in 1992, when staying in a mountain hut in the Austrian Alps I met a German who worked for Mannfred Rommel, the Field Marshal's son and now Oberbürgermeister of Stuttgart. I said that I had fought against his boss's famous father in North Africa. About a month later I received a letter from Mannfred Rommel sending greetings and enclosing photographs of his father and himself!

In November I was joined by Robert Irving (Commander, RN) as Naval Attaché. His main brief was to report on Russian naval movements into and out of Alexandria, no easy task as the dockyard was strictly out of bounds.

That first Christmas the children again flew out and we drove up the Nile to Luxor and Aswan in the Land Rover, and then through the mountains to the Red Sea at Hurghada where we camped for a day or two on the beach and spent most of the time in the sea. Our faithful followers found it quite difficult to hide on that barren open coastline but they stuck it out whilst we enjoyed ourselves.

Looking back on my first year in Cairo I wondered what had been achieved. What did I know about the Egyptian military? Had they learnt the lessons of the Six Day War? What was really happening at the front on the Canal where Egypt was still officially at war with Israel? How many Russian military 'advisers' were there in Egypt, and to what extent did they control affairs?

These were the questions to which the MOD in Whitehall wanted answers, and frankly I did not know them. I could only guess. I had not been allowed to visit a single army unit; the Canal Zone was completely out of bounds. The Egyptian communiqués were obviously inaccurate. If one was to believe them, the Israeli Air Force had almost ceased to exist.

I was obliged to rely more and more on views expressed by other Service Attachés: the French and Canadian who were on their own, and the three Italians were probably the most useful. Although I drove extensively over the parts of the country that were in bounds, there was little of military interest to see. SAM sites were visible at long range but we had little idea to what extent they were manned by Russians. We often saw long military vehicles in the streets covered with drapes which concealed missiles — not particularly informative. It was all very frustrating.

In the spring of 1969 Ted Hamilton (Wing Commander, RAF) joined Robert and me, and we became a complete inter-service team. Both Robert and Ted were inquisitive and not unsuccessful. I daresay the Egyptian Military Office that was supposed to look after attachés regarded us as a pain in the neck; however they were pretty successful at preventing us seeing or even hearing about anything of real military significance.

During his summer holiday down at Agami that year Robert Irving's car was stolen one night from its garage under the house whilst he and his wife were asleep. It was recovered a week later having been totally stripped: roof-lining, window-linings, floor coverings, all were torn open, presumably because the authorities suspected that Robert had a secret transmitter set in his car, which of course he had not. Our Embassy registered an official protest, the Egyptians regretted the incident, and that was that.

On another occasion an Egyptian Service Attaché was caught red-handed in London indulging in espionage and declared *persona-non-grata* (PNG) which meant that he had to pack his bags and leave within a week or so. I was warned by our Ambassador that my post would be at risk as a tit-for-tat. Sure enough, the Egyptian authorities suddenly claimed that I had been seen taking photographs in areas which were out of bounds.Fortunately I was able to refute this charge, and we heard no more. But incidents like these showed how careful one had to be.

In 1969 Sir Harold Beeley retired and was relieved as HM Ambassador by Sir Richard Beaumont. The Cairo Embassy ranked as probably the most important in the Arab world. Both men were very able in their different ways, Beeley as an academic, and Beaumont as an Arabist. Beaumont had been up at Oriel just before me which established a link. We used to play golf together before breakfast at Gezira, which was an excellent way of getting to know each other. There was a tennis court at the Embassy and I had a regular mens' doubles with the Italian and Mexican Ambassadors and a very charming senior American official, John Dorman. The Mexican, Manuel to all his many friends, was one of the most popular diplomats in Cairo throughout our time. As with our neighbours downstairs from Peru, I never really understood why Mexico had an Embassy in Cairo but Manuel was a definite asset at any party and knew better than most diplomats what was going on behind closed doors.

Riding was also very popular. The AA stables at the Pyramids had a number of horses for hire and several Embassy families became regular patrons. It was possible to hire one's own special horse on a long-term basis; Simone took advantage of this scheme and was lucky enough to acquire a very nice pony. There were occasional Sunday expeditions into the desert combined with picnic lunches or evening barbecues and one year the Embassy had a gymkhana.

The ancient monuments of the Lower Nile valley and Upper Egypt, in particular those at Luxor, Aswan and Abu Simbel assumed considerable interest to us partly because my old friend Brian Emery, who even before the War was a well known archaeologist, had been elected to the Chair of Egyptology at University College London in 1951, and was later Field Director of the Egypt Exploration Society. His special interest was Saqqara, not far from the Giza Pyramids, and we often joined him during the digging season. He died quite suddenly in Cairo early in 1970; many Egyptians attended his funeral and paid tribute to his work.

We visited Upper Egypt on several occasions by air, rail and road, both officially and with relations out from home. I had to meet Prince Philip twice: at Luxor in 1968 when his aircraft refuelled *en route* to Ethiopia and again in 1970 when his plane refuelled at Aswan. This time the Egyptian authorities showed him the High Dam of which they were immensely proud, built with Russian aid at the time of the Suez crisis. HRH let drop an innocent remark to the effect that he had visited other dams, which did not go down too well while the guide was explaining the wonders of Aswan.

My return journey to Cairo after this visit was slightly alarming. For some reason the regular United Arab Airline service was cancelled (we unkindly called it 'Use Another Airline') and I was offered the last seat in a large Russian transport which was packed with pilgrims returning from the *haj* in Mecca. I was required back in Cairo and so accepted. When I finally squeezed in somewhere near the tail I found that the pilgrims had mountains of luggage of all descriptions parked in the alleyways, and wherever there was a square inch of space. It all looked horribly unsafe, and I began to wish that I had waited for another flight. However, we landed safely at Cairo. The next day an identical Russian transport, also packed with pilgrims, crashed on taking off from Aswan, and there were no survivors. Later, the cause was said to be overweight.

On another occasion, returning from a visit to Cyprus in a scheduled UAA jet, I noticed as we neared the Egyptian coast that we seemed to be rather off course to the east. In no time we were almost over the Canal, the out of bounds front line with Israel. As I craned to get a better view of this strictly forbidden territory the pilot banked sharply to starboard and we were back on course.

The High Dam at Aswan, pride of Egypt in the 1950s, has over the last four decades caused problems that no one seems to have foreseen. Before it was built the Nile flooded annually after monsoon rain hit the

Ethiopian Highlands. I can well remember during the summer of 1940 watching the river rise dramatically and rush under the Cairo bridges on its way to the Med. It brought with it precious silt which was deposited in the flood plain. It also washed away many of the snails which cause bilharzia, a debilitating disease from which Egyptian farmers suffer.

The dam created a huge lake above Aswan (approximately the length of England and half its width), submerging Nubian villages and the original site of the Abu Simbel temple. This famous rock temple was dismantled, cut into separate pieces and rebuilt on top of the rocks above the high water mark. It was a remarkable engineering feat completed in 1968 by an international team of technicians and financed by UNESCO.

The annual flood is no more, farmers in the narrow Nile Valley have to use fertilisers, and bilharzia has increased because snails are thriving in the stagnant water. We now read that winter Nile steamer cruises are at risk because the river is dangerously low, particularly between Luxor and Cairo, where the silt has built up. At diplomatic cocktail parties we used to speculate sometimes, if the High Dam were to burst its banks, how long it would take for Lake Nasser to empty and for the resultant mountain of water to travel the 650 miles to Cairo. Commenting recently, *The Times* talked of the folly of mucking about with nature and added: 'If Isis and Osiris had wanted a dam at Aswan they would have built one'.

For our last year I was offered a detached house in Gezira, one of four owned by the Embassy. They were white Regency style residences with their own gardens in quiet roads lined with jacaranda and flame trees. The house allocated to the Head of Chancery had been occupied twenty-two years earlier by the notorious spy Donald Maclean.

A very colourful personality whom we came to know well was Patricia, the English wife of Hassan Nashat, the former Egyptian Ambassador to Berlin and London in the late 'thirties. He claimed to have known Hitler quite well. On posting to London he met and married Patricia Priest, then a London *débutante*, and took her back to Cairo where they lived in considerable style — the Nashat family had extensive interests in cotton.

When we arrived in Cairo the Nashats were living in a penthouse suite overlooking the Gezira club. Tragically, at the Queen's Birthday Reception in the Embassy garden in June 1969, Hassan collapsed, hit his head on a stone patio and died on the way to hospital. We saw a good deal of Patricia after that. She had four attractive daughters and we attended a wedding reception for one of them in the penthouse flat on one of the hottest days ever experienced in Cairo. In the afternoon the temperature suddenly shot up to 47°C as a hot wind blew through the city. By 9 p.m. when we were due at the reception it was a mere 35°, which was quite hot enough when one had to be smartly dressed.

Much the most dramatic event of our three years in Cairo was Nasser's sudden death on September 28th, 1970. We all knew that he had been in poor health but I don't believe that anybody in the diplomatic circle thought that he was dying. We were at one of the inevitable cocktail parties that took place practically every evening when his death was suddenly announced on the radio. Everybody was thunderstruck.

Nasser's state funeral was one of the most remarkable public occasions that I have ever attended. Heads of State and Heads of Government from all over the world poured into Cairo. HMG was represented by Sir Alec Douglas Home, then Foreign Secretary in Edward Heath's Government; George Brown represented the Labour Party and Sir Richard Beaumont, HM Ambassador, represented the Queen. I was required to be a member of the British delegation.

George Brown was well liked in Cairo despite his human weaknesses. He told me with a chuckle that when he had arrived at his hotel and been taken up to his room by an official, a bottle of Scotch was discreetly produced.

On the day of the funeral we all assembled at the former Egyptian Officers' Club on Gezira Island in the middle of the Nile, where Nasser had originally founded his revolutionary council of officers. It was from here that the coffin, borne on the shoulders of his closest friends, was to begin its long journey through the streets to the mosque in the north-eastern suburbs where it was to lie in state. The hundreds of foreign dignitaries were told that they would be expected to follow the coffin across the Kasr-el-Nil bridge; they could then disperse.

I found myself walking with George Brown. We had barely left the Officers' Club when there was a minor stampede ahead of us and we suddenly saw Anwar Sadat, Acting President of Egypt and Nasser's closest confidante, being carried over the heads of the crowd back to the Club. Apparently he had collapsed from emotion, and was only semi-conscious. Doctors were summoned, the funeral procession was halted and we all wondered what would happen next. Sadat was taken to a private room for medical attention, and a 'receiving line' of senior Government ministers was hurriedly formed, to whom we were expected to express our condolences. That was the end of the funeral as far as foreign delegations were concerned. The Cairo crowd now took over, the coffin was carried by a milling mob across the river and away. Eventually an armoured car was summoned to prevent complete chaos and Nasser completed his journey to the mosque on its top. At least two million people followed the funeral procession, of whom some forty were drowned in the Nile, having fallen off lamp posts or railings. My staff car was commandeered to transport an injured spectator to hospital. Judging by the dents in the roof which we found afterwards, it seemed that he was laid out there, and must have been a heavy man.

For me the day ended with an invitation to join a small lunch party at the Ambassador's residence to meet Sir Alec Douglas-Home. Afterwards I drove members of his staff to the airport. They flew home by VC10 that afternoon and Sir Alec caught the night sleeper to Edinburgh to launch a book that he had just written. Such is a day in the life of a senior government minister.

There was of course immense speculation amongst the diplomatic corps about Nasser's successor. Anwar Sadat, one of the original revolutionaries and Nasser's own chosen successor, seemed a broken reed. But against the betting he recovered quite quickly and came to be regarded by the West as a brave and far-seeing President who had the courage to strike a deal with Israel and end the state of war. Interestingly, we had at one stage during World War II interned him on espionage charges. Sadly, he was assassinated at a military parade in 1981, eleven years later.

Just before Christmas 1970 two crews representing Oxford and Cambridge Universities flew out to take part in the first Nile Rowing Festival. They were to race abreast against crews from Egyptian Universities and the National Police at Luxor. We put up several crew members and I remember that David, out for the Christmas holidays, had quite an evening on the tiles with them. The occasion was later described in the *Times* under the heading: 'Where the Nile flows a lighter shade of blue':

The race experienced problems with the stake boats and the start. The stake boats, a cross between a dhow and a sailing boat, dragged their anchors when the crews were attached to them in the fast-flowing Nile. To counteract the pull of the stream, and the added weight of the boats, the sails were unfurled. A strong head-wind immediately billowed the sails: crews and sailing boats set off in the reverse direction towards Aswan.

After a false start by Oxford, and with a threat of wash from a barge crossing the course, the crews were as ready as they could be in the conditions. The umpire . . . allowed the crews to take a free-standing start. By this time Cambridge were half a length down on Oxford, who found themselves half a length behind the Universities, but a canvas ahead of the Police eight.

... Cambridge came home, rating 33, with Oxford and the Police crew a length farther back providing an exciting finish opposite the Savoy Hotel.

The winning crew were to carry their boat back to Luxor temple as the priests carried the sacred barge with the god Amon to the temple's holy of holies for three weeks' residence during festivities 3,500 years ago. On account of the enthusiastic crowds this exercise was wisely abandoned.

The most interesting non-military personality whom we met frequently in Cairo during 1969-'70 was Claire Hollingworth, then reporting for the *Daily Telegraph*. Claire knew Cairo well as she had arrived from Turkey via Crete in 1941 and had covered the Desert War, managing somehow to visit the front line almost as often as the old hands like Alan Moorehead and Christopher Buckley. After the War she was also in Cairo at the time of Donald Maclean's defection and knew him and his wife well. In her autobiography, *Front Line*, she describes those momentous days though does not reveal whether at the time she believed Maclean was up to no good. Knowing how inquisitive and tenacious she is, I would be very surprised if she did not suspect something.

Two very different personalities lunched with us during our last year: Anthony Nutting who had resigned from the Eden government during the Suez crisis and was researching a book on Nasser which he published in 1972, and Miles Copeland, a former CIA officer and journalist who had been in Beirut when Philby defected and had dined with the Balfour-Pauls that evening. Both were charming and interesting guests.

Among politicians who I was asked to brief in the Embassy were Roy Hattersley who had been a junior Defence Minister in the Wilson government, and Christopher Mayhew (now a life peer) who was to become the chief Liberal Party spokesman on Defence. As far as I can remember there was not a lot that I could tell them that they did not know already.

My tour of duty as Defence Attaché ended in March 1971, exactly three years to the month. I was succeeded by an old friend Tony Lewis, the Commander of the Sultan's Armed Forces in Oman whom I had visited several times from Sharjah. Tony took over the Gezira house and I heard that our relations with the Egyptians gradually improved. Anwar Sadat was moving towards an understanding with Israel and a gradual shift away from Soviet domination, both measures very much in the British interest.

CHAPTER 25

End of Empire in the Gulf

I OFFICIALLY retired from the Army on my fifty-fifth Birthday in 1971, very shortly after returning from Cairo.

We had decided to settle at Gaddesden as my sister-in-law Kitty Pryor had bought the somewhat derelict Old Vicarage from the Church Commissioners, and invited us to be her tenants after it had been redecorated and the roof retiled. We accordingly sold our house at Potten End (unfortunately just before the property market took off) and I got a job as a civil servant in London.

Hardly had I started commuting that summer than I was rung up by the Foreign Office. They asked whether I would consider returning to the Gulf on a contract appointment to act as a link between the Trucial States Rulers and HMG in the purely military field during the removal of British military establishments from the Gulf, which was to be completed by the end of the year as part of a general withdrawal from commitments east of Suez.

It was a very attractive offer which I knew that I would find difficult to refuse though from the domestic point of view it did not suit at all.

To explain the situation in the Gulf in late 1971 I need to put the clock back briefly: during the four years that had elapsed since I handed over command of the Scouts in 1967, dramatic changes in the politico-military scene had been taking place.

HMG's decision to withdraw from Aden by 1968 meant the disappearance of the base on which Britain's military responsibilities in the Gulf had hitherto depended. Yet despite repeated assurances that she had no intention of abandoning the Gulf HMG suddenly announced in January 1968 (just after the final withdrawal from Aden) that a similar withdrawal from the Gulf would be completed by the end of 1971. To quote from Glen Balfour-Paul's recent book, *The End of Empire in the Middle East*[*]: 'This clearly implied, though no formal notification was given at the time, the end of the special relationship which had preser-

[*]Cambridge University Press, 1991, p.124.

ved the Gulf States for 150 years', and caused considerable consternation among the Rulers.

In June 1970 a Conservative Government was, a little unexpectedly, returned to power by the British electorate and was committed by its election manifesto to review the proposed precipitate withdrawal from the Gulf in consultation with Rulers. My former boss, Sir William Luce, was recalled from retirement and instructed by Sir Alec Douglas Home, the Foreign Secretary, to consult the Rulers and Governments concerned and to report his findings on the most appropriate policy to adopt.

No one in my view was better qualified or suitable to carry out this very difficult task. Luce's initial reaction was that the withdrawal announcement made over two years earlier was probably irreversible; and indeed this view was proved correct during his shuttling to and fro in the following eighteen months.

The next step was to encourage the seven Trucial States, and Bahrain and Qatar if possible, to form some sort of union. Luce had to consult not only the Trucial State Rulers but also the Emirs of Bahrain and Qatar, King Faisal of Saudi Arabia and the Shah of Iran. Saudi Arabia had a long standing frontier dispute with Abu Dhabi, and the Shah not only considered that Bahrain was a province of Iran but also laid claim to three islands off the Trucial coast, Abu Musa and the Tunbs, which had been occupied by the Qawasim for over 200 years.

In the event, the Shah was persuaded to relinquish his claim to Bahrain which together with Qatar opted for separate sovereignty and joined the UN; King Faisal came to recognise the value of the union (although he had originally hoped that Bahrain and Qatar could be included), and it was agreed with the Shah that he would share Abu Musa with Sharjah and that the Tunbs would go to Iran. In terms of a median line between the two coasts the Tunbs were on the Iranian side whereas Abu Musa was on the Arab side.

These delicate negotiations were conducted with great skill and endless patience by Luce over some eighteen months and enabled the establishment of a Union of the seven Shaikdoms to be announced amid general jubilation on November 25th, 1971, whilst simultaneously the old individual treaties with Britain were terminated and replaced by a joint Treaty of Friendship. The United Arab Emirates, now generally known as UAE, was admitted to the Arab League on December 6th and to the UN on December 9th.

Oil had now been flowing in Abu Dhabi for nine years and production, both off and on shore, was fast increasing. Dubai's oil income from her one off-shore field was much less but she was the commercial centre of the Lower Gulf and very affluent. There was still a vast difference between the haves and the have-nots; the other five Shaikhdoms were still almost penniless.

To return to the phone call from the Foreign Office: I did not take long to say yes, I would go, even though we were in the middle of moving house, and I had already accepted a lay appointment as County Chairman of the Scouts and the Governorship of a private school, as well as the London job. Sir William Luce briefed me in the Foreign Officer where he said that I could — within reason — take on any rank I chose: would I like to call myself a general?! We agreed that I would be a brigadier and the appointment was initially that of Director Military Liaison Office (DMLO), later to become Chief of Staff to the Minster of Defence UAE.

Antony Acland (later Head of the Diplomatic Service and British Ambassador to Washington) was then Head of the Arabian (later Middle East) Department in the FO. He drew up my contract which was to be signed by Shaikh Zaid, Ruler of Abu Dhabi and President-to-be of the UAE and Shaikh Rashid of Dubai, Vice President-to-be. My salary was agreed at £10,000 p.a. paid in the Gulf and tax-free. At the time it seemed an enormous amount; today a Corporal in the British Army earns more but is taxed. The appointment was initially for one year.

On the way to Sharjah (where I was to be based) I stopped overnight in Bahrain where I was met and put up by my old friend from Cairo, Patrick Wright, then Deputy Political Resident. I was also briefed by Roly Gibbs, then a Major General and Commander British Forces Gulf, who was responsible for the final withdrawal.

The concept of a Military Liaison Office had first been mooted by another old friend, Major General John Willoughby, who had been GOC in Aden for most of my time as COMTOS and had stayed with us in Sharjah on several occasions. He had stressed, and this was repeated to me in Bahrain, that there must be a clear distinction between DMLO and COMTOS; the latter must concentrate on keeping his command intact. It was a delicate situation and I soon realised that I must exercise maximum tact. Roy Watson was now commanding the TOS, and though kind and hospitable he inevitably viewed my sudden appearance as a brigadier with suspicion.

The TOS were about to become the Union Defence Force (UDF). I was required to recommend its shape and size on Independence Day (only two and a half months away) to the Rulers, and to estimate what it would cost as they and not HMG would be paying. There was not much time.

I was also required to recommend the composition of my office which must be Arab in character and include only a small British element, a Ministry of Defence in embryo. It was quite a daunting task, and several times I wondered whether my rightful place was not at the Old Vicarage, and the 8.25 to London. Watson and I agreed that the future UDF needed to be about the size of a brigade in strength, certainly no larger, and should include an armoured reconnaissance squadron of Ferret scout cars (which had in the past been provided by the British armoured car regiment from Aden): say about 3,000 men. We also recommended that about £1m worth of new four-wheel-drive vehicles should be bought. I put these proposals to the Rulers (in effect Shaikhs Zaid and Rashid as they held the purse strings) in late November and they were agreed.

During the first half of December the last British troops, both Army and RAF, left Sharjah, and on December 22nd the TOS were formally handed over to the newly-formed UAE and became the Union Defence Force. Shaikh Muhammad bin Rashid (third son of the Ruler of Dubai) had been appointed Minster of Defence, and visited all UDF camps on 'handover day', watching soldiers swearing loyalty to the new state. All Arab ranks were given a thank-you bounty by HMG and an incentive bounty by the new Government.

All this sounds quite straightforward and sensible; however, in reality there were all sorts of complications which could only occur in a very small independent state just created out of seven mini-Shaikhdoms, of which two were very rich and five were not. The problem in a nutshell was that though rulers agreed that the former TOS should become a federal force of about brigade strength, several wanted to copy the Abu Dhabi example* and have their own small private armies as well. It made them feel safer now that the British umbrella was removed. I could only stand on the touch line and advise on shape and size.

In January 1972 the Military Liaison Office duly became the embryo MOD of the UAE and my appointment changed from DMLO to Chief of Staff to the Minister of Defence (Shaikh Muhammad bin Rashid).

Shaikh Khaled of Sharjah's agreement to share the island of Abu Musa with Iran was unpopular with some of his more warlike Qasimi cousins, as was dramatically shown on January 24th, 1972, barely three months after my arrival. The former ruler, Shaikh Saqr bin Sultan, who had been living in exile in Cairo, suddenly appeared in Sharjah, having landed further up the coast, stormed the Palace and shot the Ruler dead

*See p.194.

21. Sir William Luce talking to locals in the Liwa, *c.* 1965

22. Caroline climbing date palm at Khor Fakkan, *c.* 1966

23. Departure from Sharjah Creek, our Land Rover already on board. 1967

24. German memorial, Alamein. Sir Harold Beeley and Author at the annual ceremony, 1968

25. Shaikh Muhammad bin Rashid, Minister of Defence, saluting on Independence Day, 1971

26. Gaddesden Place, David and
Caroline in foreground, 1958

27. Author planting commemorative
tree at Sandridge on Golden Jubilee
of Scout Group, 1977

11

28. HM The Queen Mother at St Paul's
Walden for Golden Jubilee of the Hertfordshire Society, 1986

29. Judge Kingham with Venture Scouts at 2,600 m. in the Alps, 1976

30. The next generation: our grandchildren with Caroline at 3,000 m. in the Austrian Tirol, 1991

before the National Guard could intervene. It was an extraordinary event which showed only too clearly the fragile structure of the new state.

Shaikh Muhammad bin Rashid quickly took charge. The Palace was surrounded and Saqr in due course surrendered. He was handed over to Shaikh Zaid, now President of the UAE, who put him under house arrest at Al Ain (Buraimi).

The only redeeming feature of this act of piracy (one might say in the tradition of the Qawasim) was the way in which young Shaikh Muhammad, then in his early twenties, took charge of several squadrons from the ADDF, the Sharjah National Guard and the UDF and forced Saqr to surrender. The leadership that he displayed boded well for the future. Though I was in the wings throughout this drama, I of course played no part.

Shaikh Sultan bin Muhammad, one of Shaikh Khalid's six brothers, was immediately proclaimed Ruler of Sharjah, and happily (at the time of writing) is still on his throne.

In June 1972 another event which somewhat undermined the authority of the UDF took place. The UAE has a sixty-mile long coastline on the Indian Ocean, sandwiched between the Musandam Peninsula to the north and the main Batinah coast to the south, both part of the Sultanate of Oman. Tribal fighting suddenly broke out between the Qawasim and the Sharqiin, the ruling family of Fujairah, which in the view of experienced observers was the worst outbreak since 1959. Although neither side was blameless we suspected that Shaikh Muhammad of Fujairah had decided to rock the boat in order to make his presence felt and settle local scores. Of the seven Rulers he was probably the poorest, and badly needed aid. The UDF was unlucky in having new and inexperienced British officers in charge of the two squadrons who first went in to try and restore law and order, and as a result were not very effective. Abu Dhabi quickly heard that something was wrong and sent three squadrons post-haste to 'sort things out', as Shaikh Faisal Sultan (formerly TOS and now Under-Secretary for Defence Abu Dhabi) put it. These reinforcements remained under Shaikh Zaid's command, and we had an absurd situation on the east coast where the UDF force was under MOD UAE and the ADDF force under MOD Abu Dhabi. Only excellent cooperation between the British officers in both forces prevented complete chaos.

Shaikh Muhammad was unfortunately on a short visit to the UK during this tribal flare-up, and Abu Dhabi lost no time in drawing his attention to the alleged shortcomings of the UDF, in their eyes still a

British-run force. As long as Shaikh Zaid remained the paymaster for the UDF and all private armies (except the Dubai Defence Force) it was difficult to see how this military absurdity could be resolved. However, there were redeeming features such as the newly-formed Abu Dhabi Military Academy at Al Ain which took cadets from the UDF, DDF and SNG.

During the year an UDF Sea Wing was planned under a RN officer who joined us in May. Abu Dhabi already had nine Vosper boats which patrolled the Gulf and Batinah coasts on a roster basis. Illegal immigration was as much a problem as ever, hundreds of Pakistanis and Iranians flooding the *suqs* looking for work.

The UDF Air Wing was also beginning to take shape, consisting initially of three Jet Ranger helicopters 'cast' by Abu Dhabi with new and more powerful engines. Shaikh Muhammad was already a qualified helicopter pilot himself and I often used to fly round visiting outlying stations with him at the controls.

In February 1972 a very unpleasant air crash occurred in the UAE. A Danish airliner full of tourists returning by night from Colombo to Copenhagen, and due to refuel at Dubai, apparently started the descent too early and flew straight into the Hajar range of mountains at a height of about 2,500 feet and still seventy miles from Dubai. There were no survivors and the UDF, directed by Jack Briggs, then Commissioner of Police Dubai, had a grisly job picking up the pieces. What was left of some 200 passengers and crew had to be brought down to Sharjah for identification. I flew over the crash scene in a helicopter and saw the wreckage spread over a wide area. The Danish Government flew out a team of pathologists and coffins to take the remains back to Denmark. A memorial service, which I attended, was held in the old RAF hangar at Sharjah and we lived with the sadness, the horror and not least the smell for some weeks.

By the summer of 1972 I was beginning to think seriously about whether I should leave after my one-year contract ended in October, or perhaps stay for a further six months if I was wanted. Sir William Luce had asked me to keep in touch after the UAE had formally become independent in December 1971 and his own special role in the hand-over had ended. My position was unusual to say the least. My bosses were officially the Rulers of Abu Dhabi and Dubai with whom I had a contract. I did not see them very often; Zaid in particular was besieged by businessmen and entrepreneurs from all over the world trying to cash in on what *The Times** described as the richest country in the world in *per capita* income. He had his own private army which was already considerably larger than the UDF, and left defence matters in the hands of his son Khalifa and Faisal Sultan, so that he could devote more time to the development of the country in other fields: these included ports, roads, communications, education and agriculture. Shaikh Rashid was much more approachable, not least because I worked directly to his son Muhammad, but again he too was surrounded by advisers of all sorts; as long as I got on with Muhammad, and adopted a fairly low profile, that suited both of them.

I was strangely alone. The British Embassy (which on Independence had replaced the two Political Agencies) was friendly but kept me slightly at arm's length: it was important that they were not seen to be publicly backing me. It was equally important that I was not seen to be taking instructions in any way from them.

The UDF and the four Rulers' private armies were friendly because of their British officers, but again went their separate ways. I was in practice my own master and could within reason adopt any line that I chose.

In April Luce had written saying that there was no certainty that the UAE Government would want the post of Chief of Staff to lapse after one year, and that if I went, Shaikh Zaid might want to replace me with an Arab. Luce felt that this would be very unfortunate 'if it happened so early in the formative stage'. He added that his personal view would be that if the option existed I should stay on into 1973. As always, I greatly valued his advice and was able to see my job in better perspective. My Arabic had never been other than 'Lower Standard Colloquial' (to use official terminology), and virtually all my discussions with Rulers were conducted through interpreters such as Jack Briggs. Jack was an enormous help. He was a close confidant of Shaikh Rashid and a personal friend of my Minister, Muhammad. More importantly, he was not viewed as part of the British presence, as was for example Tim Budd, being a British officer in the UDF.

Writing to Sir William Luce in August 1972, I said that the MOD UAE now totalled thirteen Arab civil servants (I am not at all sure what they did), three British officers and one British Civil Servant (Finance). Lieutenant Colonel Keith Shapland of the Somersets was seconded as my principal staff officer. I doubt whether any other MOD in the world was smaller! I added that Shaikh Zaid's views on whether to retain British officers to run local forces were 'somewhat obscure.' Jack

*May 23rd, 1974.

Briggs told me that Shaikh Rashid thought that Zaid wanted to get rid of them as quickly as possible, but Jim Treadwell, HM Ambassador UAE, assured us that this was not the case at all. In his view Zaid wanted a ratio of forty per cent British, forty per cent Pakistani and twenty per cent Jordanian in the ADDF. Shaikh Rashid's view on the other hand, echoed by his son Muhammad, was to retain British officers (and virtually no other expats) until the UAE Government could run the forces itself. I urged Roy Watson to 'arabise' the senior appointments in the UDF as quickly as possible, and to this end one third of the key posts were held by Arab officers by the end of 1972.

As part of the withdrawal plan in 1971 HMG had left behind a small Military Advisory Team (MAT) in Sharjah, responsible for handing over buildings and equipment to the UDF or other local bodies in need; the MAT also provided a purely military link with Bahrain and MOD UK, and an administrative base for British troops training in the UAE. It totalled about 100 British troops and was commanded by Lieutenant Colonel Derek Carson, who with his wife Pauline were most hospitable and provided a valuable safety valve where I could let off steam when feeling particularly frustrated.

Oil had now been flowing in Abu Dhabi for ten years and annual income in 1972 was approaching £1.5 billion. In addition, the oil was of high quality with a low sulphur content, and could be assured of a continuing market. By comparison Dubai, with its one off-shore field some sixty miles out into the Gulf, was producing only about one twentieth of the colossal Abu Dhabi figure. However, unlike Abu Dhabi, Dubai's wealth did not depend only on oil. Its low tariffs, liberal policies and gold smuggling had attracted trade for many years and it was now the supermarket of the Gulf.

Off-shore oil is usually piped ashore by a long pipe-line laid on the sea bed. As Dubai's field was so far out into the Gulf a decision was taken to load the oil direct into tankers on site. An American company designed and built a completely new type of off-shore storage unit at Dubai, consisting of three huge steel tanks shaped like inverted champagne glasses. Known as *khazzans*, they were sunk on the sea bed with the neck of the 'glass' protruding above sea level and having a production deck on top. As oil was pumped into the tank sea water was forced out through vents in the bottom.

In June 1972 the first of these *khazzans* was towed out, full of air, to the field and then submerged through the release of air and the addition of water. I was one of many spectators who were invited to witness this 'first' in off-shore oil production. We boarded an extremely comfortable private yacht late on a June evening, slept on board and the following morning were able to watch the *khazzan* tilt over to 34° as air escaped. We were warned that there would be a loud burp at maximum tilt, caused by air escaping from beneath the tank at a velocity of about 400 mph. The whole operation — until the tank was resting on the sea bed with just the neck of the 'champagne bottle' above sea level — lasted about an hour. We then sailed back to Dubai, having quenched our thirst with the real stuff.

In October Port Rashid, an artificial sixteen-berth deep-water harbour (later to be increased to thirty-seven berths) was completed thirteen months ahead of time, and formally opened by the Ruler. Again I was among the many guests. As though this were not enough, work started almost immediately on a massive ship repair complex consisting of three dry docks, one of which would be large enough to accommodate a tanker of one million tons deadweight. I discussed this project with George Chapman, head of Gray Mackenzies, the leading shipping agents in Dubai, and one of Shaikh Rashid's trusted expat. advisers. George had reservations about the need for such a large dock, especially as no million-ton tanker had yet been built (nor has been built at the time of writing, twenty years later), and a similar facility was being constructed in Bahrain.

The many other developments that have taken place in the UAE during the last two decades include new dual carriageway roads to Al Ain in the Buraimi oasis and through the Hajar range to the Indian Ocean coast, more hotels than can possibly be needed, four international airports when only one is really needed, desalination plants to provide much-needed extra water, a university, schools, an aluminium smelter, a liquid natural gas plant on Das Island and an earth satellite station at Jebel Ali.

As the military potential of Abu Dhabi increased it seemed logical that MOD UAE should be located there, along with most of the other federal ministries. However, Shaikh Muhammad had no intention of leaving his home in Dubai, and in July 1972 he moved my small staff from the old TOS camp in Sharjah (where we had been since I arrived the previous October) to lavish new offices in Dubai alongside the Ruler's *majlis*. I drove over from Sharjah every day in a new Mercedes provided by Shaikh Muhammad, who spent a lot of time coping with arms dealers who wanted to sell him anything from a tank to a brass hat. On one occasion Hawker Siddeley arrived with their new executive jet, the HS 125, and invited Muhammad to try it out. He took me and we flew both high and very low over the Straits of Hormuz in considerable comfort. He also test flew the Pilatus Porter, a modern version of the German Fieseler Storch which could land on a postage stamp. Whenever possible he would escape into the desert, driving a Range Rover over the dunes, piloting his own helicopter or just riding an Arab pony. He was the most Anglophile of Shaikh Rashid's sons, spoke good English (unlike his father who hardly spoke a word) and was well liked by us all. He had a natural dignity, a nice sense of humour and displayed considerable qualities of leadership.

By the autumn of 1972 I had told Shaikh Muhammad that I would stay if he wished until April 1973, thus extending my contract from a year to eighteen months. This was agreed.

President Numeiry of the Sudan visited the UAE that summer and discussed military matters both in Abu Dhabi and Dubai. Though I was not informed at the time, it must have been arranged during this visit that a retired Sudanese brigadier would take over from me when I left. The appointment was to be that of Adviser as opposed to Chief of Staff, Muhammad having decided to deal direct with Heads of Departments. In a letter home at the time I wrote that the pressures on Muhammad from Abu Dhabi were such that a non-Arab Chief of Staff as my replacement would not have been acceptable. The Sudanese, another Muhammad, was a very pleasant man who had attended the American Staff College and had been a contemporary of Numeiry in the Sudanese Army. He had retired in 1971 aged forty-six.

Amongst many visitors that winter two stood out: HRH Princess Alexandra, accompanied by her husband Angus Ogilvy, called *en route* home from Afghanistan. I suppose that I must have given the impression that I was an old hand, for Ogilvy thought that I lived in the Gulf and asked whether I often visited the UK. The other VIP was King Hussain of Jordan, for whom Shaikh Rashid gave a huge feast to which I was invited. Hussain was simply on a fact-finding tour of the now independent Lower Gulf states, possibly hoping for some financial aid as Jordan has no oil and is dependent on external aid.

On the military side the most distinguished was Mike Carver, now a Field Marshal and about to become Chief of the Defence Staff. We had last met when he was commanding 6 Infantry Brigade in Germany and I was visiting the KSLI. He questioned me closely on security in the Lower Gulf in the wake of the British withdrawal, and training facilities.

April 1973 soon came, I handed over to Brigadier Muhammad and flew
home with as little fuss as possible. It had been an extremely interesting
eighteen months which in retrospect I would not have missed for
anything. My job hinged on the fact that I was on a short contract with
no private axe to grind, and could therefore be regarded as impartial, to
the extent that any non-Arab official was thus perceived in the Gulf at
that time. I knew the area and most of the leading personalities, both
Arab and expat, and they knew me. I was not an Arabist in the strict
sense of the word, nor could I be accused of trying to feather my own
nest. The fact that Sir William Luce had sponsored me, and that the
Rulers knew this, undoubtedly helped.

Yet I left feeling that the defence picture was confused and that there
appeared to be no short term solution. Abu Dhabi's vast oil income,
and Dubai's tendency to look after herself (which she was well able to
do) and not bother too much with federal affairs were at the root of the
problem. There was no serious external threat and Rulers preferred to
run their own private armies for self-protection. A federal army needed
to be seen to exist for prestige and political purposes. Shaikh
Muhammad bin Rashid was without doubt the right man to be Federal
Minister of Defence but his place ought logically to have been at Shaikh
Zaid's right hand.

One could almost present this to the Staff College as a hypothetical
problem and invite students' solutions.

Three years later, in 1976, the Armed Forces of the UAE were formerly
'unified' (whatever that means) and in 1978 Shaikh Zaid appointed his
younger son Sultan, aged eighteen, as C-in-C without, it seems,
consulting either Shaikh Rashid or Shaikh Muhammad, his federal
Minister of Defence! Shaikh Rashid promptly withdrew his own private
army from the unified command and put them on one-hour alert. As
Henry Stanhope, Defence Correspondent of The Times wrote: 'it set
back the process of welding the UAE forces into one big happy
family'.*

Today the UAE Armed Forces are said to total some three divisions
of which two are based in Abu Dhabi territory and one in Dubai.
Shaikh Muhammad bin Rashid continues as Minister of Defence and he
and his brothers of the al Maktoum family are close to Shaikh Zaid,
President of the UAE and Supreme Commander. The 'Northern Rulers'
still have their own small private armies. It is a far cry from the TOS
as the only federal force thirty years ago.

*The Times, February 23rd 1981.

CHAPTER 26

In the Right Place at the Right Time?

LOOKING back and trying to put my soldiering days in perspective, it is not difficult to pick out the highs and lows. Those thirty-six years fall naturally into three parts: first, seven years which include most of World War II in operational Intelligence; second, a more conventional period when I was a brigade major, an instructor at the Staff College and a regimental officer at company commander and second in command level, and finally fifteen years in the Arab world as a staff officer, commander and a diplomat-soldier.

I was certainly lucky to become involved in Intelligence at the beginning of the desert war as I had received no training in this field and had only been commissioned two years. My three years in the desert were hard work and exciting, and a period of which the stuff of history is made. Much of that time we were the only active theatre of operations and always in the news, good or bad.

The conventional period was essential if I was to get anywhere, and I was certainly in the fast stream for much of that time. My second short spell in the front line as the Allies closed up to the Rhine might have led to a command if the War had dragged on. Happily it did not. The command for which I was selected in Aden heralded the beginning of a long and extremely interesting spell in the Middle East which I don't regret but quickly realised was bad for promotion.

Commander TOS was undoubtedly the highlight of my career: I was lucky to be involved in stirring events and working alongside and under very able diplomats with whom I got on well.

Perhaps the fates decided that I should follow in the footsteps of my father and grandfather by witnessing the end of empire in India, Aden and the Gulf. Maybe I was in the right place at the right time after all.

PART V, 1973-1993

CHAPTER 27

New Horizons

UNLIKE many people I was not particularly looking forward to retirement. I had no special hobbies, was not much good at DIY and, at fifty-seven, wondered what I was going to do.

The Old Vicarage that Simone had lived in whilst I was on my second Gulf tour welcomed me with its new roof and interior redecoration. I was also invited back to my civil service job in London.

It happened that the Hertfordshire Scouts had been looking for a new County Chairman, a lay appointment which required no previous experience of the Scout movement (I had none), and I had been invited to take this on. It was to open up an involvement with Scouting which continued for over twenty years and proved most satisfying and enjoyable. I quickly got to know the county and a large number of public-spirited people who were connected with the movement, either in uniform or as lay-helpers. Also, I had been invited to become a governor of Abbots Hill School at Hemel Hempstead, a private boarding school for girls where Simone and other members of her family had been educated. This commitment was also to last some twenty years and prove interesting and instructive, not to mention time-consuming.

By 1975 I found myself Chairman of Governors at Abbots Hill and a year later, when Tony Burgess the Scout County Commissioner retired, I was asked to take over from him though I had never worn scout uniform in my life. Both were challenging jobs in which I had no experience at all.

To sharpen me up on Scouting I attended a one-week residential course at Gilwell Park, Essex, the home of the movement, which proved very valuable. After that, it was leaning on senior Scouters who probably had at least twenty-five years experience, and reminding myself that I was dealing with a voluntary youth movement and any form of military discipline would not go down at all well. It was a question of striking a balance between turning a blind eye on boys looking scruffy in scout uniform and persuading them to adopt a minimum standard of smartness.

James Kingham, Circuit Judge at Luton, was my Deputy. He, in partnership with a former Guider, Marilyn Hudson, also ran at Harpenden one of the first and certainly the largest mixed Venture Scout Unit in the U.K. Their average numbers were over 150. James and Marilyn had tremendous flair with teenagers and it was a joy to watch them at work.

I was also lucky enough to recruit a high-powered business executive who was just retiring from being Chairman of Haden Carrier, heating and air-conditioning engineers. Sir Alan Pullinger had been climbing mountains ever since his Oxford days and didn't take much persuading to take over as County Chairman. He was to prove a most valuable lay leader for the next fifteen years.

Most of my scouting business inevitably took place after working hours: I would be out perhaps twice a week, driving up to twenty-five miles each way to visit a troop on a cold winter's evening, or attending an executive committee meeting of the County Scout Council.

For a week after Christmas each year, I and other leaders took a mixed group of Venture Scouts and Ranger Guides skiing in Austria and later Italy. We would travel by coach, hire a self-catering chalet, and cram in up to seventy-five. In the summer we took up to 100 in the same age group (sixteen-eighteen) to Switzerland (usually in the Valais Canton), for a fortnight's high walking, based in a large chalet. These county expeditions were extremely popular with all concerned, not least me. For those who could not afford the slightly more expensive expeditions abroad, we ran activity centres in an old mill at Bethesda, North Wales, sleeping forty-four, the former railway station at Lochearnhead in central Scotland sleeping seventy, and more recently, a rented farmhouse in Staffordshire sleeping sixty.

My five years as County Commissioner were hard work and rewarding. Hertfordshire was, and still is, one of the strongest counties in England in terms of boys in Scouting — some 15,000 and I considered it a privilege to be involved.

When, in 1976, local government was reorganised into districts, each looking after about 100,000 people, I was asked to stand as a Conservative representing Great Gaddesden, and later, two other villages on the newly formed Dacorum District Council. It was a very safe seat and I won it without much canvassing. But it meant giving up the London job which was disappointing at the time, but probably a good thing in the long run. I had quite enough on my plate.

Local government work was not very exciting. Practically all the population of Dacorum lived in the New Town of Hemel Hempstead and most council business concerned housing, planning controls and leisure activities for the 80,000 people concentrated there. The villages looked after themselves. It was a completely new field for me to begin with, and therefore interesting, but after attending endless evening meetings which did not concern my villages, I became bored and rather disillusioned, and stood down after seven years.

When in 1976 I was officially 'unemployed', aged sixty, I visited the Volunteer Bureau in Hemel Hempstead and asked whether they could suggest some voluntary work. They sent me to the Citizens' Advice Bureau (CAB) which I had never heard of before.

This call started a ten year commitment, (in those days only three hours per week, now it is six,) in a very busy office, prepared to advise the public on almost any problem from completing an income tax return to the intricacies of social security benefits, from making out a will to how to plead when summonsed, and from unfair dismissal to a broken marriage.

We were, of course, given training, but in 1976 you were thrown in at the deep end and told to get on with it. After a 'sheltered' life in the Army, I had to learn quickly how the less fortunate live. It was extremely interesting and rewarding in the sense that clients were generally grateful and went away feeling better. For much of my time we had a rather special retired police officer as Manager. Ron Hoar was a large but gentle man who had started as a guardsman. He had a lovely sense of humour and was enormously popular with us advisers, most of whom were women. Sadly, he died of a heart attack whilst in office, a devastating blow to everybody. I still have many friends in Dacorum CAB and am told that they now handle about 18,000 enquiries a year.

The Old Vicarage was to prove an ideal and happy home for us. Simone became much involved in parish affairs and Meals on Wheels (which she has enjoyed doing for twenty years). Both our children were married in Great Gaddesden Church (as were we in 1944), and in 1975 my parents came to live with us in a flat of their own on the first floor. Simone tended to their every need; they were both to die peacefully at home aged eighty-eight and ninety. Kitty Pryor then joined us from Gaddesden Place and we shared the house for nine years until she died aged ninety.

In 1975 I was appointed a Deputy Lieutenant for Hertfordshire by Major General Sir George Burns, our very popular Lord Lieutenant. Over the last eighteen years I have stood in for Sir George, or his successor, Simon Bowes Lyon, (first cousin of HM The Queen), on several occasions. I received the Princess Royal at Abbots Hill when she opened a new hall, and Princess Margaret at the opening of an NSPCC centre in Hemel Hempstead. The duties of a DL are not at all onerous: it is said by some, tongue in cheek, that our main duty is to attend each others' funerals.

In 1979 I was invited to become Director of the St Albans Abbey Roof Repair Appeal. This was a full-time salaried post which I took on with some misgivings for one year as fund-raising is never easy, particularly when it is for bricks and mortar as opposed to human beings. The Abbey dates back to Norman times, (some of the brickwork is even Roman,) and the nave is 550 feet long, second only in length to Winchester. Over a million pounds was needed to re-lead the roof and build a modern Chapter House linked to the South Transept.

I answered to the Dean, Peter Moore, a charming and highly intelligent man, and worked closely with Michael Kyrle Pope, who, like me, had recently retired from Service life and was Administrator to the Dean. Robert Runcie was then still Bishop of St Albans and became Archbishop of Canterbury in 1980 amid, as can be imagined, much local excitement.

My 'parish' covered the whole diocese (Hertfordshire and Bedfordshire); I was on the road a great deal and met folk from all walks of life. After a year I was running out of new ideas to raise money and was much relieved to hand over to Sir Eric Cheadle who had been with the Thomson Organisation all his working life and was extremely experienced in all forms of fund-raising. He also lived in St Albans, close to the Abbey. Happily, the necessary funds to repair the roof and build the new Chapter House were raised and it was opened by HM The Queen in 1982.

In 1981, again almost by chance, I was invited to run the Hertfordshire Society as Honorary Director, and my ten years in this job, following on five years as County Commissioner of the Scouts, were to prove far and away the most satisfying and rewarding of my retirement. The Hertfordshire Society, a registered charity, was concerned entirely with protecting the countryside, and in particular the Green Belt, and not with being a snob dining club as some cynics thought. We represented the Council for the Protection of Rural England (CPRE) in the county and were, in modern parlance, a pressure group. Our limited funds came from some 1,500 subscribing members living in Hertfordshire. I ran the show from a small office in Welwyn: it was manned throughout the week during office hours and I was there three days a week for perhaps twenty hours.

My experience as a district councillor in Dacorum certainly helped, particularly as I had served on the planning sub-committee. Theoretically, I dealt with planning departments in all the District Councils and the County Council, in a county of one million people.

In practice, of course, we only became involved in major issues such as applications to take over a large area of the Green Belt for housing, by-pass alignments, gravel extraction, and Stansted Airport, (just inside Essex but much involved in Hertfordshire airspace).

The Society was founded in 1936 and there is no doubt that over fifty years it has done much to help preserve large areas of beautiful countryside very close to the London fringe. We also ran the Best Kept Village Competition, an extremely worthwhile scheme open to all villages every summer. In 1982 HM The Queen honoured us by visiting Great Wymondley, which had just won its class, and in 1986 HM The Queen Mother attended a Garden Party to commemorate our fiftieth Anniversary, at St Paul's Walden, home of the Bowes Lyon family, where she had spent much of her childhood.

I was lucky enough to recruit several public-spirited ladies who for a basic wage manned the office on a part-time basis. They were led for seven of my ten years by Georgina Palmer, (who first appeared as a temp. while having a break from journalism,) and included Valerie Harding, Sue Edsall, and Sheila Townend. Heather Bardner took over the good work from Georgina, and her husband Richard helped us to unravel the mysteries of computers in his spare time. It was a very happy team, greatly helped by Michael Kyrle Pope, who, having been largely responsible for inviting me to take over as Honorary Director, became Chairman for most of my time and worked very closely with all of us.

One of the nice things about voluntary work is that people say thank you and within reason you can take time off whenever it suits you.

Scouting introduced me to long distance walking and I quickly became very keen. In 1977, my second year as County Commissioner, I completed the Lyke Wake Walk across the North Yorkshire Moors, par for the course being forty miles in twenty-four hours in order to qualify for the coffin badge and 'condolences' on the crossing. Simone and I repeated the dose two years later supported by Scouters who saw us off at about 6 a.m., took down our tent, drove our car to the finish, pitched our tent and welcomed us as we crawled in at about 10 p.m. that evening. Scenically I do not recommend the walk, nor can I think of any other reason for submitting oneself to this particular form of torture (except perhaps the challenge?).

The middle ninety miles of the Pennine Way, from Gargrave to Garrigill, which we completed over seven days in 1981 was quite a different matter: lovely scenery and comfortable bed and breakfasts. Perhaps some sections proved longer than we had anticipated, but we made it. The following year we walked through the famous Lairig Ghru Pass in the Highlands, from Deeside to Speyside, and back over two days, (eighteen miles each way). I had intended that Simone would rest at Glenmore whilst I walked back to fetch the car and drove it round. She decided, however, to come with me and unfortunately slipped on a rock and broke her wrist when we were almost down. We slept in the car that night on Braemar golf course and the next day Simone went into Bridge of Earn Hospital to have her wrist set under an anaesthetic. Our last major walk together was the West Highland Way in 1987, ninety miles from the northern suburbs of Glasgow to Fort William. Magnificent scenery and again comfortable bed and breakfasts.

Between 1984 and 1988 Alan Pullinger kindly invited me to join him and two old climbing friends on three memorable walks in the Highlands. A journey across the waist of Scotland from the west-coast main line at Corrour (the highest main line railway station in Britain) to the Inverness main line at Dalwhinnie, over five days and four nights camping, was followed the next year by driving to Glen Affric from Inverness and then walking north to Achnashellach on the Kyle of Lochalsh line, again over five days. My only complaint was that Alan insisted on us all carrying forty pounds on our backs, which I found very hard.

The third expedition was much more civilised in that a very comfortable house on the coast of the Knoydart Peninsula, opposite Skye, was taken for a fortnight and the other three took their wives. I joined them on my own for the second week, sleeping in a tent in the garden and took part in some marvellous high walking.

In 1983 I organised a Himalayan trek from Katmandu to the Everest Base Camp, following in the footsteps of John Hunt thirty years earlier. This may sound rather ambitious but over the last fifteen years or so trekking agencies have mushroomed in Nepal and all you have to do is cough up about £1,500 and walk, carrying practically nothing, for three to four weeks from 5,000 feet near Katmandu to the Base Camp at 18,000 feet. You then walk down to Lukhla airstrip at 9,500 feet for the return flight to Katmandu. Our party totalled eight: my cousin Jacqueline Elgood and her Sapper brigadier husband, Bruno, another cousin, Meg whose father had been in the Gurkhas and who particularly wanted to visit Nepal near where she was born, Spike and Jansis Barker-Wyatt, Sapper friends of the Elgoods, (he was another brigadier), Esme Bott, a cousin of Simone's, and finally my old friend Michael Kyrle Pope. Our average age was around sixty.

We had a splendid team of Sherpas who carried virtually all our kit, put up our tents every evening and cooked all meals. After twelve days we got our first view of Everest from near Namche Bazaar at about 12,000 feet. The following day, the pony which Esme, a keen horsewoman, had hired to ride, suddenly died of colic, and she had to transfer to a yak, which proved a much slower mode of transport and rather uncomfortable.

We had further fine views of Everest from the famous Thyangboche Monastery, before the Nuptse ridge obscured a closer look. Our target view-point was Kala Pattar, a rather insignificant looking 'hill' at 18,000 feet from where you can look behind the Nuptse ridge, into the Icefall and the Western Cym, up to the South Col, and of course straight at the summit. Sherpas normally take you to Lobuje at 16,000 feet where two nights are spent, and you walk to Kala Pattar and back.

In our case, Meg had to be flown back to Katmandu on Day 11 as she was not well, and Esme and Jansis decided not to venture further than Pheriche at 14,000 feet where there was a tiny cottage hospital, manned by a young American doctor who was on a sabbatical year studying mountain sickness. Five of us went on to Lobuje where I, too, began to feel rather unwell and had to walk down accompanied by one Sherpa to Pheriche after a very restless night. How lucky I was that a doctor was there. He gave me an injection and told me to lie down in a nearby tent. I was clearly suffering from a mild form of altitude sickness. Fortunately I was better by the evening and the next morning walked up again to Lobuje, passing the other four coming down. It turned out that only Spike climbed Kala Pattar and the other three went as far as Gorakshep. I slept on my own that night and climbed Kala Pattar the next day very very slowly, having to stop about every fifty paces. It was the altitude, not the terrain, which was the problem. The view was marvellous when I got there and I remember sharing a tin of sardines with a young Aussie from Sydney and a Scot from Glasgow who appeared to be back-packing on their own.

I caught up with the others after a couple of days and we all flew out of Lukhla on Day 25 as planned. It was a wonderful trip in nice company and an experience that I shall never forget.

In 1986 Michael Kyrle Pope introduced me to 'hutting' in Austria through the UK Branch of the Austrian Alpine Club, conveniently based in Welwyn Garden City. Joining was easy, thanks to the helpful and efficient secretary Doreen Dorward and, membership entitled one to reduced charges in club huts in the Austrian Alps together with expert advice on routes and the supply of maps.

Simone and I went out on our own two summers later, and thereafter it has become a family affair involving David and Caroline and our six grandchildren. The huts are mostly perched on cols at about

2,000 metres and are very well equipped. The atmosphere in the evenings in the *gaststube* and the communal bunk rooms is very special.

In the last nine years I have been on seven separate trips and am planning an eighth this summer as I write.

If readers are still with me they may well wonder how I fitted in all these different activities over the years and was still reasonably sane at the end. To put things in perspective, I was seldom under pressure, except perhaps for short periods during my salaried jobs in London and St Albans, but they only totalled three and a half years out of the last twenty. Scouting was fun and I greatly enjoyed my time with the Hertfordshire Society. Three hours a week at the CAB was very interesting, so was being a school governor. I met a lot of very nice people and made many new friends. It is true that busy people can always find time to do what interests them.

I sometimes think that the last twenty years of retirement have been more fulfilling in the sense of pulling one's weight in society than all my previous thirty-six years in the Army. The voluntary work in which I have been involved has been really worthwhile.

If Hertfordshire is a fair example, too few retired service officers take this view. As it happened, my old friend Rear Admiral Michael Kyrle Pope representing the Royal Navy, Air Commodore Ian Stockwell the RAF, and I all retired about the same time, were appointed Deputy Lieutenants about the same time, and have worked together over the last fifteen to twenty years in several different fields. But we are very much in a minority. As I write only five out of thirty six DLs have held regular service commissions.

I hope that any serving officer contemplating retirement who reads this far will ponder. A second full-time job is often not the answer.

Supported by my wife, the lovely environment of the Gade Valley, and our children living nearby, my retirement years have been enjoyable and rewarding, and I have much to be thankful for.

BIBLIOGRAPHY

Glen Balfour-Paul, *The End of Empire in the Middle East*, 1991, CUP
C.N. Barclay, *Against Great Odds*, 1955, Sifton Praed and Co
Anthony Beevor, John Murray, *Crete - The Battle and the Resistance*, 1991
Lord Belhaven, *The Uneven Road*, 1955, John Murray
Monkey Blacker, *Monkey Business*, 1994, Quiller Press
Christopher Blake, *A View from Within*, 1990, Mendip Publishing,
Hugh Boustead, *Wind of the Morning*, 1971, Chatto and Windus
The British Army Review, 1961, No. 12
Arthur Bryant, *The Turn of the Tide*, 1957, Collins
Arthur Bryant, *Triumph in the West*, 1959, Collins
J. Bulloch, *The Gulf - A Portrait of Kuwait, Bahrain and the UAE*, 1984,
  Century Publishing
Michael Carver, *Harding of Petherton*, 1978, Weidenfeld & Nicholson
Winston S. Churchill, *The Second World War*, 1949, Cassell Vols. III, IV, V, VI
John Cloake, *Templer - Tiger of Malaya*, 1985, Harrap
John Connell, *Wavell - Scholar and Soldier*, 1964, Collins
Robin Dunn, *Sword and Wig*, 1993, Quiller Press
Bernard Fergusson, *Portrait of a Soldier*, 1961, Collins
David Fraser, *Knight's Cross - A Life of Field Marshal Erwin Rommel*, 1993,
  Harper Collins
William Gibson, *Early Irish Golf*, 1988, Oakleaf Publications, Naas, Co. Kildare
Freddie de Guingand, *Operation Victory*, 1947
Nigel Hamilton, *Monty: Master of the Battlefield*, 1983, Hodder & Stoughton
Donald Hawley, *The Trucial States*, 1970, George Allen & Unwin
M.C.A. Henniker, *Red Shadow over Malaya*, 1955, William Blackwood
Tom Hickinbotham, *Aden*, 1958, Constable
David Holden, *Farewell to Arabia*, 1966, Faber & Faber
Claire Hollingworth, *Front Line*, 1990, Jonathan Cape
Alistair Horne with David Montgomery, *The Lonely Leader - Monty 1944-1945*, 1994,
  Macmillan
Brian Horrocks, *A Full Life*, 1960, Collins
David Hunt, *A Don at War*, 1966, William Kimber
Hammond Innes, *The Doomed Oasis*, 1960, Collins
Charles Johnston, *The View from Steamer Point*, 1964, Collins
Brian Lapping, *End of Empire*, 1985, Granada Publishing
Margeret Luce, *From Aden to the Gulf - Personal Diaries 1956-66*, 1987,
  Michael Russell Publishing
Michael Mann, *The Trucial Oman Scouts - The Story of a Bedouin Force*,
  Michael Russell, 1994
Penderel Moon OUP, *Wavell - The Viceroy's Journal*, 1973
Barrie Pitt, *The Crucible of War I, Wavell's Command, II Year of Alamein*,
  1980 and 1982, Jonathan Cape
David Rissik, *The DLI at War*, 1952, The Depot, DLI, Brancepeth Castle, Durham
David Shepherd, *The Man who loved Giants*, 1975, Hodder & Stoughton
Peter Snow, *Hussein*, 1972, Barrie & Jenkins
Wilfred Thesiger, *Arabian Sands*, 1959, Longmans
Edited by Dick Vernon, *Strafer Gott 1897-1942*, Culverlands Press, Winchester
Philip Warner, *Auchinleck - The Lonely Soldier*, 1981, Sphere Books Ltd
Philip Warner, *Horrocks - The General who led from the Front*, 1984,
  Hamish Hamilton

Appendix 1

LILI MARLENE

Vor der Kaserne, vor den grossen Tor,
Stand eine Laterne und Steht sie noch davor;
Da werden wir uns wiedersehen
Bei der Laterne werden wir stehen
Wie einst, Lili Marlene, wie einst, Lili Marlene.

Schon riefen die Posten, sie bliesen Zapfenstreich
Es kann drei Tage kosten, kamerad ich komm sogleich
Da sagten wir aufwiedersehen
Wie gerne möcht' ich mit Dir gehen
Mit Dir, Lili Marlene, mit Dir, Lili Marlene.

Deine Schritte kennt sie, deinen schönen Gang,
Alle Abend brennt sie, doch mich vergass sie lang;
Und sollte mir ein Leid geschehen
Wer wird bei der Laterne stehen
Mit Dir, Lili Marlene, mit Dir, Lili Marlene.

Aus den stillen Raume, aus der Erde Grund
Hebt mich wie in Traume dein verliebtes Mund
Wo sich die späte Nebeln drehen
Bei der Laterne werd' ich stehen
Wie einst, Lili Marlene, wie einst Lili Marlene.

Appendix 2

THE SOLDIER'S PRAYER

The desert breeze blew a slip of paper into a slit trench at Alamein just before all hell broke loose. A soldier picked up the piece of paper, saw it had a poem written on it and that there was a reference to God — he put it in his pocket — days later when things had quietened down he decided to give it to his Padre - who in turn read it and later gave it to Monty. I heard Monty read it at a Chaplains' gathering.

The author is unknown.

Bob Davies, former Bishop of Tasmania

Stay with me, God. The night is dark,
The night is cold; my little spark
Of courage dies. The night is long;
Be with me, God, and make me strong.

I love a game: I love a fight,
I hate the dark: I love the light,
I love my child: I love my wife,
I am no coward. I love life.

Life with its change of mood and shade
I want to live. I'm not afraid,
But me and mine are hard to part;
Oh, unknown God, lift up mine heart.

You stilled the waters at Dunkirk,
You saved your servants. All your work
Is wonderful, dear God. You strode
Before us down that dreadful road.

We were alone, and hope had fled;
We loved our country and our dead,
And could not shame them; so we stayed
The course, and were not much afraid.
Dear God, that nightmare road; and then
That sea; we got there. . . We were men.

My eyes were blind, my feet were torn,
My soul sang like a bird at dawn;
I know that death is but a door.
I knew what we were fighting for;
Peace for the kids, our brothers freed,
A kinder world, a cleaner breed.

I'm but a son my mother bore,
A simple man, and nothing more.
But — God of strength and gentleness,
Be pleased to make me nothing less.

Help me; Oh God, when death is near,
To meet the haggard face of fear,
That when I fall — if fall I must —
My soul may triumph in the dust.

PERSONAL MESSAGE FROM THE ARMY COMMANDER

To Be Read Out To All Troops.

1. The Allied Armies landed in Sicily, on Italian soil, on 10th July, magnificently supported by the Royal Navy and the Allied Air Forces, and are, today, in possession of the whole island except for the north-east corner, where the enemy is now hemmed in.

2. I want to tell all of you, soldiers of the Eighth Army, that this has been a very fine performance. On your behalf, I have expressed to the Commander of the Seventh American Army on our left the congratulations of the Eighth Army for the way the American troops have captured and cleaned up more than half the island in record time. We are proud to fight beside our American Allies.

3. The beginning has been very good, thanks to your splendid fighting qualities and to the hard work and devotion to duty of all those who work in the ports, on the roads, and in rear areas. We must not forget to give thanks to "THE LORD MIGHTY IN BATTLE" for giving us such a good beginning towards the attainment of our object.

4. And now let us get on with the job. Together with our American allies we have knocked MUSSOLINI off his perch We will now drive the Germans out of SICILY.

5. Into battle with stout hearts. Good luck to you all.

B. L. MONTGOMERY
General,
Eighth Army.

SICILY.
July, 1943.

Monty's message to the Eighth Army in Sicily before the invasion of Italy.

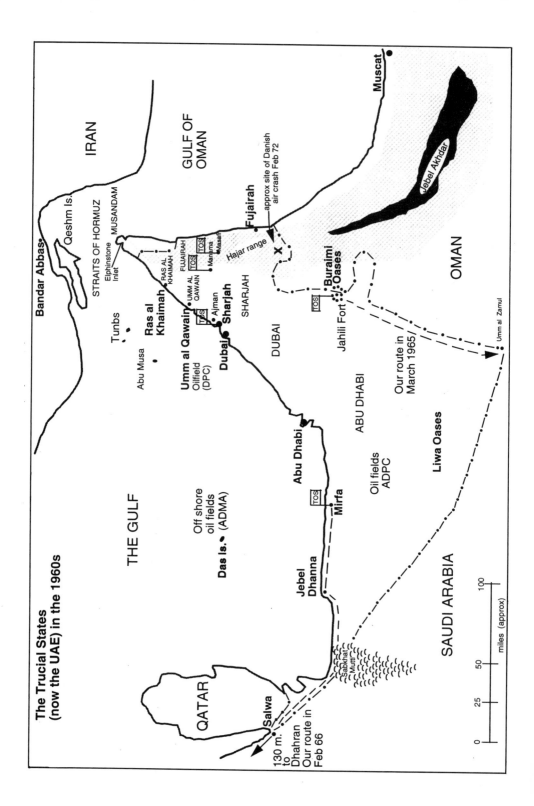

The Trucial States
(now the UAE) in the 1960s

IRAN

Bandar Abbas

Qeshm Is.

STRAITS OF HORMUZ

MUSANDAM

Elphinstone
Inlet

GULF OF
OMAN

Muscat

Jebel Akhdar

approx site of Danish
air crash Feb 72

Fujairah

Hajar range

X

OMAN

Tunbs

Abu Musa

Ras al
Khaimah

RAS AL
KHAIMAH

FUJAIRAH

TOS

TOS

Manama

Masafi

UMM AL
QAWAIN

TOS

Umm al Qawain
Oilfield
(DPC)

Ajman

Dubai

Sharjah

SHARJAH

DUBAI

Buraimi
Oases

Jahili Fort

TOS

Our route in
March 1965

Umm al Zamul

THE GULF

Off shore
oil fields

Das Is. (ADMA)

Abu Dhabi

ABU DHABI

Oil fields
ADPC

Liwa Oases

Jebel
Dhanna

TOS

Mirfa

SAUDI ARABIA

Sabkhat
Mutti

QATAR

Salwa

130 m.
to
Dhahran
Our route in
Feb 66

0   25   50   100

miles (approx)

INDEX